THE
VATICAN
CONNECTION

THE
VATICAN
CONNECTION

· · · · · · · · · · · · · · · · ·

Richard Hammer

C. 1

HOLT, RINEHART AND WINSTON
New York

364.163

HAMMER

Library of Congress Cataloging in Publication Data
Hammer, Richard, fl. 1969–
The Vatican connection.

Based on the recollections, files, and records of
Detective Sergeant Joseph J. Coffey, JR., commanding
officer of the Organized Crime Homicide Task Force,
New York City Police Dept.
1. Swindlers and swindling.   2. Securities theft.
3. Coffey, Joseph J.   4. Counterfeits and counterfeiting.
5. Mafia.   6. Catholic Church.   Curia Romana—Corrupt
practices.   I. Coffey, Joseph J.   II. Title.
HV6691.H34   364.1'63   82-1044   AACR2
ISBN: 0-03-060146-0

Designer: Joy Chu
Printed in the United States of America
10 9 8 7 6 5 4 3 2

ISBN 0-03-060146-0

FOR BARNA OSTERTAG
AND JOSEPH COFFEY, SR.,
AND PATRICIA COFFEY

"It was without a compeer among swindles.
It was perfect, it was rounded, symmetrical,
complete, colossal."

—Mark Twain,
Life on the Mississippi

C O N T E N T S

• • • • • • • • • • • • • •

A U T H O R ' S   N O T E

. . . .

The events described in this book are true and the characters are real. Except for certain interpretations and conclusions, which are the author's responsibility alone, the story is based on the recollections, files and records of Detective Sergeant Joseph J. Coffey, Jr., commanding officer of the Organized Crime Homicide Task Force and special assistant for organized crime affairs to the Chief of Detectives of the New York City Police Department.

It also relies heavily on wiretaps and electronic surveillance done under court order in the United States and the Federal Republic of Germany, and on reports, files, records and documents of the New York City Police Department, the New York County (Manhattan) District Attorney's Office, the Federal Bureau of Investigation, the United States Department of Justice and its Organized Crime Strike Force in New York and elsewhere in the United States, other government agencies, subcommittees of the United States Congress, Interpol, the Munich Criminal Police and other investigative bodies in the Federal Republic of Germany and elsewhere in Europe, court proceedings, and the recollections and statements of certain of the participants in these events.

Those conversations that have been re-created are either taken directly from transcripts of legal wiretaps and electronic eavesdropping devices or are based on the recollections of one or more of the participants in them.

—R.H.
New York, February 1982

T H E
VATICAN
CONNECTION
. . . .

M U N I C H , M A Y 1 9 7 2

● ● ● ● ● ● ● ● ● ● ● ● ● ●

Matteo de Lorenzo was in a mellow and nostalgic mood. It was late on a warm spring night and he had spent the evening on the town. His aide and traveling companion, Vincent Rizzo, had shown him the sights of Munich and together they had toured the best of the Bavarian capital's night spots, had perhaps eaten a little too much heavy German food, had washed it down with a little too much good liquor. By midnight, back in their suite at the Bayerischer Hof Hotel, they were flushed with the glow of satiety, and with the anticipation of great financial success.

They paused for a nightcap and then went to bed. Despite the fatigue, sleep did not come easily. All that good food and liquor, combined with jet lag, sat heavily on the stomach and frayed the nerves. And, at least for Marty de Lorenzo, there was a trace of homesickness. He was far from his modest house in Bayside, Queens, and at sixty-one, like many men his age, he found it hard to adapt to radical change, had grown accustomed to a regular routine. His normal orbit did not usually include an expensive suite in a deluxe European hotel. A short, somewhat overweight man, looking older than his years, with a round, open and often smiling face, he would have seemed more at home behind the counter in a small neighborhood grocery, surrounded by a dozen grandchildren for whom he would always have had an inexhaustible supply of pennies and candy, and by a group of old cronies with whom he'd be trading an inexhaustible repertoire of tall stories during idle hours.

To pass those hours that night in a strange bed in an unfamiliar city until sleep came, he mused softly into the darkness, talked reflectively across the night table that separated his bed from Rizzo's. He talked about the past, about how things had been in the old days when he had been young and ambitious. It was a monologue, broken now and then by some drowsy comment from Rizzo to indicate that he was still awake and listening.

"It's always been a tough world to make money," de Lorenzo summed up in those final moments before drifting into sleep. "Things has to get better and, you see, we are using our heads. We started using our brains a little. Of course, a lot of people never had the brains to use, so they . . . But some of us . . . There was bootlegging, right. Then from bootlegging, we went into numbers; numbers to horses. But you had to have a brain to go with it. It goes from one thing to the other. Then into shylocking. Then legitimate business. That means it took us a long time to realize that legitimate business is the best thing. When I got into legitimate business, it was stocks."

Marty de Lorenzo was, indeed, into stocks and bonds, and a lot of other things, too. Vincent Rizzo was overseer of many of those de Lorenzo interests. He was the man who had put the portfolio together and was charged with its safekeeping, with making it produce ever-increasing profits. It was a portfolio that might have been the envy of any investor, of even the sharpest Wall Street trader. It was worth close to a billion dollars and it was filled with such choice blue-chip investments as United States Treasury bills, bonds and notes, bonds of the Federal Intermediate Credit Bank and the Federal National Mortgage Association, common stock and bonds in major corporations such as National Aviation Company, Unishops, Inc., General Portland Cement Company, International Business Machines, Beneficial Finance Company, California Computer Corporation, First Union, Inc., Capital Holding Corporation, Coca-Cola Bottling Company of Los Angeles, Occidental Petroleum Corporation, Norton Simon, Inc., Chrysler Corporation, Pan American World Airways, Inc., American Telephone and Telegraph Company, General Electric Corporation and more.

There was just one trouble. De Lorenzo and Rizzo were neither ordinary investors nor sharp speculators. They did not watch the ticker tape, calculating whether to buy or sell or hold on the movements of fractions of a point. They had only a cursory interest in what happened to the price of their shares on the stock markets. Their definition of stock trading and legitimate business was unique to them, could be found in no dictionary unless it was one they wrote themselves. They had not bought their stocks and bonds, notes and bills in the ordinary manner, through brokerage houses or from banks. They had accumulated them from the mail sacks of the United States Postal Service, from private homes, from the vaults of such major banks and brokerage houses as Manufacturers Hanover Trust Company, Bankers Trust Company, Security Pacific Bank, Continental Illinois Trust Company, Blair and Company, Shearson Hammill, Merrill, Lynch, Pierce, Fenner and Smith, and a lot of others, and from the private engravings and printing presses of their friends, allies and employees. They had never paid the going market price for a single share in their portfolio; if they had paid anything at all, it had never been more than a fraction of the market value.

What de Lorenzo and Rizzo were, in fact, were major figures in the world of organized crime—men respected and honored by those at the very top, and held in awe, and no little fear, by those below. They owed their positions not so much to the use of the traditional muscle and force, though they were not afraid to use violence when they thought it necessary (indeed, Rizzo thought it necessary more often than not), but more to the fact that they were prime earners. They had the instinct to smell where the main chances lay and seize them. They knew how to take a dollar and turn it into ten or more, and so enrich themselves and their organization. They had their hands in everything. They were the men who controlled the distribution of stolen and counterfeit American securities throughout the world. And that was what had brought them to Munich that spring night.

De Lorenzo may have looked like everybody's kindly uncle (indeed, he was known as Uncle Marty throughout the syndicate), but there was little softness beneath that surface. He had climbed from the poverty of his native Cerignola in Foggia Province and the slums of New York's Lower East Side, had survived and even thrived during the internecine wars of the 1930s, 1940s and 1950s, to emerge as a *capo* in the crime family once ruled by Charles "Lucky" Luciano and Vito Genovese. If he had not driven for the very top, it was because he knew the perils of the throne; he was satisfied to be a man close to the top, a friend to all, making money for all and so cherished by all.

Twenty years his junior, Vincent Rizzo was smart, shrewd and ruthless. His tensely coiled body seemed put together with steel wires; his pockmarked face looked like the inside of an open can of nails; his cold brown eyes were so terrifying that few could stare into them for more than a moment before cowering and shrinking away. His world was filled with people who had learned to their sorrow that he was a very dangerous person. He was de Lorenzo's man and the word was that he feared no one and was in awe of no one but his patron.

That May night in Munich, waiting for sleep, both de Lorenzo and Rizzo felt safe and secure, convinced that all that lay ahead was more success, greater riches. Their business had been booming, operating with hardly a setback for the last several years. They were certain that there was nothing that could disrupt it.

They did not know that every word they spoke that spring night was being picked up by a microphone planted in the lamp between their beds, was being transmitted to a tape recorder and into the ears of two New York City detectives and several Munich police officers hovering in a room down the hall. They did not have any premonition that a net was beginning to close around them, and around scores of others, some until then considered reputable businessmen, men beyond reproach. They had no idea that the strands of that net were stretching across the world, from New York to Los Angeles to Tokyo to Panama to Buenos Aires to London to Munich to Vienna to Rome. They had no way of knowing that the first strands had been woven seventeen months before by some Playboy bunnies.

Part One

• • • • • • • • • • • • • • •

THE PLAYBOY BUNNIES

1

• • • • • • • • • • • • • •

Christmas Eve, New York, 1970. By the middle of that cold, bleak afternoon, what little remained of the holiday spirit had begun to dissipate in the angry heat rising from the shoving crowds of frantic shoppers filling the stores and sidewalks, among the staggering drunks spilling out of office buildings after a little too much partying, even in the scowls that had replaced the broad smiles of the street-corner Santa Clauses whose ringing bells and loud "ho-ho's" had begun to take on a threatening timbre, demanding that passersby drop something into the pot.

That afternoon there were not many detectives in the offices of District Attorney Frank Hogan's rackets bureau on Leonard Street in downtown Manhattan. Some of the sixty-odd investigators assigned there were on vacation and many more had somehow managed to break away early. The few who straggled back after lunch scratched away at paperwork, one eye fastened on the clock, wishing the hours away until it was time to quit work, go home to the kids, maybe finish trimming the tree and putting out the presents and have a couple of days to forget about work. In that nearly empty office, about the last thing anybody wanted as dusk settled over the city was to see somebody walk in with a problem he wanted solved right away.

So there were inward groans when Assistant District Attorney Gerard Hinckley strode through the door. Just behind him was a man who had the look and the smell of an expensive lawyer, the kind who doesn't show up at the district attorney's office bearing holiday largess, or even season's greetings; the kind who appears only when there is trouble. That he was the bearer of bad tidings was apparent from the look on his face, from the purposeful, tight way he walked. Hinckley and the attorney headed directly for the private office of Inspector Paul Vitrano, the commanding officer of the detectives in the rackets bureau, and disappeared inside, closing the door behind them.

A few minutes later, the door opened, and Vitrano stepped outside. His eyes moved slowly around the room, searching. Nobody wanted to meet that gaze. "Carey," he called. "Montello. Come in here. I want to see you. Now."

Detectives John Carey and Lou Montello looked at each other and sighed, rose slowly from their desks and crossed the room to Vitrano's office, followed him inside. "We've got a little problem," he said. "I want you guys to get on it."

He introduced them to a very disturbed and angry lawyer who wanted action and who wanted it immediately. He represented the Playboy Club on East Fifty-ninth Street in Manhattan. Some tough punks, he said, had been making a lot of trouble and they had to be stopped. Though he had just learned about it, and, of course, had immediately brought the news to the district attorney's office, the hoodlums had appeared at the club a few months before, had forced their way in and, through threats and violence, had been trying to take it over and had come very close to doing just that. They had the club management so terrified that they were able to do just about anything they pleased. Their friends had been named to positions of trust and control. Anytime they walked in, they demanded, and got, free meals and booze. With no interference from the frightened management, they sold marijuana, cocaine and pills right out in the open and operated a flourishing loansharking business at the bar and from a center table. Anyone who tried to interfere, who even voiced a mild complaint, was bullied, threatened and beaten. This open and arrogant display had been enough to drive some customers away.

Even the bunnies were not immune. They were, in fact, special targets. The hoodlums had been supplying them with drugs and pills, had been forcing narcotics on them, turning some of them into users. And they had been pressuring some of the bunnies into becoming high-priced hookers, part of a stable for which they pimped, this despite a rigid club policy against any bunny even dating a customer. A few of the girls had objected and threatened to carry their complaints to the authorities if they weren't left alone. The result had been beatings so severe that the girls had been unable to work for days afterward, and warnings that this was only a sample.

The situation had become so serious that unless something was done immediately, the future of the Playboy Club itself could be placed in jeopardy.

It was not a new story to Carey or Montello, or to anyone in the rackets bureau. They had been hearing numerous tales for years of young toughs loose in the city shaking down nightclubs, restaurants and bars, extorting protection money, taking clandestine control, building stables of expensive prostitutes from among the girls who worked or hung out in those places. For some of the young hoodlums, this seemed a good way to make a reputation, to impress the bosses of the city's Mafia families and so win themselves entrance into the organized crime syndicate. Though essentially a free-lance operation, it was carried out with at least the tacit approval of the syndicate rulers, who, naturally enough, expected a share of the take. It was lucrative, but it was also more than a little dangerous for those who tried it, especially for those who figured they didn't have to cut the bosses in, who thought if nobody knew they were scoring or how much they were scoring, they could pocket the take. A few who had tried had ended up in the trunks of abandoned cars.

Putting their holiday plans aside, Carey and Montello went up to the Playboy Club to see what they might learn. It wasn't much. Most employees wouldn't talk to them. Those who did merely denied that anything out of the ordinary had been going on. The club, they said, was operating just as it always had. The idea of anyone trying to step in and take over was ridiculous. But the bunnies, nearly all of them, were terrified, some so frightened they refused even to talk to any cop. Most of those who agreed to be interviewed insisted, like the others who worked the club, that there was no trouble; nobody had been offering them drugs or pills, nobody had been trying to force them to use narcotics, and, certainly, the idea that anybody had been trying to turn them into prostitutes or call girls was too absurd even to discuss. The bruises that were evident on some? They hadn't come from fists or blackjacks or any weapon; they were the result of easily explained accidents—a fall down a flight of stairs, a stumble on some uneven pavement, something like that.

But there were a couple of bunnies who were angry and upset enough so that their fear receded just a little, far enough so they talked in private and off-the-record. Though they would not name any names and refused to look at mug shots in the police files, they did confirm what the Playboy attorney had said.

If the bunnies, out of that very real fear, would not cooperate, then perhaps something could be learned just by hanging around the Playboy Club at night and pretending to be customers. That was the next course Hinckley and Vitrano decided to follow. Carey and Montello were ordered, and it was an order they accepted without much reluctance, to go up to the club and eat, drink, take in the entertainment—and watch what went on. To give this the air of a party—a group of unattached men out for a good time on the town—a couple of other detectives would get a chance at the fun along with them.

One was Joseph Coffey. In his four years on the rackets bureau squad, he had emerged as one of the stars—a detective whose memory for people, events, dates and linkages was almost photographic, a detective who seemed always to find himself in the right place at the right time, a detective whose hunches seemed to pan out and who had that innate and essential ability to see through bland surfaces to the hidden core. He had already played major roles in several investigations into organized crime, had been instrumental in the investigations of Cuban terrorists and violence by the Black Panthers. At six feet four inches, with curling black hair and rugged Irish good looks, moving with a litheness and grace, he looked more the professional athlete than the cop. Coffey could act the part of a Playboy regular with ease, could probably pass undetected in that circle, and with his memory he might be able to spot, recognize and catalogue any of the hoodlums who showed up.

"Be our guests," the Playboy attorney offered. "Everything is on the house. If you can stop this thing and put those guys where they belong, it will be cheap no matter what it costs us."

"Go on up there," Hinckley said. "Pretend you're having a good time. See what's really going on and if anything happens while you're there, make a summary arrest, on the spot. But the Playboy Club pay the bill? Never. The district attorney's office will pay. Nobody picks up the tab for the men who work for Frank Hogan. He wouldn't stand for it."

"That's ridiculous," the detectives said. "A night at the Playboy Club could cost a small fortune, and if this thing lasts a while, it could cost the office a large fortune. Why not let the club pay the bill? Who's it going to hurt?"

"No way," Hinckley said. "That would be corruption, to let somebody else pay for our men during an investigation. This office will pay the bill no matter what it costs."

One night soon after Christmas, Carey, Montello, Coffey and a couple of other detectives had a little party at the Playboy Club. They ate, they drank, they enjoyed the entertainment and the ambience. And they learned nothing they hadn't known before. When the bill arrived at Leonard Street, it turned out that Hinckley's unbending attitude, his insistence that the rules in Hogan's office were unbreakable, had cost the district attorney more than $400. There was some grumbling, especially since the office was on a meager budget. Still, the office paid and, despite the continuing offers of the Playboy Club to pick up all the costs no matter how high, it continued to pay all during the month-long investigation, though after that initial party, only Carey and Montello enjoyed the club's food and booze on a regular basis.

Although those evenings at the Playboy Club were little more than watchful relaxation for the detectives, they were a welcome break from the office's complex and difficult investigation into racketeering in the city's meat industry. They got to know the bunnies well, though despite that increasing familiarity, the bunnies did not bend enough to offer any help. It hadn't taken more than a few minutes from their initial appearance for the word to spread that the cops were in the place, looking into the rumors and reports, looking for confirmation and evidence, ready to make an arrest at the first sign of trouble. So, whenever the detectives were at the club, the hoods were not, and on those nights when something kept them away, the hoods invariably turned up and the trouble erupted again. It was frustrating. It was a pattern the detectives could see no way of breaking. As long as they were there, everything would be peaceful. The moment they were gone, there was going to be trouble. But there was no way they could be there all the time. The office didn't have enough detectives to handle all the other work. What they needed was a break, perhaps somebody who would not be afraid to open his mouth before a grand jury and at a trial.

It was more than a month before the break finally came. Carey and Montello were off on another job. The toughs put in their appearance and went into their usual act. A group of West Point cadets was having a little celebration in the club that night. The hoods decided the cadets deserved their special attention. There were some sarcastic comments about Boy Scouts. They were ignored. The remarks got rougher, more pointed, more personal until the cadets could no longer ignore them and began to respond. That was what the hoodlums had been waiting for. One of them went after a cadet with his fists, broke a whiskey bottle over the cadet's head and left him on the floor, bleeding and unconscious.

This was not, of course, the first time something of the sort had happened. In the past, though, the battered patrons of the club had decided the best course was to tend to their bruises and stay away from the club rather than risk another confrontation with people who were obviously looking for just that. Indeed that was the cadet's first reaction. But, unlike most customers of the Playboy Club, he was vulnerable because of what he was—a cadet at the United States Military Academy and a future officer of the United States Army. A couple of days after the beating, Carey and Montello heard about it, passed the news to Vitrano and Hinckley. Hinckley made a call to officials at West Point. They called the cadet in, advised him strongly to cooperate with the Manhattan district attorney, ordered him to New York to tell his story and identify his assailant. With obvious reluctance, he obeyed his orders. The man he identified was Donald Viggiano—a small-time punk with a record of minor crimes, a Mafia hanger-on who was out to make an impression that would win him favor with the bosses.

On February 8, 1971, a grand jury handed down an indictment of Viggiano for criminal assault. But Viggiano was nowhere to be found. For about three weeks, the cops looked for him but he showed up in none of his usual hangouts. Then, early in March, on a miserable winter day, Viggiano was spotted. It was early in the evening and someone who recognized him called in to say that he was sitting alone in a car on Mulberry Street in Little Italy. Carey and Montello went out to get him. The car was still parked at the curb, Viggiano still behind the wheel when they arrived. They pulled open the door, told him he was under arrest, and read him his rights.

Joe Coffey looked up from his desk and spotted Carey and Montello as they brought Viggiano into the office. He and several other detectives had been working late, trying to decide whether it was time to venture out into the miserable night for the trip home or wait it out and pray that the rain would begin to taper off. The quiet of the office was broken by the appearance of Viggiano in custody. Coffey and a couple of others rose and wandered over to watch as he was booked, fingerprinted, photographed.

"About your car, Viggiano," Carey said.

"It's not my car," Viggiano said.

"No? Where did you get it?"

"Borrowed it from a friend."

"Yeah? What's the friend's name?"

"Crespino. Philip Crespino. It's his car."

Coffey nudged Carey. "What's with the car?"

"In the back," Carey said. "We found a blackjack, a bunch of credit cards and airline tickets. You know they're hot. Also a little junk." If the car had been Viggiano's, he would have been in serious trouble. That it belonged to somebody else meant he couldn't be touched because of what had been found in it, and neither could the owner.

But the name Crespino touched something in Joe Coffey's memory—a faint notion that he had heard that name before. A quick check of police department files turned up a yellow sheet, but it contained little of importance, only a record of a few minor offenses. Coffey was sure there had to be something more. He made a few phone calls, asked a few questions and a picture of Crespino began to take shape.

He was a tall, hulking man in his early forties, with a perpetual sneer. ("The kind of guy," Coffey would say a long time later, "who when you meet him you want to punch his lights out on first sight.") He was a mechanic for the New York City Transit Authority, taking care of the buses in a garage on Manhattan's Upper East Side. He also took care of a few other things: he ran a shylocking operation for transit workers out of that garage, and had a piece of another in Little Italy, where his swaggering presence was cause for fear and concern among his customers. He seemed to enjoy using his massive fists, sometimes with a club or blackjack in them, on people who were slow in their payments almost as much as he enjoyed collecting his vigorish. He was, the story went, a low-level soldier in good standing in the Genovese family, knew his place, split his take fairly with those in power above him, and carried out whatever strong-arm errands he was assigned.

That Viggiano was using Crespino's car and claiming him as a friend obviously linked the two, and what had been discovered in the back of that car tied them to things of considerably greater moment than a little extortion and assault at the Playboy Club; it tied them to people on a level above them in the syndicate hierarchy. This was a lead that might point somewhere and Coffey wanted to follow it. He went to Inspector Vitrano.

"We have to call this guy Crespino and tell him we've got his car," he said. "Why don't we tell him to come down now and pick it up, and when he gets here, put a tail on him and see what turns up?"

Vitrano considered that for only a moment. "Good idea," he said. "Get on it. Pick a couple of guys and move."

The call was made. The detectives in the office split into teams, went down to the street, got their cars, parked them pointing in different directions around the spot on the street where Crespino's car had been parked, so that when he drove off at least one team would be able to pick him up and follow. Then they waited.

Crespino appeared about an hour later, went up to the district attorney's office, signed the release for his car, got the keys and made his way out of the office toward the elevators. The call went out to the detectives: "He's on his way down."

Crespino appeared, saw his car, got in, sped out into the rain and the blackness of the night, heading north. A block behind, Coffey and his partner, Anthony Saraniero, kept pace. Crespino had no sense that he was being tailed, made no effort to shake his pursuers, drove directly through the rain-slicked streets to the Columbia Civic League Club on Twelfth Street just east of First Avenue. He parked, got out, went into the club. Coffey parked directly across the street. He and Saraniero slumped down, watched and waited.

Within a few minutes, Crespino, wearing the now-soaked three-quarter-length black leather coat he favored, emerged from the club. With him was a man in a white raincoat. The beam from a street-light on the corner caught their faces for that moment, until they moved beyond it, into the shadows. The moment was long enough for Coffey to recognize Crespino's companion. He was Vincent Joseph Rizzo.

Though a known member of the Genovese family, Rizzo was not then considered a man of particular importance or especially high rank. "We knew him," Coffey says, "but we didn't think he was anybody special. He was around a lot. We knew he was a wheeler-dealer. We knew he was a good earner for the mob. We knew he was into a lot of different things, like shylocking, running guns to South America back in 1967, other stuff. But we didn't think he was very high up."

Watching Rizzo and Crespino as they came out of the Columbia Civic League Club, as they stood talking in the rain, Coffey had a sudden intuition that everybody had underrated Rizzo and that they had stumbled onto something of considerable importance. He and others who were investigating organized crime were very familiar with the Columbia Civic League Club. It was not just a standard Mafia hangout; it was one of the few places where members of all five New York families, especially those in the upper echelons, were wont to gather, talk, drink, make their plans in some measure of safety, away from prying ears and eyes. Strangers were not welcome.

Knowing that there was no reason Crespino and Rizzo could not have remained inside where it was dry and comfortable and secure, where they would be among friends and cohorts, Coffey tried to understand why they had decided to go into the freezing rain to have their talk. What was so important, so confidential that they could not talk about it inside?

For ten or fifteen minutes, Rizzo and Crespino stood in the shadows, in that drenching rain, talking intently. The conversation ended abruptly. Rizzo gave some orders to Crespino, then watched as Crespino got back into the car and drove off.

"The hell with Crespino," Coffey said to Saraniero. "Let's sit on Rizzo and see what he does."

Rizzo stood at the curb, watching as Crespino's taillights grew dimmer and then vanished into the darkness. He started back toward the club, stopped, turned and strode diagonally across First Avenue to a drugstore, went inside, and headed for a telephone booth. It was another anomaly. Why would Rizzo go to the drugstore to make a phone call? Why not to the club?

Coffey looked at Saraniero. "Tony," he said, "get over there, go into the next booth, and see what you can pick up. What number he calls, what he says, anything."

Saraniero stepped into the booth next to Rizzo's just as Rizzo was beginning to dial. He had a clear view of Rizzo's back, of the phone, and was able to see the numbers as Rizzo's finger spun the dial. When it was checked out later, the number turned out to be that of the L and S Coffee Shop at 201 Avenue A, only a block away; it turned out, too, that Rizzo owned the coffee shop, owned the entire building as well, and lived there with his wife. Saraniero was able to pick up only a few broken phrases from the conversation: "I'll be over in a little while. . . . No, it doesn't look too bad. . . . Yeah, he was just here. . . ." Then Rizzo hung up, left the phone booth, recrossed First Avenue, went back into the Columbia Civic League Club.

Coffey and Saraniero remained in their car for another half-hour. Rizzo did not reappear. There was nothing more for them to do, so they drove back to the office, checked in, and went home for the night.

The next morning, Coffey went in to see Inspector Vitrano, made his report, and concluded, "I think we ought to get on Rizzo right away."

"Why?" Vitrano asked.

"I've just got a hunch something big is going down."

"What have you got besides a hunch?"

"That's all. But I'm sure of it. I'm sure we ought to sit on Rizzo and see what develops."

Vitrano shook his head. "It's not enough, Joe. We've got too much to do in this office right now and you know it. We can't spare a single man. I think we'll just stand on the Viggiano indictment and let it go at that, get back to work on the meat thing."

Coffey argued. Vitrano would not give. "Forget it," he said. "Let's get on with what we have to do."

2

• • • • • • • • • • • • • • •

Joe Coffey did not forget it. He went back to work on the meat racket as he was ordered, but his hunch that they had underestimated Vincent Rizzo, that Rizzo was into something big, kept eating away at him. Even years later, he was not sure why. He remembered only that an alarm had sounded in his brain; that some basic instinct, the indefinable mark of the good detective, had convinced him that something was wrong, was out of place, in the scene he had witnessed that rainy March night; that he had caught the edge of something it would be perilous to ignore.

If he couldn't forget it, he was determined that nobody else would either. "I made a pest of myself," he says. "Every couple of weeks, I'd go in to see Vitrano and bug him about Rizzo. I was bugging Hogan, too; everyone." And everyone kept telling him, "Not now, the office is too busy, there isn't the manpower to spare to play a hunch." Though he could not convince them then, his persistence made it certain that when the time and the manpower were available, the name Rizzo would not be forgotten.

It may have been inevitable that the paths of Joe Coffey, detective on the rise, and Vincent Rizzo, organization criminal on the rise, would one day cross at a crucial moment, and that crossing would have consequences of unexpected dimensions, would change forever their lives and the lives of many others. From childhood, they had traveled different roads, but those were not diverging roads; they edged ever closer until they met and the two men were joined in a deadly conflict.

If there was a single passion that dominated Joe Coffey's life from the time he was a small boy, it was to play some vital role in the war against organized crime and perhaps win a major victory. Organized crime had been around him all the years of his growing, had been part of his development, and had played an important role in making him what he was.

Joseph Coffey, Sr., was a truck driver, born and raised on New York's Lower East Side. His closest boyhood friend was Eddie McGrath—the man who became during Prohibition the leading Irish mobster in the East, close friend to Meyer Lansky and other rising young syndicate bosses. While McGrath was rising to the top in the underworld, Coffey, possessed of deep religious and moral convictions, tried to make it in the straight world. He faltered only once: jobs were hard to find during Prohibition and about the only work a young truck driver could get was driving a beer truck for the bootlegger Arthur Flegenheimer, better known as Dutch Schultz. The older Coffey hardly considered that a slip—he was no bodyguard and did not carry a gun; he just drove a truck for a wage that certainly did not make him rich. When Prohibition was over, he took his driving skills to the city's department stores—Macy's, Saks Fifth Avenue, Gimbels.

By 1938, when his second child, first son and namesake, Joseph, Jr., was born (there would be two more children, both boys, in the next eight years), he was driving for United Parcel Service, which had taken over deliveries for most of the city's retail stores. He, his wife, Margaret, and the children were living then in a tenement at 569 Third Avenue, between Thirty-seventh and Thirty-eighth streets, in the shadows of the looming, and soon-to-be-doomed, Third Avenue El. But for $28 a month, which was about all the Coffeys could afford, it would have been hard to find anything better than that three-room railroad flat. It was not a bad place in which to grow, for it was a home filled with love and concern, ruled by parents determined above all to guide their children along a moral and religious path. And there were some very real advantages. Most of the neighbors were, like the Coffeys, devout Catholics. And the apartment was only a couple of short blocks west of the UPS garage on East Thirty-eighth Street out of which the elder Coffey drove his truck every morning.

For young Joe, those were good years. "We were poor, only we never knew it," he says. "We always had a roof over our heads and enough to eat on the table, so none of us—my older sister, my two brothers, me—realized that we were poor and always living right on the edge."

There were twin centers to his life, overlapping and meshing— his family and his church. In each he found a hero, someone to influence his thinking and his very existence in the most basic ways.

At home, there was his father. Every evening at dusk, standing on the corner near the apartment house, he watched for him to appear a block away, striding wearily home from the UPS garage. He would run to him, throwing a ball when he was close enough, and they would play together as long as there was light, or sometimes just talk and be together until it was time to go inside.

Around the family table, he listened with fascination to tales of another world and another time—his father's world, beyond his own experience, almost beyond his imagination, where life was hard and not so pleasant or safe as the world in that warm kitchen. There were always friends from his parents' childhood around, and they were men who lived on both sides of the law. Sometimes, McGrath showed up, along with those who had traveled with him. Young Joe's uncle (his mother's brother) was there often with his own stories, and he had many, for he knew and was a friend to everyone; he was the man who supplied theater, fight and ballgame tickets to those in power in the organized underworld. Those evenings and those Sunday afternoons, the air reverberated with tales of adventure and daring, of the perils of existence on the fringes and in the center of the Prohibition wars and the battles that followed repeal when so many were faced with a crucial choice. Listening, watching, young Joe encountered the very men who were the myths of the time; he came to see them not as distant heroes or ogres, but as human beings.

By the early 1940s, Joe Coffey, Sr., was deep into union affairs. The International Brotherhood of Teamsters had chartered Local 804 to organize the drivers at UPS. He was a founding member of that local, a trustee, active in spreading the gospel of solidarity, and instrumental in turning the unorganized drivers into a strong and unified force. Now the men who gathered around the Coffey table were not just the old friends from early days, that mixture of the honest and the shady, but men committed to the union, and the stories they told were about the struggle with management. But something else was creeping in, something frightening and fascinating to a boy of seven or eight: there were new skirmishes, for organized crime was trying to seize the local.

Word of the success in organizing the drivers of Local 804, and the scent of the lucrative potential that lay within the local with its deliveries for the city's retail stores, had not escaped the racketeers. They had already muscled in and taken control of other teamster locals. Now they took aim at Local 804.

It was 1946 and young Joe Coffey was eight, and the moment was approaching that would dictate his future.

There had been many opportunities for the older Coffey to take a turn from his path and throw in with his old friends. There were moments when he was tempted, but those moments passed quickly. "One thing I have to give my father credit for," Joe Coffey says, "is that he never sold out to them. He could have, easily, a dozen times, and maybe if he had he could have put us all on easy street for a while. But, on the other hand, if he had, he could just as easily have been dead and we could have been dead, too. But I don't think he ever thought about selling out for more than maybe ten seconds. It wasn't in him."

In 1946, the temptations were there once more, and the demands that he sell out grew stronger. The underworld wanted Local 804. Increasing pressure and lucrative offers were directed at those who ran the local. One of those most insistent was John "Cockeye" Dunn, sometime boss on the waterfront and a merciless killer who would one day die in the Sing Sing electric chair. He was another of the older Coffey's childhood friends and, if not friendship, at least a certain warmth had lasted between them despite their moral differences. A message was sent to Coffey: "Your old friend, Cockeye Dunn, wants to meet with you to discuss a little union business."

Dunn calculated that the threat would be enough to win compliance. He should have known better from childhood days. The senior Coffey might be a physically unprepossessing man, a bare five foot eight inches and only 125 pounds (in later years, he would stare at his sons with amazement and amusement, wondering how he had managed to sire three men who all towered more than eight inches above him and outweighed him by more than a hundred pounds), but he was a tough Irishman with an unbending code of honor. He sent back a sharp reply. "Tell the son of a bitch I don't want to meet with him. We don't have anything to talk about."

A few evenings later, Coffey and his wife, then pregnant with their fourth and last child, were returning home from a shopping expedition. They had just passed through the glass front doors into the shadowy hallway of the tenement, illuminated by only a single dim bulb in a fixture in the ceiling on the landing, and were on their way up the stairs when a sharp report, followed instantly by a second, destroyed the quiet of that narrow space, and echoed through the stairwell. Coffey felt a sudden gust and a searing heat between his sleeve and his body. Behind him, the glass panes of the door shattered, a spider web of cracks spreading from two overlapping holes in the center. He heard the rapid clatter of feet racing up the stairs from the landing above. Someone had fired two shots at him. He understood immediately that they had been intended to kill, that they had missed and that he and perhaps his wife and unborn child, as well, had been saved, only because of a trick image, an illusion created by the rays of the light and the glass of the door. The light struck that pane in such a way that it always appeared that anyone on the stairs, between the light and the door, was actually standing just inside the door. The shots had struck the center of that image.

The shaken Coffeys rushed into their apartment, closed the door tightly behind them, then sat around the kitchen table trying to understand what had happened and what they could do about it. It was obvious that Dunn had put out a contract on Coffey's life and an assassin had waited on the landing to fill it. That the shots had missed did not mean there would not be a second attempt. Indeed, Coffey knew that there would be and probably very soon. Dunn was out to get him, and now the reasons were doubled: he had not only spurned Dunn's demands for a meeting, and capitulation, but he had become a very real danger to the killer. He had survived an attempt on his life and so he would have to be silenced before he could talk to anyone.

As his parents talked and worried, young Joe Coffey stood near them, listening. He was frightened by what had happened and he was outraged as only a child can be outraged. He wanted to hear that his father would do something, would take some action himself against those people. "But my father was very low-key, philosophical," he says, "and he was inclined to wait and see what happened. My mother, on the other hand, was a real firebrand. She always wanted to do something right away, take some steps. She was never one to wait." From the discussion that evening came the realization that they had only a single hope: an appeal to an old and still-close friend with more power and influence than Dunn. She called Eddie McGrath and told him what had happened. McGrath listened, told her they should take it easy and he would see what he could do.

The Coffeys waited, hoped, prayed, feared and watched their every step. Dunn made no further move. Then the word came back from McGrath. It had been taken care of. The contract had been killed. There was nothing more to worry about.

But Joe Coffey would never forget. From the moment he learned of the attempt on his father's life, of the reasons for the attempt and who had been behind it, Joe knew what he would do with his life. "I was going to be an FBI man," he says. "That's where the action against the Mafia was. At least, that's what I thought then. Those people, they did a number on my father and, as a result, they did a number on the rest of us. I was going to get back at them and going into the FBI was the best way I could think of."

He knew firsthand about the Irish Mafia, from those conversations across the kitchen table, and from the answers to the questions he now began to pose to his father's friends. He began to learn all he could by reading about the Italian Mafia, the Jewish Mafia and the rest of the organized underworld. "I must have read every book ever written about the mob and the FBI and the DA's office. I was pretty impressionable when I was a kid and I believed everything I read. Some of it, though, was pretty accurate, even if it was flamboyant, so I learned a lot about those people and the ways they operated."

If Joe Coffey's home and his admiration for his father was one of the twin centers of those years, the other was the church. And in the church, there was the other hero of Joe Coffey's youth—Fulton J. Sheen.

As devout Catholics, the Coffeys were determined that their children would be trained in the disciplines of their church. When he was six, Joe was enrolled in Saint Agnes Parochial School, an easy six-block walk north of his home. His parents would have it no other way, though they could ill afford it and needed help from a relative to make it possible.

From those first days at school, his education was always under the strict discipline of the church—first the Sisters of Charity at Saint Agnes, then the Jesuits at Xavier High School, a Catholic military academy he attended for three years, then the Marist Brothers at Saint Agnes High School for his final year, and again the Jesuits at Fordham University. He was a good student and a good athlete, flourished under the tutelage of the nuns and the brothers, absorbing lessons from his books and the lessons implicit in that cloistered world. Some he would never forget, reinforcing what he had learned at home: there are things in the world that are inherently good and things that are inherently evil and a man must learn to know them and so be able to choose the right course. And some lessons would take him years to see as fallacies, years and trauma before he could shake them: that priests are not ordinary men; that they have a vocation—they have been chosen by God from among the common herd to perform a mission, to carry the word of God to man; and so priests are without blemish, are not tempted or swayed by the passions and desires of ordinary men.

No single man exemplified more that sense of priestliness to the young Joe Coffey than Fulton J. Sheen. Coffey was thirteen when he met Sheen for the first time. He had been an altar boy at Saint Agnes Church since he was seven, had assisted visiting priests in their tasks, had served them mass every morning at one of the side altars before going on to school. Sheen, then a monsignor and making a mark as a writer, philosopher and vocal church advocate and proselytizer, had been relieved from the usual parish assignments to carry on his other work, and he used Saint Agnes as the church where he said his daily mass. Young Coffey was assigned to assist him and soon the monsignor and the boy became close, Sheen requesting his services for those daily rituals. When Sheen was named to head the Society for the Propagation of the Faith in late 1951, and so moved into the society's headquarters on East Thirty-ninth Street, he asked Coffey if he would be willing to come to the office every morning as his personal altar boy and serve him mass at his private altar there. For the next eighteen months, Coffey did just that, and after every mass, Monsignor Sheen forced a five-dollar bill into his hands.

"I would have to say he was the finest man I ever met in my life," Coffey says even now. "He was a fabulous man, a truly holy man. I mean, he wasn't a phony. He was truly dedicated to what he believed in. He's probably the only priest I ever met in all my years that I can say that about. Sheen was everything a priest was supposed to be. You could talk to him. You could go to him if you had a problem and he would try his damndest to help you out. He was a man full of wisdom. You'd leave after you spoke to him and you'd say, 'This guy is dynamite.' You'd feel good when you left him."

With the influence of home and father on the one hand, and church and Sheen on the other, Coffey had both the determination and the impetus to move hard toward the goals he had set for himself, to do the things in school and out that were necessary to attain them.

When he went to Fordham after graduation from high school, it was as a prelaw student; he knew that to be an FBI agent, he would need a degree in either law or accounting, and since he wanted to be in the field, where the action was, he was sure law was the better route. But he kept that ultimate ambition to himself. He knew well enough that his father, from bitter experience in childhood and in union affairs, had little affection for either the police or the FBI. Joe explained only that it was his desire to be a lawyer, which was fine with his father, who was certain he could steer him into labor law.

The dream of the law and the FBI died within a year, a victim, ironically, of organized crime. A Senate subcommittee, under John McClellan of Arkansas, with Robert F. Kennedy as chief counsel, was deep into public hearings on labor racketeering and corruption and the links between the labor movement and organized crime. The main target was the Teamsters Union, and particularly its strongman, James R. Hoffa. The senior Coffey and other officers of Local 804 were subpoenaed to testify about their battle against underworld infiltration. But the night before they were to appear, the local's president and one of Coffey's closest friends, Leonard Geiger, was found dead behind the wheel of his car. The official diagnosis was a heart attack. The appearances of Coffey and the other officers were initially postponed and then canceled.

The death of Geiger spurred newer and younger men to move to seize control of the local. The elder Coffey had been in too many battles to relish another, especially one that might tear his local apart. He abandoned the union office with its comfortable salary and benefits, and went back to driving a truck, at reduced pay.

Without the financial support of his father and, indeed, with the family now needing help from him, Joe Coffey dropped out of Fordham. If the FBI was, then, beyond reach, still he did not abandon the idea that somehow, someday, he would find a way to the battlefront. Until then, he would do what he had to do. He became a mailroom clerk at Western Electric and was quickly advanced into the data processing department, becoming an expert computer programmer.

And, at Western Electric, he met and fell in love with Patricia Flynn. "She didn't want the best part of me at first," he remembers. "She thought I was just a wise kid because I was two years younger." She ignored his advances, even laughed at them, until a year later, on Saint Patrick's Day, they happened to be at the same party and started talking. "It was one of those things. Something clicked and pretty soon we were talking about marriage. But we were pretty practical kids in those days. I had the service hanging over my head and we decided that there was no way we would get married until I got that out of the way."

He pushed up his draft, went into the army in September 1957, when he was nineteen, did his two years, most of it in Germany. It was, except for missing Pat, not a bad time. Since he'd been an outstanding athlete in school, the army tapped him not for his abilities with computers and electronics, but for his talents on the football field and basketball court. And he played hard enough and well enough for service teams in Germany to gain some notice; when his two years were up, he was offered football scholarships to a couple of colleges and an appointment to the United States Military Academy at West Point. "Because I was in love and wanted to get married, I didn't go anywhere but home. I turned them all down. Maybe if I'd gone to West Point, my life would have been different. But I haven't really got many regrets, not the way things turned out."

A civilian once more, he was back at Western Electric, back programming computers, and early in 1960, he and Pat Flynn were married. By the time their first child, Kathleen, was born a year later, he was doing well—he'd been promoted to systems analyst, was setting up and directing computer flows, had been transferred to the Western Electric operation in Yonkers, in Westchester County, and was earning $12,000 a year, which was very good pay, indeed, in the early 1960s.

But the old dream to fight the syndicate would not die. It was, he was sure, the thing he really wanted to do, the thing he had been born to do. A few months after Kathleen was born, he took the examination for the New York City Police Department, passed high on the list, and was offered an appointment. "I wanted it. But at the same time, I had a wife and a child and responsibilities and I was earning a fairly good living at Western Electric, about twice what I'd be making if I became a cop. I thought about it and I figured I couldn't do that to my family. I had to turn it down."

Fifteen months later, the police department summoned him again, offered him that appointment a second time. Again he thought about it and again came to the same reluctant conclusion. "I thought it just wasn't in the cards for me, so I said no."

He thought then that the dream was dead and he would have to settle for what he had. But early in September 1964, the offer was extended a third time. "Now I was really up against the wall. There was a rule in the police department that if you turned them down three times, that was it. Three nos and you were out for good. So, this was my last shot. I had to make up my mind whether I was going into the police department and maybe get a chance to do what I always wanted to do through them, or just forget the whole dream and spend my life with the computers at Western Electric or some other place."

He and Pat talked about it, thought about it, explored it from every angle. "We made a decision. Not me. Both of us. She told me, 'Joe, money isn't going to do that much for us if you're miserable with what you're doing. You have to do the thing you believe in. If being a cop is what you have to do, then you'll be a cop. Maybe someday, if we're lucky, the salaries in the police department will get up to the level of private industry. But even if they don't, we'll make out some way.' "

So Joe Coffey quit Western Electric and on October 2, 1964, became a New York City cop. The luck that would mark his years on the force began almost immediately. He was part of a class of 150 new cops, the first class to be trained at a newly opened Police Academy. The department decided that this class would be a model one, its members those who had scored highest on the department's entrance examinations and had the highest IQs of all potential new officers. For the next twenty years the bureaucracy would follow them to see what effect, if any, high intelligence has on a man's performance as a cop. In that stellar class, Joe Coffey was one of the brightest stars. He ranked near the top in marksmanship (though through his police career, he would never fire his gun at anyone), physical ability, investigative aptitude. And, at the end of the four months of training, he shared the award for highest academic achievement.

Now his real career as a cop began, and his luck continued to hold. He was assigned exactly where he wanted to go—the department's elite unit, the Tactical Patrol Force. The TPF was sent into high-crime areas, or anyplace where there was trouble that had to be handled quickly, firmly and with dispatch. "I wanted the TPF and I got it. And the reason I wanted the TPF was because I wanted to be a detective and that was the best road into the detective bureau. And not only did I want to be a detective, I knew exactly where I wanted to go: the Manhattan district attorney's office. Because, in my estimation, working for Frank Hogan was the epitome of working against organized crime. Now, it's not easy to get into the detective division. You have to work, you have to get your ass out there and make quality arrests, not garbage arrests like a two-dollar street-corner junkie or that kind of stuff, but quality arrests. And since the TPF worked Harlem and Bedford-Stuyvesant and other high-crime neighborhoods, we were bound to get quality collars." He was with the TPF for a year and four months, racking up hundreds of quality arrests—for homicides, possession of guns, dealing in heavy narcotics, other major felonies. That record did not escape the attention of his superiors.

In January 1966, John V. Lindsay was inaugurated as mayor of the city of New York. One of his first acts was to appoint Howard Leary of Philadelphia as the new police commissioner. One of Leary's first acts was to name Sanford D. Garelik, who had been assistant chief inspector, as chief inspector, the highest ranking uniformed officer in the department. And Garelik had a particular affection for the Tactical Patrol Force and its members. He considered them the pride of the department, men with courage and intelligence whose performance every cop should emulate. Garelik determined to spread some of those men around, into sensitive areas where they would show just how good they were and perhaps in so doing prod others into excellence. He ordered the commanding officer of the TPF to take 150 of his patrolmen—those with the best arrest records and the greatest potential—and make them detectives and assign them to various parts of the detective division.

"I was one of the guys they chose. And they gave us three choices of where we wanted to go in the division—narcotics, homicide, the rest. We were supposed to list them in order of preference. I wrote down the Manhattan district attorney's squad three times, period."

But the detective squad in Frank Hogan's office was small, elite and a closed shop. It had a reputation in and out of the police department for excellence and incorruptibility, for doggedness in pursuit of evidence and for results. Many chose it but few were chosen. The word in the department was that unless a cop had a rabbi, somebody to speak and vouch for him, he had no chance of being admitted into that tight circle of sixty detectives. As far as Coffey was aware, he knew nobody in Hogan's office, had nobody to put in that good word for him. Yet that was his choice and he was convinced that somehow he would manage to make it work.

He waited for an answer, and while he waited, he went about his usual business with the TPF. One afternoon, he was summoned to Leonard Street—not to Hogan's office but to appear before a grand jury, which was on the same floor, to testify about an arrest he had recently made. As he was leaving the grand-jury room, one of Hogan's veteran detectives was just leaving the office of the rackets bureau. Coffey stared and the detective stared back. They recognized one another after only a moment. "His name was Henry Cronin and I'd known him since I was a little kid. We used to spend a couple of weeks every summer out at Rockaway Beach and so did he, and he became a friend of my family."

They greeted each other warmly. Cronin asked, "Joe, how are you? How are things going? What are you doing down here?"

Coffey explained.

"Where are you working now?" Cronin asked.

"I'm in the TPF," Coffey said. "But you've probably heard, Garelik's transferring a bunch of us to the detective division."

"That's great," Cronin said. "Why don't you come to work here, then?"

"Henry," Coffey said, "that's exactly where I want to come. In fact, the DA's office is the only place I put down on my application."

"Then don't worry about it, Joe," Cronin said. "I'll put in a good word and see what I can do."

The next morning, Cronin called Coffey. He had arranged an interview for the following day with Inspector Paul Vitrano, head of the detective squad. Coffey should get himself into his finest clothes and make sure he was on time.

Coffey showed up in his best mohair suit, groomed as he imagined a Hogan detective would be groomed. Vitrano was impressed with his appearance, but more impressed with Coffey's record, which he had on his desk. "I think you'd fit in," Vitrano said. "Now, do you know anybody who can write a letter recommending you to Mr. Hogan?" Coffey still needed a rabbi.

His father's cousin was Matthew Walsh, and Matty Walsh was the general manager of the Hotel Roosevelt, a favorite watering hole of important politicians. Walsh knew everyone who was anyone, in and out of politics, and while he happened to be very close to New York Republican leaders, like Governor Nelson Rockefeller and New York County GOP boss Vincent Albano, his circle included important businessmen as well. Coffey was sure he could call Matty Walsh and Walsh would come up with one of those prestigious friends who would be willing to write a letter of recommendation that would win a talented and ambitious young cop a place on the district attorney's staff.

He decided not to wait a moment, to call Walsh from the lobby of the Leonard Street building as soon as he left Vitrano's office. Perhaps it was a portent, but on the way down in the elevator he bent over, heard a screeching rip. The seam in the seat of his trousers split. He put one hand behind him, tried to hold the split seam together, shuffled out of the elevator to the nearest phone booth. He made his call, won Walsh's promise of help, then somehow, clutching the seat of his trousers, managed to get to his car without attracting undue attention.

If there was one man Walsh should have stayed away from, it was Vincent Albano. But that was the man Walsh asked to write the letter. One of Frank Hogan's proudest boasts was that he had removed the district attorney's office from politics. He himself was a Tammany Democrat and ran for reelection every four years on the Democratic line, and on several other lines as well, and had even run in 1958 as a Democrat for the United States Senate. But where the district attorney's office was concerned, he said often and firmly, politics had no place. Any politician, Democrat or Republican, who approached Hogan looking for favors was turned away peremptorily, and more than once such requests led Hogan to take a searching look into that politician's affairs.

So, Hogan turned choleric when the letter from Albano reached his desk. He read, "It would be greatly appreciated if you would take Patrolman Joseph J. Coffey, Jr., currently a member of the Tactical Patrol Force, on your staff as a detective. I am certain you will find that his previous performance as a police officer was outstanding and that he will make a major contribution to your work." Hogan fumed. He summoned his chief aide, Alfred Scotti, and showed him the letter. He summoned Vitrano and showed him the letter, too. He ordered them to do something about this patrolman who was trying to use political influence, and Republican political influence at that, to worm his way into the office. He ordered them to conduct a complete investigation of Coffey and if they turned up anything at all, he wanted Coffey arrested, indicted and tried.

When Coffey got back to the TPF headquarters that afternoon, there was a message for him to call Inspector Vitrano. He was sure the inspector was calling to tell him that he had been accepted. But when Vitrano told him Hogan's reaction to the letter and indicated that the letter had just about ended any chance Coffey had of getting that appointment, Coffey paled and immediately rushed down to Leonard Street to try to explain to Vitrano exactly what had happened. "I want you to investigate me, like Mr. Hogan said," Coffey said, "because when you do you'll find out there was nothing behind it. All Albano was doing was a favor for my father's cousin. There wasn't anything political in it at all. In fact, the only reason Matty Walsh asked him to write that letter in the first place was because you said I had to get somebody to put in the good word for me."

Vitrano heard him out. But there was nothing Vitrano could do to smooth things over. Coffey would just have to forget his ambition. Then Sanford Garelik came down on Coffey's side. He heard about the mix-up, about the trouble one of his TPF stars had gotten into, and made a call to Hogan himself. The district attorney was appeased and withdrew his objections. Two weeks later, Coffey took off his uniform, put on a suit and was officially made a detective in the rackets bureau.

Coffey had imagined that joining Hogan's staff would immediately propel him into the war on the syndicate, that he would quickly be in the thick of an investigation into the Mafia. He could not have been more wrong. Rookies on Hogan's staff, especially those rookies who had come aboard with few if any friends (Coffey's only friend was Henry Cronin), got only those dirty, routine jobs that nobody else wanted. Coffey's first assignment was to be a bodyguard to Sidney Slater, an informer who had once been a member of Crazy Joe Gallo's mob, had broken with it and testified against Gallo. He had been under protection since 1961, and the first job given to the new detectives in the rackets bureau was to baby-sit Slater and his wife twenty-four hours a day in their Queens apartment. Working in shifts of twenty-four hours on and twenty-four off, they slept on cots in the foyer of the Slater apartment, accompanied Slater wherever he went—when he walked his Afghan hound, when he drove his car every night a few blocks to pick up a paper. They catered to the desires, whims and needs of the Slaters, made sure nobody got close to them, made sure that, in exchange for Slater's testimony, they remained safe and secure.

It was an assignment that was supposed to last for the first year in the office, and every detective who served that term later said it was the most miserable of jobs. "It took me about ten minutes to develop an extreme dislike for that creep, and his monster dog, Sheik," Coffey says, and he was not alone. There was not a baby-sitter who did not come to detest Slater. In order to make life at least a little bearable, they took what petty revenge they could: invented stories that they knew would terrify him, about contracts put out on his life, about strangers lurking in the neighborhood; planted smoke bombs in his car that exploded with a deafening bang and emitted noxious fumes when he turned on the ignition; came up with a variety of harmless practical jokes that he never found amusing and that kept him on edge. But then, Slater had little affection for his guardians and tormentors, and took his own revenge. He was constantly on the phone to Hogan's office with complaints about anything that didn't suit him, trying to make as much trouble as he could, and, indeed, he managed to get a couple of detectives transferred not just from the assignment but out of the rackets bureau.

Coffey lived in the middle of this turmoil for seven months, from May 1966 until shortly before Christmas. "The whole thing finally blew up," he remembers, "late one night in the middle of December. All that time I was miserable, not just because I really hated that guy, which I did, but because I had come on the squad to investigate organized crime, not be a bullshit bodyguard." Just before midnight every evening, Slater would take his dog and one of his bodyguards, go downstairs, get into his Chrysler Imperial, shove the dog into the backseat and drive into the center of Flushing to buy the morning newspapers. On that particular night, it was Coffey who went with Slater, sitting in the front seat beside him.

"We were coming back along Main Street in Flushing when Sheik saw another monster of a dog in the lobby of a building we were just passing. He went crazy. He started barking, leaping around, trying to get out of the car, trying to jump over the seat onto my head. I thought if I didn't go deaf from all that barking, I'd get killed when he landed on me. That was too much. I grabbed the dog and shoved his snout right against Sidney Slater and I said, 'Here, you rat cocksucker, you keep this fucking dog away from me or I'm going to kill him, and you, too. Got that?' "

The next morning, Inspector Vitrano was on the phone to Coffey. "You're off the bodyguard detail as of right now," he said. "Report back to the office tomorrow morning."

Within days, Coffey was thrust into the center of an investigation of the infiltration of organized crime into the electricians' union. He was where he wanted to be at last, and he immediately showed that it was where he ought to be. His instinct and intuition were instrumental in helping to break that case, and led to several major arrests.

His reputation began to grow. "Over the next couple of years," he says, "I kept getting better and better cases, mostly in organized crime, though I got the Black Panthers and the Cuban bombers, too, and I was lucky because I kept getting good results. One case after another—it was like every case I touched turned to gold. It was just one of those things, like I always seemed to be in the right place at the right time."

And he had what a lot of cops don't have and desperately need: he had a wife who supported him, who believed in him and what he was doing as deeply as he did, who understood the importance of his work and knew that if he were to reach the goals he had set for himself, social life and even family plans had to come second. She had been behind him from the moment he made that decision to become a cop, had worried with him and tried to shore up his confidence during the difficult times when he was uncertain. There were those first weeks as a TPF rookie out of the Police Academy, when he looked for and failed to find his first arrest, returned home more and more depressed, convinced that, as he told her, he was going to be the first cop in the history of the department to go through his twenty years without making a collar. "No matter how many times I told him not to worry, it kept getting worse," she says. "It got so I wanted to go around the corner and hold up the local bank just so he could make that first arrest. And then, of course, he made it."

There had been the first years in Hogan's office when he had waited so anxiously to receive the gold shield that would officially mark him a detective. That shield meant something, and not just the extra pay. There had been times he had made arrests and then, when he couldn't produce the gold, had been laughed at and told he was only a cop pretending to be a detective. But he could go home and talk to Pat about it and know she would understand, that her own rage would exceed his and that would calm him. She would remind him of what he already knew: that the men of Hogan's office were at the bottom of the list when it came to handing out detective shields, the feeling being that working for Hogan was reward enough in itself. And when the shield was finally given in May 1969, if it seemed almost anticlimactic to him, he could take pleasure in her righteous indignation that it had been so long in coming.

Pat Coffey believed in him totally—believed, too, that he could take care of himself. "The kids in our neighborhood," she remembers, "said that while one bullet might stop most cops, it would take at least four to stop Joe, but nobody was ever going to get a chance to get four shots at him." She learned enough about his work, by listening and sharing, not to worry too much when he was working on organized crime cases. He managed to convince her that those in the syndicate, vicious and unprincipled as they might be, nevertheless lived by a code that forbade violence against a cop, and called for actual respect for a cop who was doing his job. She knew that this combat was a game that had to be played by the rules, on both sides.

She did worry when Coffey was assigned to investigate terrorists, for she had come to know that codes, that respect for those on the other side, meant little to them. She never forgot the fears that shook her when he testified against the Black Panthers and as he left the witness stand became a target for vituperation and threats of retribution, as they shouted that he and his whole family would not escape their reach. Though he refused an offer of police protection at home, Pat was able to take some small comfort from the knowledge that for the next weeks cruising patrol cars would keep a constant watch over their house. But she kept her fears to herself. She was determined to do nothing that would communicate those fears to the children.

So, his luck held. At home, there was Pat. And on Leonard Street, he had caught Frank Hogan's eye. At first, it was because of the trouble that had been caused by the letter of recommendation from Albano. Then it was because he could not be overlooked; his very size and Irish good looks and charm made him stand out in any crowd. But, most important, it was because his name kept appearing on reports of the most important cases that passed through the office. Hogan started calling Coffey in for private conferences about those cases, questioned him closely, listened to his recommendations.

And he discovered something else in Coffey that led to the creation of a firm bond between them. Though years younger, Coffey shared much the same background and philosophy. Both were Irish Catholics from poor families. Both believed deeply in their church and its sanctity. Both were committed totally to fighting the war against the syndicate, and to winning that war no matter the odds or the difficulties.

When Coffey, through 1971, talked so vehemently about Vincent Rizzo, about his hunch, Hogan paid attention. If the time ever came when it was possible and practical, he would be of a mind to turn Coffey loose.

3

• • • • • • • • • • • • • • •

Vincent Rizzo's turf was the few blocks of deteriorating tenements, bars and small stores on Avenue A just below Fourteenth Street. But that seedy neighborhood, hemmed in on the north by Stuyvesant Town, Metropolitan Life Insurance Company's monument to the success of privately owned middle-class urban redevelopment, was home ground, as well, for a lot of small-time hoodlums trying to make some kind of reputation and win favor with the Mafia families. Those who noticed him at all considered Rizzo just another one of those hoods. He might be a member of the Genovese family, then ruled by Tommy Eboli and Jerry Catena, but he was obviously, outsiders thought, on a very low level, just another soldier without much power or standing. It was an impression Rizzo had carefully cultivated in the world outside the syndicate. Within the organization, however, he was recognized as an earner, a man on the rise, a man for whom great respect must be shown, a man to fear.

If rumors about Rizzo reached the ears of investigators, they tended to be ignored. After all, Rizzo was not some newcomer sent into the neighborhood by the bosses as their regent, nor was he one of those who had risen through the ranks, amassed wealth and power, moved to a large home on Long Island or in New Jersey and returned only to conduct his business. He had been born on Avenue A in 1931, had been raised there and had never left. If his world was the world of crime, then that surprised nobody, for crime had been the norm of Rizzo's life since the day he was born. His parents had fled the poverty of Italy only to find more and equally grinding poverty in the new world—food and clothes almost luxuries rather than necessities. His father turned to crime when he could make out no other way, and was unsuccessful even at that; for him, the prison gates were swinging doors, and when he wasn't in the small, dingy tenement apartment, everybody knew he was back in prison.

In that environment, Vincent Rizzo learned early that what you got was only what you took, and that to take by force was both necessary and pleasurable. He began before he was six. In kindergarten, he attacked his teacher with his fists and with a baseball bat, was sent to a psychiatrist by the school system. The help didn't take. Until he finally quit school in the tenth grade—and he was given a choice that year, either to leave on his own or be thrown out—there was hardly a time when he was not in some kind of trouble. In that closely knit Italian neighborhood on Avenue A, he earned the reputation as a petty thief and bully, wound up as a young teen-ager in the hands of the police for a minor theft, got a warning and was sent back to his family with the advice that he straighten out or find himself in very serious trouble and in a very unpleasant place. Warnings and advice had no more effect on him than the help offered by the school psychologist.

At sixteen, out of school, he was back on the streets—back at the old trades and getting better at them. But the scrutiny of the cops, who had begun to notice this swaggering neighborhood bully and some of those battered victims who were afraid to talk about him, and the urging of his mother persuaded him that perhaps, at least for a time, he ought to find a job—at least as a cover. Over the next few years, he delivered newspapers, worked as a butcher's apprentice, an auto mechanic, a longshoreman, an unskilled factory hand. He never lasted more than four months at any job. By the time he was nineteen, it really didn't matter; he was making a reputation in the right places as a strong-arm man and thief. But he was still just a punk kid and those who came to know him, who held out promises of the future to him, who encouraged him, laughed when he approached and put him off. He had a lot to learn before they would take him on, he was told, and a lot more to do. Maybe he showed promise, but promise was not enough. He would have to ripen, perform.

A month before his twentieth birthday, the Korean War boiling at a violent heat, demanding more and more men, he enlisted. The idea of engaging in direct action, in being given a license for violence, appealed to him, and since he was certain that the Marines was where the real action was certain to be, he became a Marine.

With an unintentional irony, the Marine Corps sent him, after boot camp at Parris Island, not across the Pacific into the battle he craved, but to stateside duty as a guard at the brig at Camp Lejeune, North Carolina. Giving Vincent Rizzo a rifle or a shotgun and telling him to keep the peace was like sharpening the claws of a lion and then putting him into a cage with a herd of deer and telling him to see that no harm came to them. Rizzo's career as a prison guard lasted only a few months. A prisoner said something to him he didn't like, gave him an argument. Rizzo took his shotgun and beat that prisoner senseless with the butt, nearly killing him. The only reason he hadn't shot, he told Marine Corps superiors, was because the gun jammed when he pulled the trigger.

Relieved from duty and confined to barracks while the corps tried to decide what to do with him, he paused only long enough to collect a few belongings and go over the hill, back to the streets of New York's Lower East Side. Something happened on those streets within days of his return, something serious enough, he said later, though never explaining precisely what, to convince him that the cops would be after him. His mother persuaded him that his only course was to return to the Marines and turn himself in. Six days after departing, he showed up at the gates of Camp Lejeune, was promptly put into the brig, and now was the one under guard instead of doing the guarding.

In the brig, he snarled at his superiors, fought with the guards, refused to obey any orders, tore apart the seclusion cell into which he was confined. The warden had him put under restraint, then moved him to the brig hospital for psychiatric observation. There, he fought with the corpsmen, began to rant and rave that he had been tricked, that everyone was putting a noose around his neck, that everyone in authority was a Communist, part of Stalin's NKVD. And then, when the medical personnel finally managed to calm him, he began telling a doctor that he had invented a secret weapon that would revolutionize close-in combat and proceeded to diagram the weapon—a combination pistol, knife and brass knuckles.

Anyone in the streets who had dealt with him could have told the Marine Corps what now became apparent to psychiatrists: Rizzo was not ideal Marine material. Said one psychiatrist: ". . . he sounded off too much . . . losing his temper often got him into trouble . . . he displayed inappropriateness of his affect in that he laughed in a silly fashion at his transgressions of regulations and social rules." Added another: "This patient is definitely paranoid and psychotic. . . . He has a longtime asocial personality with strong delinquent trends and was definitely a threat to society because of his behavior." Said a third: "He is sullen, surly and almost snarling in his responses. . . . The man was immature, impulsive, motivated solely by a pleasure-pain principle."

He was studied and analyzed and tested, and the tests found that his IQ on the Wechsler-Bellevue Intelligence Scale was a mental defective 58. But long conversations with him convinced the doctors that the IQ score was meaningless. "The patient shows very inadequate judgment and reality testing," they said. "He is confused and disorganized and his reasoning is schizophrenic-like. Much bizarreness of content is noted. Social intelligence is grossly impaired as is the ability to differentiate between essential and unessential details. Projective tests reveal a strong paranoid trend . . . has made a poor social adjustment and has developed into an adult with low sexual drive. . . . Confusion and disorganization predominate. . . . His form and verbalization indicate a much higher IQ than that obtained. . . . His inappropriate affect is better described as 'wise' and there does not seem to be any gross disturbance of his affect in conversation with him."

This "delinquent," this "asocial personality," this "threat to society" was, then, considered not fit to be a Marine. The thing to do with him, it was suggested, was to turn him over to a social-service agency somewhere, anywhere but in Marine jurisdiction, and let them try to deal with him. And so, in September 1952, eleven months after his enlistment, Vincent Rizzo was given a bad-conduct discharge and shipped back to Avenue A.

His adventures as a Marine had toughened and sharpened him. He was no longer a punk kid; he was a driven man, and those in power soon saw it. So did the police. Between 1952, when he returned to New York, and 1967, his name appeared on police records a dozen times, and his yellow sheet ran to several pages. He was arrested for car theft, transportation of stolen bonds in interstate commerce, robbery, possession of guns and, on several occasions, for felonious assault with his feet and fists, with blackjacks and guns.

What apparently escaped any searching notice, though, was the slowly accumulating evidence, some subtle, some not so subtle, that

Vincent Rizzo had gained entrance into a wider and more profitable world, an organized world, and was on his way up. The clues were there had anybody bothered to look for them:

- Despite all those arrests—and in several the evidence against him was overwhelming—he did not spend a single day in prison. In every case but one, the charges against him were dismissed, and in that sole exception, when he was arrested for transporting stolen bonds (a federal offense), he was merely put on probation for five years and his constant violations of that probation were ignored.
- He had found powerful patrons, was often at their side, but his presence in such company, along with the signs of his increasing importance and closeness to those high in the syndicate, was neither recognized nor understood by those on the outside. He had been discovered and his value appreciated by the de Lorenzos—Matteo, the elder statesman, the earner, the man satisfied with his position of safety just beneath the top in the Genovese family; Uncle Marty's nephews, Gerardo "Jerry" de Lorenzo, a man who seemed to turn up everywhere and in everything, and Anthony "Hickey" de Lorenzo; as ruler of the Metropolitan Import Truckmen's Association, Hickey had a near monopoly on hauling air freight, gasoline and food to John F. Kennedy International Airport, and had been spreading his influence nationwide through his close and working friendship with Jimmy Hoffa and other leaders of the Teamsters Union; he had also become instrumental in leading the syndicate into Wall Street, showing the profits that could be made in stolen and counterfeit securities; and he was considered the man most likely to succeed Tommy Eboli as head of the Genovese family until, in 1971, he was sent to prison as the mastermind behind the theft of more than $1 million worth of IBM stock. (Prison did not hold him long, however. A year after going behind the walls, he was given permission to visit his outside dentist, unaccompanied by guards; he was not seen again for several years.)
- Those on the inside were whispering his name as a central figure in a dozen different deals of increasingly larger scope, though somehow the whispers rarely got to the authorities, and even when they did they were dismissed. Rizzo was, it was said,

behind a ring that moved stolen weapons to South America. He was one of the city's major loansharks, supplying money to businessmen, restaurant owners and other big borrowers all over New York, and he employed a crew of strong-arm men to make sure that the payments came in on time. He was dealing in a very large way in the importation and distribution of narcotics, especially cocaine. He was into stolen and counterfeit securities, as well as counterfeit money, and he had outlets all around the world.

· Though he did not dress particularly well and kept his wife in meager circumstances in their apartment at 201 Avenue A, he had become very rich. He owned the building in which he and his wife lived, and owned a country estate in Wurtzboro to which he rarely brought her. He drove a Mercedes, though it was registered in the name of a Philadelphia underling. In suitcases and attaché cases in his Avenue A apartment and on his Wurtzboro estate, he kept hundreds of thousands of dollars in cash, not to be spent except in an emergency. In the syndicate, he was mentioned, though not directly to his face, as a cheapskate, a man forever looking for a bargain, who, as one of his associates later said, squeezed the dollar until the eagle screamed.

What was moving Rizzo ever upward in the syndicate, and what had brought him the favor of the de Lorenzos and won him their patronage, was a golden touch. As the Marine Corps had noticed and commented upon twenty years before, his interest in women was not great; he took them as he needed them and discarded them casually when he was finished, without much passion. (He made no secret of his occasional affairs, and told his wife if she didn't like it, she could move out, but she'd better not expect a penny from him if she did.) Rizzo's passion was stirred by money, and the things that fascinated him most were those things that implied big money—stocks and bonds, loansharking, narcotics. He knew where the best deals were to be found; and he knew how to develop them, it seemed, better than anyone else.

Vincent Rizzo had become a man to know, a man to see, a man to fear. For years, that had been something of a secret from the world outside the syndicate. Now it was to come into the open.

4

• • • • • • • • • • • • •

Another Christmas. After more than a year, the investigation into the meat racket had finally wound down. There had been some good arrests and indictments, and the racket had been set back. But, as the cynics in the district attorney's office knew, as experience had shown only too well, it was a small victory that would not last; before long, the racket would be operating just as broadly as before and one day they would have to go after it again.

With the investigation over, Joe Coffey went on vacation the first two weeks of December—not to play and rest but to moonlight as a truck driver to earn enough extra money to pay a few outstanding bills and maybe be able to buy Pat and their three children some Christmas presents. On the Monday morning he returned to work, Inspector Vitrano called him into his office.

"Have a good vacation, Joe?" he asked.

Coffey shrugged. "Okay. About as good as you could expect, considering."

"You ready to get back to work?"

"Sure."

"Are you still interested in that guy Vincent Rizzo?"

Coffey stared hard at him, leaned forward in anticipation. "What do you think I've been breaking my balls about for the last ten months? Of course, I'm interested in Rizzo. You know it."

"Good. We've been talking about him. We've decided it's time to give it a shot. Go pick yourself a partner and get on him and see where it leads."

Coffey wanted somebody who would share his own enthusiasm, a younger man anxious to make a mark. He approached Larry Mullins and Mullins, who had just come into the rackets bureau, agreed the moment he sensed Coffey's excitement. But, that afternoon, before they could start out, Mullins got a phone call from home. His wife had suffered a miscarriage, had been rushed to the hospital. Mullins looked at Coffey and told him what had happened. "I want to work with you on this thing, Joe," he said. "But, you understand. . . ."

"Sure, Larry," Coffey said.

"Look, Joe," Mullins said, "don't pick anybody else. Just let me make sure my wife's okay, get her out of the hospital and back on her feet, and then you can count on me."

"Sure, Larry," Coffey said. "Whenever you're ready."

"What are you going to do in the meantime?"

"I don't know. Maybe take it solo."

Coffey would wait for Mullins, would until then move after Rizzo on his own. He drove up to the Columbia Civic League Club where he had first had that hunch, parked, and waited for his target to appear. The wait was not long. Rizzo came strolling along the street, walked into the club, remained there an hour, emerged and headed east. Coffey tailed him to the L and S Coffee Shop, knowing now that Rizzo owned it and the whole building, and waited outside while Rizzo went in and talked to several people in a manner that indicated he was giving orders. When Rizzo left, he started north, went not even a block, and entered Jimmy's Lounge, a sleazy bar at 211 Avenue A, between Twelfth and Thirteenth streets.

Coffey continued his lone surveillance over the next several days, past New Year's, 1972, sitting on Rizzo eighteen hours a day. He began to discern a pattern of behavior, to see Rizzo in a new light. Picking up Rizzo outside his apartment house in the morning, he would follow him to the Columbia Civic League Club, the first stop on the day's rounds. There was no way Coffey could follow inside; it was tightly sealed against intruders. But he could sit in his car across the street and watch, make note of the license plates of the Cadillacs and other expensive cars that drove up and parked, make note of those who entered. His notes read like a listing of the hierarchy of all the New York Mafia families. Into the Columbia Civic League Club those winter days went Joseph N. Gallo, Aniello Dellacroce, Vincent "The Chin" Gigante, Phil Tartaglia, Nicholas Frustachi, the regents of the fallen Joseph Colombo, and more— the men who ruled the rackets in New York. From his distant vantage, Coffey watched as they huddled together, and noted that

Rizzo seemed always somewhere near the center. Though he heard none of the words they said, Coffey understood something clearly and without a doubt: Rizzo was no minor Mafia soldier. He was accepted into these rarefied circles as an equal. He was treated with the respect due a man of standing. He was somebody very important, indeed.

Rizzo never stayed at the club long, only long enough to make his presence felt. When he left, he invariably headed for Jimmy's Lounge. The police had not suspected it was a hangout for the organization; but that function came clear to Coffey almost immediately. Rizzo was using it as an office. He was in and out several times during the day and long into the night. He met people there and on the street outside. He made and received a steady stream of telephone calls. And those who frequented Jimmy's Lounge were men Coffey recognized, men on the middle and lower levels of the syndicate. There was Vincent "Popo" Tortora, an important man in the Genovese family, a notorious gambler, loanshark, and dealer in narcotics, with an arrest record dating back to 1943, when he was twenty; despite nearly yearly arrests, he had spent hardly a day in jail. There were soldiers and hangers-on, like Freddy Mayo, Jimmy Heimerle, Tommy LaManna, Pasquale "Patty" Marino, Joe Calgano, Rizzo's brother, George, and more. If there had been any doubts before about Coffey's intuition of Rizzo's importance, they were now dispelled. These men, coming and going, hanging out at Jimmy's Lounge, were into crimes of all kinds, and they were taking orders from Rizzo.

Day after day, long into the night that freezing January, he sat in his car across the street from Jimmy's Lounge, hunched down behind the wheel to make himself inconspicuous, invisible, and watched, saw crimes committed in the open with a nonchalance that said no one cared and no one would intervene to stop them. Hardly a day passed when young Puerto Ricans, blacks, Italians did not appear before Tortora, receive small packages, carry them away. Coffey had been a cop long enough to know exactly what was going on. "Tortora was dealing street-level junk," he says. "There wasn't any question about that. I could have made an arrest right then and there. But I didn't make a move because we were after something else, something a lot bigger, even if we didn't know what, and I wasn't going to tip our hand."

If he could see and chart what was happening in the street and on the sidewalk in front of Jimmy's Lounge, what was going on inside remained a mystery. The bar was open from ten in the morning until four the next morning, every day but Sunday, when it closed early. Inside, there were clandestine meetings, conversations, phone calls. "I had to get in there," Coffey says. "The only way we were ever going to know what was going on was to put an informant in there—and the chances of that at that stage weren't very good, to say the least—or plant a bug or a wiretap on the phones. I wanted to build up enough information so we could go to court and get an order to put the place up. So, even though I was working by myself until Mullins got back, I made up my mind that I'd go undercover, go in and take a look. There was a time when I used to moonlight as a steamfitter to make a little extra money. What I did was to put on those old clothes, like I was still a steamfitter, and start going into the place on a regular basis, about six o'clock, and hang around the bar, drink some beer and see what I could pick up."

Unlike the Columbia Civic League Club, which was out-of-bounds, Jimmy's Lounge was open to outsiders, though why any outsider should have wandered into it and stayed more than a minute was an enigma. It was an Augean stable, filthy and repellant; it had not been painted in years, or even cleaned since the day it opened; the walls, furnishings—everything—was coated with thick layers of dirt, grime and grease, and roaches and vermin played undisturbed games in the litter. Had anyone bothered to complain, the health department could have closed it on a dozen different grounds. Yet it had its customers, and they were not just Rizzo, Tortora and their friends and underlings. Laborers in the neighborhood were wont to drop by after work for a beer or two before going home, and even some of the cops from the local precinct stopped in now and then, some on a regular basis. Thus, Coffey did not appear totally out of place at the bar in his worn, dirty steamfitter's clothes. Still, he was a stranger and no one exactly welcomed him or tried to strike up a conversation. The other patrons, the regulars, moved away, left a space around him at the bar, pretended he was invisible. And that suited him.

The first evening he strolled in, and every evening thereafter, he made sure he found a vacant spot at the bar opposite the telephone, ordered a beer, spent the next couple of hours sipping, watching and listening, though his expression was bland, distant, uninterested. He noticed several things immediately.

Rizzo and Tortora were engaged in a hushed conference at one of the tables. The phone had an Out-of-Order sign on it, but it rang continuously. The barmaids, Loraine and Tootsie, were usually the ones who answered it. The calls were almost always for Rizzo or Tortora, and though Coffey could not hear what the caller said, he heard distinctly Rizzo and Tortora's end of the conversation. They acted as though they had total privacy, as though nobody could possibly be listening in, as though that tall, muscular steamfitter at the bar did not exist. What Coffey heard was enough to add weight to his assurance that his hunch had been right and he was on to something very big.

"Yeah," he heard Rizzo say one evening, "well, you tell that fuckin' ragpicker if he doesn't come up with the dough he's gonna end up with two broken kneecaps. . . . I don't give a damn about his alibis. You tell him I don't make no jokes. I mean it. You tell him, pay up and no more crap or he's got broken legs, busted kneecaps, maybe worse."

Outside, in the street, Coffey had seen narcotics. Now, inside, he was learning about extortion and more. His time drinking beer at the bar in Jimmy's Lounge came to an end, though, the night Rizzo picked up the phone, said, "Yeah, I agree. We got to have a meet. When? Tomorrow. Ponte's. I'll be there. You be there."

Ponte's restaurant was the antithesis of Jimmy's Lounge. Near the piers on Manhattan's Lower West Side, it had a reputation for good and expensive Italian food and a fashionable clientele, was a gathering place for important people from the worlds of business, finance, politics, society and the underworld. If Rizzo was going to meet somebody there, Coffey would tail him and find out who. He would not, of course, go inside; he would wait and observe from the outside. "All he would have needed was to see me, the steamfitter from the bar at Jimmy's, walk in and that would have blown it right there and then," Coffey says. "But I figured I'd pick up something just watching who went in and who came out."

Those who went in, Coffey observed from his car in the cold and the dark near the waterfront, were Phil Tartaglia, a major figure in the Joe Bonanno crime family, Jerry de Lorenzo and several others. About two hours after all had entered, Rizzo came out. With him was

Jerry de Lorenzo. They were talking with considerable animation and intensity. And Coffey was struck by the repetition of what was becoming a very familiar pattern. The discussion was one between equals, or, if one was more equal than the other, it was Rizzo. De Lorenzo was listening with absolute concentration, his attitude one of respect shown only to a man of importance.

Watching that, watching them drive off, Coffey knew that whatever was happening was spreading and growing rapidly, that it had become far too big for a single detective operating alone, or even for two men (Mullins was about ready to join him). The next morning, he was back in the office, closeted with Vitrano and then with Hogan. They listened, agreed it was time to bring more men onto the scene, time to take official notice. An assistant district attorney named Ronald Goldstock was assigned to oversee the case and try the case when it came time to present evidence to a grand jury and go to trial. In addition to Mullins, several other detectives, including Mario Trapani and an older veteran, Fred Casey, joined the investigation. Now Jimmy's Lounge, the Columbia Civic League Club and Ponte's would all be under observation.

Ponte's was to be the province of Coffey and Trapani. They went undercover. Coffey, hanging his steamfitter's clothes back in the closet, put on a good suit and became a teamster lawyer from Chicago, visiting New York on union business. Trapani, a hulking, tough-looking man, put on his good suit and became a teamster official from the same city, hooked up with the Midwest syndicate. They moved in, became regulars at Ponte's. They had only a single concern, and it was a slight one. Rizzo might appear at the restaurant and if he did, he would probably recognize Coffey despite the change of clothes. But Ponte's was not part of Rizzo's normal orbit, so the chances that he might show up again were not great, and if he did, Coffey and Trapani could be warned by the other detectives who were keeping watch on him and so have time to get out before he appeared.

It took a little time and some lavish spending on drinks for the regulars and tips for the help, but soon Coffey and Trapani were accepted. Nobody doubted that they were what they claimed to be. They played their game every evening—sat at the bar, drank, talked to the bartender and others, picked up bits and pieces of information, enough to give them leads in a dozen different directions. They watched and listened as Jerry de Lorenzo, Tartaglia and other Ponte regulars made frequent trips to the nearby phones to conduct business and they heard plenty about extortion, loansharking, stock deals and a lot more.

By the third week, information was pouring in to them without any effort on their part. They had become so familiar, so much a part of the atmosphere that they were being fed confidences. And then Gino Galina walked in. He had once been an assistant district attorney on Hogan's staff. He knew Joe Coffey. He had been defrocked by Hogan—summarily fired when the district attorney discovered that Galina was violating many of his strict rules, was not up to the standards he demanded, had perhaps been corrupted by those he was supposed to be prosecuting. Out of the office, he had gone into private legal practice representing some of the leading New York mobsters and there were rumors that he was something more than just a mob lawyer. (A few years later, Galina was murdered because of his knowledge of and participation in the business of his clients and because of reports that he was prepared to talk about that business to a grand jury.)

Coffey saw him, jabbed an elbow at Trapani. "Mario," he whispered, "we're going to be made."

Galina's face froze when he recognized Coffey. He nodded, just a slight movement of the head. "Hello, Joe," he said softly.

Coffey glared at him, made an obscene gesture.

Galina ignored it, walked down to the end of the bar and motioned to the bartender and several mob figures nearby. They gathered. Galina leaned toward them, whispered, gestured toward Coffey and Trapani. The bar went silent. The group around Galina stared down the bar, tense, poised.

"Now," Coffey says, "Mrs. Coffey didn't raise any stupid kids. Nobody had to put up a neon sign telling us what was going on." He grabbed Trapani's arm. Together they rose from the bar, those glares like knives against their backs. If there was one thing they could find some comfort in it was that they were in Ponte's, with its respectable clientele, and not in Jimmy's Lounge. Still, they did not take their time. They walked directly to the exit and did not feel completely safe until they were in their car and blocks away.

5

• • • • • • • • • • • • • •

*I*t was the beginning of February 1972 and the moment for decision had come. It was time to put aside total reliance on undercover work. The confrontation at Ponte's dictated that. Nobody doubted that an alert had been sounded within the mob to be wary of strangers. Long-distance surveillance had done about all it could. It was time, then, to move a little closer.

The morning after that episode at Ponte's, there was a meeting in the district attorney's office with Goldstock, Vitrano, Mullins, Casey, Trapani, Coffey and the other detectives who had joined the hunt. The investigation had been in progress for five weeks, and in those weeks a lot of hard evidence had been uncovered about a variety of crimes, and hints had emerged about many more. "We've got enough," Goldstock said, "to go to court and get an order to wiretap all those spots—Ponte's, the Columbia Civic League Club, Jimmy's Lounge, the L and S Coffee Shop, Rizzo's apartment. There's just one trouble and you guys know it as well as I do. Money. We don't have enough to tap every location. We've got enough to put up one spot and that's it. So, we've got to make a choice. Where do we go?"

There was near unanimity. It had to be Ponte's. It was a fashionable place. Important leaders of the syndicate gathered there almost every night. They used the phones to conduct their business. If Ponte's were wiretapped, the arguments went, then important information incriminating those at the very top would certainly emerge, and what everybody wanted, of course, was to get to those at the top.

Goldstock and Vitrano went around the room, and one after the other, the detectives chorused, "Ponte's." But, when they reached Coffey, he said, "Jimmy's Lounge. That's the place we ought to put up."

"You're out of your head," somebody said. "Ponte's is the place. It's a natural." There was general agreement.

But Coffey would not give. He argued, explained, insisted. "A lot of people think that if you start in a place like Ponte's, which is a very nice place where the big guys go," he says, and it was the argument he used that day, "you're going to get a Carlo Gambino or a Funzi Tieri, the really important guys, the heavies. But, when you really think about it, you know we aren't going to get them, at least not that way. They're too well insulated. In this business, things don't trickle down. In this business, you have to start at the bottom, you have to start with the shit and hope it flows up."

Coffey was persuasive enough so that by the time he fell silent, Vitrano and Goldstock, at least, were convinced. It would be Jimmy's Lounge. Goldstock would draw up the papers, go into court and ask Judge Harold Birns for authorization to tap the phones in the bar.

The order, granted by Judge Birns, was good for only thirty days, though, and in order to have it extended for another month, evidence of crimes had to be amassed through the wiretap. Nobody had any doubts that such evidence would come over the phones, and that it would be solid enough so there would be no difficulty in winning judicial extensions every thirty days. The only problem was in placing that tap. Mobsters have little compunction about talking on the telephone and make only minimal efforts to disguise what they are talking about—so long as they are convinced that the phones are safe. But they are forever on the alert for any sign that somebody might be listening. Rizzo was a man who took special care to see that his phones remained clean. He paid people to do little but sit in their windows and watch the telephone terminals in the backyards of any building where he frequently made phone calls, paid them to report to him any suspicious movements near those poles, the appearance of strangers, the arrival of telephone men at odd hours. He had technicians who checked the terminals, wires, boxes, every aspect of the telephones on a regular basis, who ripped out anything that looked suspicious. Most important, he had telephone company employees on his payroll so that he could get the word from inside about whether he was being tapped.

A way had to be found to escape that scrutiny. Hogan's people went to the telephone company's security officers, and after a long discussion, they hit on an idea. An unused telephone line on the central frame in the telephone company's main office, a frame that handled all the phones within a fifty-square-block radius that included Jimmy's Lounge, was leased, at a cost of $3,000 a month. The tap was placed on that unused line. Behind the frame, the phones in Jimmy's Lounge were bridged to it. Thus, all calls to and from the bar traveled their normal route to and from the central frame. But, instead of following the normal route in and out of the frame, they were bridged onto the unused line, split into two channels. One sent the calls along their usual route; the other diverted those same calls to the eavesdroppers. Unless someone came across that bridge—and that someone would have to know exactly where to look and what to look for—the tap was undetectable.

The bridge was in place, the phones tapped, the leased line wired into a listening post in an unused room in the basement of one of the buildings in Stuyvesant Town, a block and a half from Jimmy's Lounge. In that dark and dingy basement plant—without windows or adequate ventilation, furnished only with a few cots and some battered chairs and tables the cops brought in, and wired with specially installed electricity to provide both lights and power for the equipment—the tape recorders, monitors and the rest of the electronic gear were set up, manned by a crew of detectives who would sit there eighteen hours a day, all the time that Jimmy's Lounge was open, and even longer if necessary. And there were many times in the months to come when Coffey and other detectives did not leave that basement plant for days on end—sleeping there, eating there, never emerging into the daylight and fresh air.

About noon on February 8, 1972, exactly a year to the day after the grand jury's indictment of Donald Viggiano for assault of a West Point cadet at the Playboy Club, a switch was thrown and the first tape recorders and monitors began to hum. Surrounded by a jungle of wires and cables leading to those machines, Coffey, Trapani and a couple of other detectives waited anxiously for something to happen. Their wait was a short one, and when it was over, there was no worry about getting a judicial extension of the wiretap order.

Somebody named William B. "Billy" Benjamin kept picking up the phone in the bar, dialing numbers in the New York area, and asking urgently, "Is he in? I've got to talk to him." Just who Benjamin was calling he never said, and apparently it wasn't necessary. He never succeeded in reaching his man, and he was finally forced to leave a message: "Tell him Mr. Benjamin called and I'm going back to Philly and I'll call him tonight." By four-thirty that afternoon, Benjamin abandoned his search. Detectives watching the bar saw him leave with Vincent Rizzo.

Those might, of course, have been only innocent calls and the departure in company with Rizzo might have been just a meeting of two casual acquaintances. They might have been, except for who William Benjamin was. A short, fat man from Philadelphia, then sixty-three years old, he was a familiar figure, in name and person, to those who knew the inner workings of the syndicate. Benjamin's criminal record dated back to the 1930s, and his prison record included terms in federal penitentiaries and Sing Sing. He was an accomplished forger, a dealer in stolen and counterfeit securities; he had long worked with the leaders of the organized underworld all over the United States, and there were rumors that he had recently moved into heroin and cocaine. On the files of the Pennsylvania Motor Vehicle Commission, he was listed as the owner of a new Mercedes. He never drove it. The man who drove it was Vincent Rizzo.

If nobody knew who or what Benjamin was seeking with such urgency all the day, there was no doubt what Vincent "Popo" Tortora was up to when he picked up the phone a little while later. He called Freddy Mayo, reached Jimmy Heimerle instead. Heimerle would serve as well, for he and Mayo were sometime partners. Tortora was sending two guys to Florida on a job, he told Heimerle. "I need two things for Miami on Tuesday."

No trouble, Heimerle assured him. The airline tickets would be prepared and delivered in plenty of time. Indeed, there was no reason why Heimerle or Mayo would have any difficulty supplying two airline tickets, or a thousand if they were asked for that many. That was their business, among other things. Heimerle had been arrested two years earlier by Las Vegas police—he was using the alias "James Farrell," and he was carrying a suitcase full of stolen airline tickets, credit cards and traveler's checks; he and Mayo had been picked up a few months later in Queens with another bundle; and in 1971, Heimerle had wholesaled more than 10,000 stolen and counterfeit tickets. It was a big business and a lucrative one, and he and Mayo were the travel agents for Rizzo and a lot of others in the syndicate. The listeners in the Stuyvesant Town plant would hear a lot more about that business in the days, weeks and months to come.

Rizzo returned alone, in time to take a long-distance call.

"Vinnie?" asked the caller.

"Yeah. How are you? I've been waiting for your call."

"I saw the guy."

"You went to L.A., personally?"

"Yeah. No, I sent somebody. He owned up owing you. He admitted owing it to you."

"Yeah," Rizzo said. "He knows he owes it. Twenty-five grand."

"I'll take a trip in with a friend of mine."

"Yeah, you do that."

"Do you want me to lean a little bit?"

"You . . . oh, just so far, you know."

"Yeah. You don't want nothin' physical?"

"No, no," Rizzo said. "A lot of abuse. But that's about it."

"Maybe a little slap job?"

"Well, if he steps out of line. I hadda throw a few, you know."

"Yeah."

"You collect the twenty-five," Rizzo said, "you keep five for your trouble."

"Right."

"You'll let me know?"

"Right. Or you can call me. You got the number?"

"Home or at the salon?"

"At the salon."

"You'd better give me the number again, to make sure."

The number was given, though not with an area code.

"Got it," Rizzo said. "How are things out there otherwise?"

"Great. Hot as hell."

"Just like New York."

There was a laugh. "You gotta come out here."

"One of these days. Right now, I got other things."

"Sure."

"So, you'll take care of that matter?"

"You bet. I'll be in touch."

Standing in the plant next to the monitor, Coffey knew immediately that he was listening to something that went beyond the jurisdiction of the New York district attorney's office. He was hearing a conversation about extortion and assault, and maybe more; the crimes crossed state lines and so were in the federal jurisdiction.

That could be a major break. Though he considered this his personal case, and one he wanted to hold on to until he reached an end, still, the federal government, and particularly the Federal Bureau of Investigation, had the resources and the money that Hogan's office did not. If the FBI could be brought in, then maybe sharing the case, and the glory that might come from it, would be worth the price.

But Coffey did not then know the identities of either the victim or the man Rizzo was contacting to collect what was owed, and he wasn't even certain where the call had originated. Something in what had been said made him think of Las Vegas. Acting on that hunch, he dialed Las Vegas information, asked for the telephone numbers of the beauty salons in all the hotels he could think of—the Sands, the Flamingo, the Sahara, Caesar's Palace and others. He prayed silently while the numbers were recited, his eyes fixed on the pad on which he had scribbled the digits given to Rizzo. He hit a winner. There was a match. The number was that of the Salon di Pompiea at Caesar's Palace. Its owner: Isadore Marion. Coffey had heard that name before.

Forty-year-old "Izzy" Marion was a man of many faces and several careers. Swarthy, muscular, always meticulously groomed and dressed in the latest Hollywood styles, he was a ladies' man, a man who knew what women wanted and how to give it to them. He pampered and curried and catered to them in the beauty salon he owned at Caesar's Palace, which his clients called "Izzy's Place" and where his very expensive personal services were in constant demand. He owned, too, the beauty salon at the Playboy Hotel in Great Gorge, New Jersey, and had made it flourish, its appointment books filled from morning till night despite the exorbitant fees he demanded. His appeal to women was not merely the outgrowth of his expertise with scissors, combs and all the other tools of the beautician. There was something about him, something earthy and sensual and menacing, that appealed to certain types of women, and he was always surrounded by the most beautiful ones. He had been married for a time to the pop singer Connie Francis, but that marriage had come to an end when another side of Marion appeared: he beat her so badly the night before she was scheduled to open at the Copacabana that she had to cancel that appearance. Marion was more than a beautician and more than a lover. He was a tough guy, a strong-arm man, a man with his hands in a multitude of rackets. He was originally from Detroit and was very close to the boss of the Detroit Mafia family, Joe Zerilli.

Coffey took that news and a tape of the Marion-Rizzo conversation back to Goldstock and Vitrano and suggested that they call in the federal people. That was the only way they were going to move in on this particular crime, since Marion was in Las Vegas, his victim in Los Angeles and the New York police on their own would have no way of discovering his identity and so, perhaps, preventing an assault on him, or worse.

Goldstock called Daniel Hollman, then head of the Organized Crime Strike Force for the Department of Justice in the Southern District of New York, and told him something very hot, with federal implications, had come into the hands of Hogan's detectives. They ought to meet to talk about it.

Hollman and his chief assistant, William Aronwald, himself an assistant district attorney in Hogan's office before moving on to the Strike Force, showed up the next day in Goldstock's office and listened while he and Vitrano went over what had been discovered. When they finished, Hollman and Aronwald rose, shook their heads, said it had been a pleasant meeting, but that they were not really interested. They had bigger things to do, more important people to go after than a couple of small-time hoods in New York and Nevada.

So, Hogan's office was still on its own. The Rizzo-Marion extortion lead had to be put to one side and the detectives in the plant had to look for something closer to home that they could deal with. They could only keep watching and waiting and listening to see what happened next.

What happened next was totally unexpected, totally bewildering. Shortly after noon on February 11, three days after the plant went into operation, Rizzo picked up the phone in Jimmy's Lounge and called Lufthansa Airline. "I want to make a reservation on a plane to Munich, Germany, on the twenty-sixth," he said. "That's in two weeks, two weeks tomorrow."

"We do have a flight that day. Flight 409, leaving John F. Kennedy Airport at five forty-five in the evening."

"Yeah, that sounds okay."

"Will that be one-way or round-trip?"

"Round-trip. I want to come back in, like, in a week, like, what would that be—oh, March fourth? You got anything then?"

"Yes, sir. We can confirm you on Flight 408, leaving Munich at eleven in the morning on March fourth."

"Okay. That sounds good."

"Will that be first-class or tourist?"

"You got a package or something? You know, plane, hotel, the whole thing?"

"Yes, sir, we have a package that would give you a week in Munich at the Palace Hotel."

"What kind of hotel is that?"

"It's a new hotel, sir, overlooking the site where the Olympic Games will be held this summer."

"How much is it gonna cost me?"

"Two hundred twenty dollars," the Lufthansa clerk replied. "Would you like me to confirm your reservations now?"

"Yeah, I want to make the reservations now. Name is Rizzo, V."

Rizzo had made his first mistake. It was a major one, but natural to him, born of his cheapness, of his eternal search for a bargain. For, listening to that conversation in the plant, Joe Coffey knew not only that Rizzo was intending to go to Germany, and when he was going and returning, but where he would be staying while in Munich. Coffey rushed back to Leonard Street, into Vitrano's office. "You won't believe this," he said, "but Rizzo's going to Munich, Germany."

Vitrano stared at him. "You know that for sure?"

"He just called Lufthansa, made a reservation, plane, hotel, the whole deal."

"What's he going to Germany for?"

"Inspector," Coffey said, "that's beyond my comprehension. But I can tell you what he's not going for, and that's for the skiing in the Alps. The only skiing that guy's ever done is on the sidewalks of New York, and you can bet he didn't have boards on his feet."

"Agreed. Then, why do you think he's going?"

"That's the trouble. I haven't got the slightest idea. But I'm sure it's got to be something big. Rizzo's not the kind of guy to take a trip like that unless it's really big. And I think we ought to go with him."

Vitrano laughed sarcastically. "You got rocks in your head."

"I'm not kidding," Coffey said. "Look, this investigation has really taken off. Everything we've done so far has paid off good. We tail the guy around and look what we came up with. We've had the tap on Jimmy's for three days and we've made a dozen cases already. Now, all of a sudden, Rizzo's doing something totally unexpected. I don't think we can just drop him and let him run by himself. We've got to go with him."

"Look, Joe," Vitrano said. "As it happens, I agree with you. I think you're absolutely right. But I can tell you right now that the chances of your getting on a plane and flying off to Europe are absolutely zero. First of all, you tell anybody you want to go to Europe to tail Rizzo, they're going to be sure what you really want is to set up a big party, have an all-expenses-paid vacation on Hogan, and chase a few frauleins. Maybe we could get around that. But the main thing is that you're up against department policy, and you know it as well as I do. You know the last time a New York cop went out of the country on an official investigation? In 1909. That was Petrosino. And you know what happened to him. He got knocked off in Sicily. No cop's been sent out of the country since then on an investigation. That's a hard-and-fast rule. No exceptions."

"Maybe," Coffey said, "after more than sixty years it's time somebody changed a few rules, or at least made an exception. Besides, Hogan's not bound by that, and we all know it. If he wants to send somebody, nobody's going to say no."

"Okay, Joe," Vitrano conceded, "I think you're right, and because I think you're right, I'll see what I can do. But I don't want to go in to the boss and tell him you want to go because you've got some kind of wild hunch. We have to give him something solid. Take a little time, do some thinking, see if you can come up with something that will make Hogan go for it."

For the next several hours, Coffey hung around the office, went out a couple of times for coffee, tried to come up with an idea that would not be too farfetched, that would be logical enough so that Hogan would believe it and agree that the time had come to break that ancient police department rule. He pulled out all the reports on Rizzo, went over them, looking through the files for something. And then he found it. "This was the time," he remembers, "when the troubles between the IRA and the Protestants were really blowing up in Northern Ireland, not that they've ever stopped, of course, but the situation was really bad then, people getting killed all over the place, practically a real war going on. Now, I know that Hogan's an Irish Catholic, just like me, and, to put it mildly, he doesn't like what's going on over there. And I know, and we can show it to him, that Rizzo had been a gunrunner, that that had been one of his rackets. So, suddenly, this real bullshit story comes to me and it looks pretty good. We'll tell Hogan that it looks like the reason Rizzo is going to Munich is to make contact with the people at Krupp over there and arrange to buy guns which he's going to ship to the Protestants in Northern Ireland to use against the Catholics. I figure if Hogan's going to buy anything, it'll be something like that."

Coffey went back to Vitrano with the story. Vitrano listened, started to grin, laughed out loud. "That's pretty good, Joe," he said. "It just might work. Anyway, let me give it a shot. I'll go in to see the boss and lay it out for him."

Coffey waited near Vitrano's office with mounting anticipation while Vitrano went in to talk to Hogan. Vitrano reappeared about fifteen minutes later, grinned at Coffey. "He didn't say yes," the inspector said, "but then he didn't say no. He said he'd think about it over the weekend and give us an answer on Monday. You're still in business."

But Monday was a long way off and a lot could happen over the weekend. Coffey knew he could not rush Hogan, that he would have to wait those days, but still he wondered if perhaps his chances might improve, become more solid, if he could enlist additional support to put more pressure on the district attorney. He sought out Frank Rogers, an assistant district attorney, the chief administrator of the office, a man very close to Hogan and someone Coffey had come to know well, and respect. Late that Friday afternoon, he asked Rogers to have a drink with him. Over a couple of martinis, he explained exactly what he wanted to do and why; he told him the story he had invented for Hogan's benefit and the reason for it, and stressed how his intuition had so far been right and there was no reason to think it would turn sour this time. "Now you have the whole thing, Frank," he said. "I would appreciate your help in getting the okay from Hogan."

Rogers nodded slowly. "I think you've got your teeth into something, Joe," he said. "I'll talk to the boss. I'll do whatever I can to help."

Coffey wandered through the weekend edgy, nervous, the waiting pressing in like a restricting garment, making it hard to eat or breathe or sleep. He took offense at even the mildest remark from Pat or the kids, found himself snapping and snarling at them. All he wanted was for Monday to arrive, for Hogan to say yes.

Monday morning, within an hour after they arrived at the office, Coffey skipping an early appearance at the plant for a change, Coffey and Vitrano were summoned by Hogan. The district attorney told them to sit down, stared at them silently, his expression blank, unreadable. "I've thought about it," he said when the waiting became unbearable. "I've come to a decision." He looked from one to the other, leaned forward. "I agree that that man, Rizzo, must be followed to Munich. I agree that we must send someone to find out exactly what he's up to. If he's trying to send arms to Ireland, we have to stop it. But I'm only going to approve sending one man. That's all we can afford. That one man is going to be you, Joe Coffey, nobody else. Joe, we'll give you a thousand dollars to cover all your expenses, and let me tell you, that's more than we can really afford. But let me warn you right now, you'd better come back with results or you can start looking for a job as a nightwatchman."

Coffey floated out of Hogan's office. Since, unlike Rizzo, he would not be traveling on a special package deal, would be paying the full freight all the way, the plane fare alone was going to cost $852 round-trip. That would leave him less than $150 for the hotel and all the rest of his expenses. That didn't bother him at all. "I was so enthusiastic about this that I didn't care if they told me they were only going to give me two hundred dollars. I wanted to go. I had to go."

Part Two

. . . .

*O*PERATION
FRAULEIN

6

• • • • • • • • • • • • •

*R*izzo would leave for Munich on Saturday, February 26, and arrive in Germany on Sunday morning. Hogan's approval of Coffey's pursuit had come on Monday, February 14, and it was Coffey's intention to leave for Munich two days before Rizzo, so he'd have time to set everything in motion in advance. Thus, even working over the weekend, he had fewer than ten days to get his passport, make the arrangements and do the thousand things that had to be done if the trip were to prove as meaningful as he hoped. It was obvious that the one sure way of learning what Rizzo was about was through electronic surveillance. The German laws on wiretapping and bugging, then, had to be researched to find out just what was possible. Coffey reached out to a friend at Interpol, Kenneth Genalis, and after a few days, Genalis sent back news that was both good and bad.

The good: the German eavesdropping laws were nearly identical with the American ones with a single exception. In the United States, a court order could be obtained to wiretap the suspected criminal, but not his intended victim. In Germany, the court could order wiretaps and bugs on both criminal and victim.

The bad: the law had been on the books since the birth of the Federal Republic of Germany in 1949, but it had never been used. The dark shadow of the Hitler years, when no German citizen was safe from the brutal arm of the Gestapo, hung over that law and anything aimed at intruding into a citizen's private affairs. A liberal press maintained a posture as watchdog, prepared to raise the alarm when and if any of those relics of the Hitler years made a reappearance. As a result, the highly sensitive German authorities had allowed the law to languish unused—only words in the book of statutes. Perhaps, Coffey and Vitrano tried to persuade themselves, if a

New York detective arrived with enough strong evidence, the Germans could be brought around to dusting off those books and putting the statutes to work.

But what evidence would be strong enough to win over those suspicious Germans? All that had been turned up so far had related to crimes in the United States. That would have little relevance for authorities in another country. The news that a member of the American Mafia, no matter how highly placed or dangerous, was about to pay a visit to Munich would not be enough. What was needed was something directly connected with the potential commission of a crime on German soil, something solid enough so the Germans could not ignore it and would realize that the only way to confirm and possibly prevent it was through electronic surveillance.

A few days before Coffey's planned departure, the wiretap on Jimmy's Lounge came up with what they needed. Rizzo was on the phone with a swindler named Harry "Heshy" Lebensfeld. He and Rizzo had worked together on a few deals and Lebensfeld owed Rizzo some money. Rizzo said they had to get together to talk about that debt.

Lebensfeld said he couldn't do it right then because he was leaving for Germany within a few days. Maybe when he got back, they could meet and settle things.

Rizzo said they could do it in Germany. He was going to Munich on Saturday himself. As long as Lebensfeld was also going to be there, then they certainly should meet and work things out. The sooner it was done, the better it would be for everyone.

If there was a certain vagueness to the conversation, still it had a menacing undertone. Given Rizzo's reputation, it was possible to read into it that Rizzo was extorting money from Lebensfeld, intended to try to collect it while both were in Munich, and would not hesitate at murdering Lebensfeld if his demands were not satisfied. That, at least, was the imputation Coffey was going to put on it. He would show the transcript of that phone call to his German counterparts, together with a copy of Judge Birns's order so they would know that it had been obtained legally, and then would give them his reading of its meaning. That ought to be enough, he thought, to turn them from their reluctance to use bugs and taps.

The days between Hogan's approval of the mission and Coffey's departure fled too quickly. Coffey rushed through those days convinced there was always something more to do, something that could not be ignored. Was there something he had forgotten to ask Genalis? Was there something essential he had not checked out thoroughly with Vitrano or Goldstock or even Hogan? Should he take sophisticated wiretap and bugging devices with him? He talked about that with Vitrano and Goldstock. They told him to forget it. After all, the Germans were electronics experts. They were certain to have everything he needed and more, and what they had would undoubtedly be better than anything he could find in New York. So, why load himself down with unnecessary impedimenta?

And of course there was the plant in Stuyvesant Town. He was drawn to it, unable to stay away. He was convinced that he had to make sure everything was running smoothly and would continue to do so while he was away. Though he was only another detective, no different in rank from the others assigned to the case, he considered it his personal enterprise. He had originated it, had done the initial work on it alone, had a deep and all-absorbing preoccupation with it. So total was his commitment that almost everyone else had come to agree that this was Coffey's case, that he was the man in charge. Now that he was about to go to Germany, some wag in the district attorney's office had begun to refer to the investigation as "Operation Fraulein," which, it was then said archly, was what Coffey would actually be doing while he was in Munich. The name had been picked up with a certain glee, and within a matter of weeks, Operation Fraulein had become the official code name for the case with all its multiplying ramifications.

Before he realized it, it was time to leave. "My wife and three kids drove me to Kennedy to say good-bye. I'm not ashamed to admit that when they left and I was alone and ready to get on the plane, I was scared shitless. First of all, I was going out on a limb with this thing and my reputation and my career were on the line. And second of all, I'd been told I'd better come back with something or don't come back at all. And third of all, I didn't speak any German, not enough to get along, and I didn't know Munich from Tokyo. And fourth of all, I'm not a big fan of flying. So, all these things combined made me a nervous wreck. I had about five martinis and then I got on the plane, and I was on it for about eleven hours before we got to Munich. I couldn't sleep a wink the whole time. When I finally got there, I was exhausted. No sleep, jet lag, the whole bit. All

I wanted was to go to bed. But there was no way that was going to happen. Rizzo would be coming in two days and there was too much to do before he got there."

When the plane landed, it was noon, Munich time, and the Bavarian police were waiting for him. They greeted him warmly, if a little suspiciously, and drove him straight to the police presidium in the center of the city, where he met with Klaus Peter, the detective assigned to work with him, and other police officials. Coffey had to win them over, convince them to cooperate. They listened without comment or commitment while he went over the documents he had brought with him, explained what he would need from them. It took about an hour for him to discover some other bad news that Genalis had not given him, probably because there was no way Genalis or anybody else could have known about it. The Munich police, Peter told him, were ready to assign sixteen of their detectives to work with him, to keep constant watch over Rizzo from the moment he arrived until he departed. They were ready to give Coffey interpreters, access to their files and records and their personal knowledge, take him around the city and show him whatever he felt he wanted to see. They had arranged for him to have a room two floors above the one they had managed to have assigned to Rizzo, and they had reserved a room two doors away from Rizzo's for use as a command post. They were prepared to give Coffey everything he needed—except one thing. They were not prepared to go along with his desire to wiretap and bug Rizzo's room at the Palace Hotel.

"Over here in the States," Coffey says, "the cops want to tap and bug everything. The minute they get even a hint of something, they want to put a tap on immediately, and then it takes days and weeks to convince the prosecutor and the judge that there's a legitimate reason for going that way. You practically have to argue yourself hoarse before they agree that's the only way to go. Over there, in Germany, it's exactly the opposite. Because they'd never used the wiretap law, they were not very anxious to do it then. In fact, it was about the last thing they wanted to do."

From noon until ten that night, haggard and beyond simple exhaustion, at the end barely able to make sense to himself, Coffey argued, entreated, did everything he could think of to convince the German police that Rizzo's room at the Palace had to be tapped and bugged. He went over all the evidence and all the reasons with Klaus

Peter and his group, went over it again for hours with those on the next level of the police hierarchy. Finally, by evening, he was ushered into the offices of Reinhard Rupprecht, the director of the Munich Police Department's criminal division, second man in the entire department and later that year to be in charge of security at the Olympics (it was he who finally directed the attack against the Arab terrorists who held hostage and murdered the Israeli athletes). Fluent in English, Rupprecht heard Coffey's tale, gradually warmed, finally agreed. The police, he said, would go along.

Coffey's concern now was that if the police had been so reluctant to use the electronic-surveillance law, then the resistance of the prosecutor and the judge would probably be even greater. Before he got the order and got the equipment in place, if he ever did, Rizzo would have come and gone and all would be lost. Escorted by Rupprecht and Peter, Coffey was taken to a meeting with the prosecutor and the judge, and all his fears evaporated. Rupprecht gave them a cursory summary of Coffey's evidence and arguments. Few questions were asked. Within ten minutes, the order was signed. Peter drove Coffey to the Palace, took him up to his room. Coffey collapsed into bed.

In the morning, with twenty-four hours to go before Rizzo's arrival, Coffey got the next piece of bad news. He had the legal order to put an electronic watch on Rizzo's room. But there was no way to do it. The Germans had no equipment. Since they had never before needed any, they had never seen any reason to develop or stock any. Even without sophisticated gear, the wiretap was no trouble. It was only necessary to hook a tape recorder onto the telephone switchboard in the hotel, though anytime anybody in the hotel made a phone call, it would activate the recorder. Still, that was not an unmanageable problem, and Rizzo's incoming and outgoing calls could be recorded.

The bug was a different matter. Captain Rudolph Pecher of the Munich police criminal division came up with a solution. He had contacts within the American Central Intelligence Agency community in Germany. They were sure to have something and, if an immediate meeting could be arranged, perhaps their help could be enlisted. Coffey, Pecher and Peter had lunch that day with several CIA officials at the United States Army's officers' club in Munich. There were some amused grins as Coffey spelled out the bind. The

CIA, the officials said, was willing to step in, would even assign an agent-technician to install and service the bug. And the bug needed plenty of servicing. Coffey saw, as soon as he was given a look at the devices, that what the CIA was using in Germany was nowhere near as advanced or sensitive as the bugs used by the police in New York, bugs Coffey might have brought with him had he been forewarned. The radius of the CIA bugs was limited, which was not a great problem in a hotel room, but, and most important, the bugs worked off batteries with a limited life, batteries that had to be changed every twenty-four hours. That meant that once a day, the CIA technician would have to gain access to Rizzo's room.

When Rizzo arrived at noon on Sunday, February 27, Coffey was waiting for him at the airport with the first of the German surveillance teams that would cling to him throughout his stay. They tailed him to the Palace Hotel, watched as he checked in, as he was assigned to room 354. An hour before, the bug had been planted in the massage unit on the bed in that room. Two rooms away, in room 350, German detectives and interpreters fluent in German, English and Italian waited, hovered over tape recorders and monitors, listening for the first sign.

Rizzo entered his room. Through the monitors came the sounds of movement, of a suitcase being opened and closed, of drawers and closet doors opening and closing. Rizzo picked up the phone, dialed a Munich number, the clicks clattering onto the tape.

"Hallo?"

"Hello, Al? Hello, is this Al? Uh, Fred?"

"Bitte?"

"Oh, I must have dialed the wrong number."

He tried again. This time there was no answer. He called the hotel operator, gave her the number he was trying to reach, asked her to try it for him. There was no answer. But it was a Sunday night and he was calling a business telephone. The number was that of a Swiss company called Interpromotions Corporation. Its director for German affairs, who was in charge of that Munich office, was a man named Alfred Barg.

Rizzo tried another Munich number.

"Hallo?"

"Hello. Could I speak to Ense, please?"

"*Bitte?* There is no Ense."

He recited the number he had dialed.

"*Ja.* That is the number."

"I'm sorry, ma'am. Somebody gave me this number in the United States and they told me to call up and ask for Ense. He's a friend of mine and—"

"There is no Ense here."

"Oh, okay. Thank you. I must have dialed the wrong number."

Two rooms away, the German cops checked the Munich telephone directory, found a Winfried Ense listed whose number was close enough to the one Rizzo had called to assure them that this was the number that he had been trying to reach. A call to the police presidium turned up the information that Winfried Ense was a businessman of uncertain reputation. He had been questioned by the police about his link to the sale in Brussels eighteen months before of a stolen $100,000 United States Treasury certificate. He was also suspected of being deeply involved in spreading stolen stocks and bonds around Europe. Not enough conclusive evidence had been gathered to indict or try him, but there was enough so that his passport had been temporarily revoked.

Rizzo gave up and went to bed. In the morning, he was up by eight-thirty, and went down to the coffee shop for breakfast. That gave the CIA technician plenty of time to get into his room, change the batteries on the bug, check to make certain that everything was operating properly. He was gone by the time Rizzo returned and once more began making telephone calls. He tried, without success, to reach a used-car dealer in Augsburg, an American named Jack Calvelle. Klaus Peter looked at Coffey, smiled knowingly and nodded. Calvelle was the object of an investigation by the German police and Interpol. He was considered an important member of a ring that sold stolen cars at cut rates to American soldiers stationed in Germany.

Rizzo also tried several times to reach Alfred Barg. He was told by a secretary at Interpromotions that Barg was out, would not be back until late in the afternoon. About three that afternoon, Rizzo finally got through.

"Herr Barg, please."

"Just a moment," a secretary said.

"Hallo?"

"Herr Barg?"

"Ja."

"Hello, Fred. Vincent."

"I am sorry," Barg said, and it was apparent that he was not fluent in English, that he had to struggle and speak slowly to come up with the right words. "He has not called me yet," Barg said.

"Okay. I'll call you back later."

An hour later, Rizzo was on the phone with Barg again. "Hello, Fred," he said. "All right, how long are you gonna stay there? How long are you gonna stay in your office?"

"I do not know."

"Well, Fred, you have to stay there 'til we see Ense. Do you understand?"

"Nein," Barg said. "I am not certain."

"Well, you'd better talk to Ense."

"I will talk to him."

"We have to meet."

"I will talk to Ense."

Rizzo hung up, tried then to call a number in Amsterdam, but could not get through. He tried to call Ense but nobody answered. It was starting to get dark when he suddenly strode out of his room, out of the hotel, and got into a cab. He led his German stalkers to Tengstrasse 38, where Interpromotions maintained its German offices. The German surveillance team could do nothing but wait outside, knowing only that Rizzo had taken the elevator to the floor where Interpromotions was located.

Rizzo strode into the office of Interpromotions, shoved his way past a protesting secretary, burst into Barg's private office. "You've been giving me the runaround," he said without preliminaries.

Barg, startled, stared at him without comprehension. "I do not know you."

"You'd better know me," Rizzo said. The way Rizzo said that caused a wave of fear to surge through the German. "I'm the guy who's come to collect the money you owe, three hundred fifty grand. I want it now. No more alibis. I want it. That's why I'm here."

"I do not know you," Barg repeated, struggling. "How can I pay to somebody I do not know?"

"Call Billy Benjamin in Philadelphia," Rizzo said. "Tell him you just saw Vincent Rizzo and Rizzo says you're to pay the money to him. Understand? Benjamin will give you the word. You make that call and then you pay up. I want the dough in my hotel tomorrow morning. Understand?"

"I will call Benjamin," Barg said.

Rizzo turned, stalked out of the office, led the surveillance team back to the hotel. He tried Ense again. No answer. He gave up, went down to dinner, returned to his room and went to bed early.

Though they had no idea yet what was going on, it was apparent to Coffey and the German detectives working with him that something important was soon to happen, that Rizzo was trying to arrange a meeting and it could take place at any time. What they hoped was that when it did it would happen in his room, so they could hear it all.

The CIA technician arrived early on Tuesday morning with his equipment, ready to dart into Rizzo's room and change the batteries in the bug as soon as the American went down for breakfast. Through the bug, they heard the sounds of Rizzo stirring, rising, washing and dressing. He picked up the telephone, asked for room service. "This is room three fifty-four," he said. "I want to order breakfast. What? Oh, orange juice, fried eggs, bacon, toast, coffee. Deliver it as soon as you can."

Coffey looked at the technician, at the German detectives. "Oh, shit," he said.

"That's what you'll get, shit, nothing," the CIA man said, "unless I can get in there pretty soon and change the batteries."

Rizzo did not leave and the sounds coming from the bug began to fade. The waiter arrived, and Rizzo's words to him were less audible. Coffey paced room 350, sweating, growing more agitated, trying to figure some way to lure Rizzo from the room. If something happened in that room and the batteries had not been changed, the whole enterprise would die with the dead bug.

At eleven, the phone in Rizzo's room rang. He picked it up. At least the tap was still working. "Hello," he said.

"This is Ense."

"Where you been? I've been tryin' to reach you for two days."

"I did not know you were coming. Nobody told me you were coming to Germany."

"Yeah, well, I'm here and we gotta meet."

"Yes."

"Now. No more delays. You get Fred and you get over here. Now."

"Yes. I will get him. We will be there at twelve-thirty."

"On the dot?"

"It might be twelve forty-five."

"You just get here. I'll be waiting."

Now it was obvious that something vital was going to happen. A call was made to the police presidium and within minutes the room began to fill with detectives and interpreters. Still, Rizzo did not leave his room, and the sounds from it over the monitor were growing fainter. Unless they could manage to get him out long enough for the technician to get in and change the batteries, they would be locked out, unable to pick up anything when Ense and Barg arrived, never to know what was going on in there. They tried frantically to come up with an idea. Could they stage a fire, an alarm, anything to get Rizzo out? If they did that, maybe he would not return, would hold his meeting somewhere else.

A little after twelve, Rizzo picked up the phone again, called the front desk. "This is Mr. Rizzo in room three fifty-four. I'm expecting two visitors pretty soon. A Mr. Ense and a Mr. Barg. When they show up, will you have me paged? I'll be in the bar. Thanks." The phone went back onto the cradle. Rizzo's door opened and closed. He padded along the carpet toward the elevator.

In room 350, there was no movement, no noise until the sound of the elevator door opening and closing could be heard in the hallway. Then there was a frenzy of activity. One German detective, carrying a walkie-talkie and a stopwatch, raced for the elevator, timed its descent, then stationed himself in the lobby nearby to alert those above the moment Rizzo started to return. They would have, he whispered through the walkie-talkie, exactly twenty seconds from the time Rizzo got onto the elevator.

Carrying his tools, the CIA technician started out the door in the direction of Rizzo's room. He stopped abruptly. The maid was just opening the door to room 354. He stepped back, looked toward Coffey. "What do we do now?"

Coffey looked around desperately. The door to the tiled bathroom was open. If something happened in that bathroom, he suddenly thought, they could call for the maid to clean it up. That would give the technician the necessary time. Coffey picked up a glass, started to drop it, realized it would need more than that. If he dropped the glass, the shards would be in a small area, could be cleaned up quickly. He pulled back his arm, heaved the glass at the tiled wall. It exploded in a thundering echo, spraying fragments all over the bathroom. He rushed to the hall door. "Maid!" he yelled.

The maid appeared in the doorway of Rizzo's room. *"Bitte?"*

"We've had an accident in here," Coffey said. "Could you come in and clean it up?"

"Bitte?" She looked at him blankly. She spoke no English.

One of the German detectives spoke to her. She understood him only a little better. She was from Italy, spoke and understood only Italian. One of the interpreters spoke to her in Italian. She understood, nodded, smiled, grabbed her bucket, broom, scrub brushes, cloths, entered the room, went to the bathroom and began to clean the shattered glass.

As she bent over her work, the CIA technician grabbed his kit, raced into Rizzo's room, unscrewed the cover from the massager, changed the batteries, checked them and the connections, hurried out. It took him less than a minute. "We're back in business," he told Coffey.

The maid finished in the bathroom, smiled at the men in room 350, went back to Rizzo's room, cleaned it, made it up. She was just leaving when the walkie-talkie sputtered to life. Rizzo's two visitors had arrived. The three men had just gotten onto the elevator.

The door to Rizzo's room opened. The switches on the tape recorder and the monitor were flipped on, the reels began to spin. For the next hour and a half, everyone in room 350 was gathered around the recorder and monitor, straining not to miss a word, an intonation, anything.

7

• • • • • • • • • • • • • •

"**Y**ou want somethin' to drink?" Rizzo's voice came through the monitor, clear, distinct. In room 350, there was a deep breath of relief.

"Scotch. I drink Scotch," Barg said.

"Okay. Any particular kind? Chivas okay?" He picked up the phone, called room service. "Send up a bottle of Chivas Regal Scotch—oh, and some ice and water. This is room three fifty-four." There was silence, broken by the sound of bodies moving, shifting, weight settling into chairs. "Now—" Rizzo began.

"I have to tell you," Ense interrupted hurriedly. "But tell me first, what is this Benjamin thing? What has transpired?"

"He had a little problem," Rizzo said. "So, what happened, Ricky had to go to Philadelphia 'cause his brother was sick. And they let him out. They made him call up Maurice while I was there. And he told Maurice, 'Release the money to Benjamin.' The two hundred thousand and the hundred and fifty thousand that he had comin'."

(Two rooms away, Coffey nodded to himself over the notebook in which he had begun furiously scribbling notes, jotting down the names as they were mentioned. The reference to Benjamin clicked. It had to be William Benjamin, the Philadelphia forger who often worked with Rizzo. And Coffey knew just what Benjamin's problem was. He had been picked up by federal agents in mid-December while carrying a package of stolen securities.)

"Now," Ense said, "you belong to the people which—"

Rizzo cut him off. "No, I got the money comin'."

"I must tell you something," Ense said. "When Ricky was here, we only had to deal with Ricky. And then when Mr. Jacobs, he was ill, he sent his son. And after then came Benjamin. And then at the moment when he came, and Benjamin was here, I got a call from the people over there and they said, 'Well, you don't have anything to discuss with Benjamin.' And I said, 'Benjamin, come here. Listen. They say I don't have anything to discuss with you. You are out of this deal.' 'Okay,' he said, 'well, I got to get back. Please help me. Give me the money I need here.' "

"And you gave him thirty-five hundred marks, somethin' like that," Rizzo said.

"I gave him a little bit more. It doesn't matter," Ense said. "And then he said, 'Okay, but first I come back. I see you soon and you get the news, and you get a letter from me or I come back myself.' "

"He didn't come because he got arrested," Rizzo said. "Ricky came in from California and got him out of jail for three or four or five days, or whatever it was. They had a meeting. I was there. That's when I said we have to resolve this thing. They says, 'Evelyn called up Maurice and says to Maurice not to release any money.' So, Ricky said—"

"I don't know whether you know the whole story from the beginning on," Ense interrupted. "You can't know."

"I know," Rizzo said with an edge. "I'll tell you what I know. We were supposed to get the money October fifteenth, then it's October thirtieth, then in November. He called up Fred twenty, thirty times. Right?"

"Correct," Ense agreed. "Oh, you are right."

"Now," Rizzo said, "I had a friend of mine call up a couple of times. Because he is a partner with me. I tell him, 'Call up and see what it's all about. Maybe he doesn't speak English at all. Maybe the only one that spoke English is Ense.' He says, 'Well, I didn't see Ense.' And I said, 'We'll get together and try to resolve things.' Well, that's all. I gotta come over here, first of all, to get some money; second of all, to make an arrangement. The arrangement that you originally were hoping to make with Jerry, Ricky's son. That was, open an account in Switzerland. Correct?"

"That's right."

"And putting the money . . . I'll do that now."

They were interrupted by a knock at the door. Rizzo opened it. It was the waiter. "Yeah?" Rizzo said. "Oh, put the stuff on the table, right there. Here."

"*Danke.*" The door closed.

The only sound for a moment was of ice and glasses and the

pouring of the Scotch. The sounds would be repeated often over the next ninety minutes. Barg did most of the drinking, Rizzo and Ense only a little.

But Barg was an alcoholic; he said later that he drank so much as a way of finding relief from the migraines he suffered, an affliction that came from the air and the winds that blow down over Munich from the Bavarian Alps.

"Listen," Ense said once the drinks had been passed around, "I tell you the story from the beginning on. The first time, this is—I met Ricky before—"

"I know," Rizzo said. "I was involved in that, too."

"Oh, I see," Ense said, and he sounded a little uncertain, a little surprised. "Well, the first time when I met Benjamin before, in London . . . before we started this deal . . ."

"You mean with Ricky and Tony?"

"Yes. Tony, Ricky, Benjamin, some people else, I don't know them, Maurice and me. The first man I met there was called Dr. Ledl. And this guy was a friend of Ricky."

"Right."

"And he couldn't speak to Ricky because Ricky doesn't speak any German and he doesn't speak any English. And Ricky said to me, 'Please ask him what does he want. What does he want for his friends in Rome?' So, I learned they had a deal in Rome, this deal would be made with his people in the Vatican, and Dr. Ledl said, 'Okay, I need this merchandise.' "

"Yeah. In counterfeit."

Ense kept talking as though he had not heard, as though it was essential that he explain as much as possible before Rizzo stopped him. "And Ricky asked me not one or two or three times, twenty times, 'Ask him again. Is he quite sure that the people in Rome, in the Vatican, his friends, that they want counterfeit?' And Dr. Ledl says, 'They want all I can get. I can only say, yes, that's what they want.' In the meantime, Ricky went away."

(Those words sounded louder than they really were, clearer, more distinct, as they came over the monitor and struck the ears of the listeners. Coffey and the German detectives stared at the monitor in disbelief, stared at each other in shock. Except for the CIA technician, they were all Catholics. Even those who understood no English caught the word *Vatican*, so similar in all languages. "Impossible," somebody whispered. "It can't be true." "Be quiet!" The words, a sharp exclamation, were an order. "We must hear it all." They pressed forward, straining, determined not to miss a syllable. But unlike those detectives, Rizzo seemed to have less than an overwhelming interest in the Vatican and those counterfeits.)

"He lost his appeal," Rizzo said casually. "He had to go in."

"Yes," Ense agreed, "that's what I mean. So, he sent his son and . . ."

"And the son grabbed five thousand dollars from you," Rizzo said. "Am I right?" Something in the way he said that convinced the listening Coffey that he was checking, testing, perhaps both Ense and Ricky's son.

"Much more," Ense said. "Much more."

"I'd like to know how much," Rizzo said. "I know, but I want to know."

Ense and Barg held a whispered conversation in German. Ense said to Rizzo, "He told me, seventy thousand marks."

Rizzo said, "He said the kid got seventy thousand marks?"

(Something registered in Coffey's memory. Seventy thousand deutsche marks was something more than $25,000. That was the amount Rizzo had told Izzy Marion the guy in California owed him.)

Rizzo obviously wanted to pursue that line for the moment. To the relief of the listeners, however, Ense was more anxious to go on with his story of the Vatican and the counterfeits. "This is not the thing we have to discuss," he said. "I must tell you the story, that you know everything from the beginning on."

"I know," Rizzo said, and again it was apparent that he had little desire to hear something he already knew.

But Ense ignored him, rushed on. "Tony, Jerry and Dr. Ledl and Maurice and me and two . . . two other German people. . . . I sent them by car to Rome. I had to pay for everybody, of course. And Dr. Ledl was expecting us in Rome, and from this moment we had only two days. We were waiting in Rome and the only word that Dr. Ledl and his Italian friends . . . They were negotiating and doing something. We couldn't check what they did. And after two weeks, I said, 'Okay, friends, we must go back. I cannot stay any longer here in Rome because the money is finished and we must go back.' And Dr. Ledl said, 'Everything is okay, only a few more days and we get the money.' How? I don't know because I could not attend the deals. I don't know what they did. I have everyone waiting there and Jerry was waiting there and so we went back to Munich. And I think three or four weeks later, Jerry called me from the States and he said to me, 'Ense, we saw in the newspaper, in the *New York Herald-Tribune*, that something happened in Rome with our merchandise.' 'Well,' I said, 'I don't know. Our newspapers, I didn't read something like that.' And he said, 'Well, believe me, it is quite clear that's our merchandise.' In the meantime, Maurice was in Rome. So, I said to Jerry, 'Jerry, Jerry, wait, I'll call you. I must first speak to Maurice. He must know something about this case and I must ask him.' Nothing had happened. I am in contact with those people every day. I am here and everything is okay. So, I said to Jerry, 'Jerry, I can't find out what happened, but they say everything is okay.' Nothing was okay. What he read in the newspaper, that was absolutely right. That was accurate. And they didn't inform us what happened. And then the Italian people, they said, 'Well, we couldn't know that the rules applied.' And then they said, 'Well, the merchandise is lost.' So, I said to Jerry, 'Jerry, I cannot help you. That is a matter of Ricky's and your matter. He is not my friend, Dr. Ledl. I don't know him.' He said, 'Please check everything as far as possible and then call Dr. Ledl. That's all. That's the only thing you can do.' Okay."

(In room 350, that outpouring was heard with total concentration, with fascination, and with a considerable lack of comprehension. There was a thirst for more, a prayer that Ense, and maybe Rizzo, too, would follow this path, would spell out the details slowly so that understanding would finally emerge.)

Without warning, Ense was off in another direction. "The other merchandise which he got," Ense asked, "it was worth nine hundred thousand dollars?" (It took a few moments before anyone realized that the "he" Ense was talking about was not Jerry or Dr. Ledl, but Barg, and that the subject was a totally different deal from the Vatican.)

"Whatever it was," Rizzo said, and his voice was hard, an undertone of menace coloring it, "I only want to make one point clear. I'm not interested in how much merchandise was involved. I'm only interested in the money that's coming to these people. There's two hundred thousand dollars, Ense, coming to these people."

"To which people?" Ense asked.

"To whoever supplied whatever you got," Rizzo said with impatience. "They got to get two hundred thousand dollars, and a hundred and fifty thousand dollars."

"Where do you know this from?"

"Where do I know this from?" Rizzo laughed, but there was no humor in the sound. "From Ricky. Where do I know this from? From Bill. From him. Bill went and asked him, 'Do you owe this money?' And he says, 'Yes.'"

"Wait," Ense said quickly. "You are speaking about the merchandise which was lost in Italy, or only this one?"

"Only this one," Rizzo said. "Yes, only this one. Maurice is a different chapter. You are not responsible for Maurice. Maurice goofed. We'll take care of Maurice ourselves. Our own way. I'm only here for one reason."

From the moment they had walked into that room, Ense had been looking desperately for an opening, something that would permit him to take the play away from Rizzo, launch a counterattack and so put Rizzo on the defensive. He knew why Rizzo was in Munich, to collect $350,000 from him and Barg. If he had had any doubts, the American had made that clear to him, and to the listeners two rooms away, within minutes after the conversation began. He had tried to divert Rizzo with talk about the Vatican, but Rizzo would not be diverted. Now, he tried another ploy. Ricky, he said, had assured him that the $900,000 package of merchandise—and he put a name to that merchandise: Coca-Cola Bottling Company of Los Angeles—"was qualified merchandise." But Ense pressed on: "Are you quite sure? It's very important for me to know."

"That isn't counterfeit?" Rizzo asked. "I will call up when I get back and verify it there." Then his voice hardened, "But what has this got to do with this right now?"

Ense went into a long, rambling and confusing explanation—confusing at least to those listening in, if not to Rizzo—about a friend of Dr. Ledl named Dr. Amato from Milan who had taken possession of the merchandise and then had not paid for it because, he said, it was "bad merchandise." This was causing a lot of trouble for Ense and Maurice, and they couldn't get their money until they were able to tell Dr. Amato "that this merchandise is absolutely okay." Ricky had assured him that the merchandise, the Coca-Cola Bottling, was okay, was qualified, but now Ense was very troubled, especially since another friend, whom Rizzo knew, named Jacques Suesans, from Amsterdam, had also told him, and not two weeks before, that the Coca-Cola was "not okay."

Rizzo dismissed all that, said, "All the stuff I got was good." The only thing he was interested in was getting what he had come for. "We'll arrange something between ourselves," he said, "and put it on paper. Ricky's involved in it, and Bill. I told Ricky whatever I do with Jacques, he gets something out of it. Whatever I do with anybody here that I represent. What I want is this, Ense. I have to check out this situation with Fred. 'Cause I have to bring these people back the money, and an answer, and a commitment. Because there's a lotta money layin' out over there."

Ense did not want to talk about that. He wanted to talk about "the merchandise," whether it was qualified or not, whether they might have to get it back from Dr. Amato, which might cost him about fifty thousand marks.

Rizzo vented a deep sigh, decided to turn to something else for the moment. "May I ask you a question?" he said. "When you cashed that bond. Ricky gave you three?"

"Yes," Ense said. "You mean, the treasury bills?"

"Yes," Rizzo said. "Why couldn't you cash the other two?"

"That was Ricky," Ense explained. "He took the other two back with him."

"How much did you get?" Rizzo asked.

"Me?" Ense said. "Forty thousand. Me, for my part."

"For your part," Rizzo said. "And what did Ricky get? He told me he only got thirty."

Ense emitted a loud laugh. "Oh, very good."

Rizzo was not amused. "What happened to the other money? That's what I wanted to find out. He says that he got beat."

"Well," Ense said, "if he would wait eight, ten days longer, I could have given him all that money, because we were in Brussels, and—"

"When he came back from there," Rizzo said, "I met him in Munich. I met him in the Bayerischer Hof. It was November 1970."

"He made two mistakes," Ense said. "When I was in Brussels together with him, he said, 'Ense, I am in a hurry. I must go.' And so my friend in Brussels gave him a check, a German check. The check he brought back several days later and he said, 'I cannot cash this goddamn check because—' "

"Yeah," Rizzo said, "he wanted to give us the check. I told him to stick it up his ass."

"The check, it was good," Ense insisted.

"I wanted cash," Rizzo said. "I don't care if it's in . . . what's that Jewish money? It's called—"

"Pounds."

"Pounds, yeah. I don't care if it's in pounds. I don't want no check."

"The check," Ense said, "was very good."

"I don't want no check," Rizzo said sharply.

"Well, all right," Ense soothed. "We took the next plane. We went to Frankfurt. He was very worried because it was a lot of money and the banker said to me, 'Please, let us go down into the cellar, there you get the money.' So, I left the lobby of the bank. And Ricky was observing the main floor. He saw me going in, not going out, and then I came out, then I put all the money in the bag and then he took the next plane and went away."

"He went to Munich," Rizzo said, and for some reason, both he and Ense found that amusing, both laughed loudly. Then Rizzo became serious again. "All right, let's get back to . . . what kind of arrangements are we gonna make with this money?"

Ense and Barg spoke briefly in German then, and Ense said to Rizzo, "Is it correct when he asked me, 'What is your position in the deal?' and I said to him—"

"I get all the money," Rizzo said. "All the money I get. Ricky's money. Bill's money. Evelyn's money. I get it all. I had to come and get it, you see. All their money."

"Yes, of course," Ense agreed quickly. "And is it right when I say that you are the man who's supplied the merchandise to the people? Is that not right?"

"No, that's not right," Rizzo said sharply. "I'm just an errand boy, Ense. Whatever my capacity is, it's immaterial. I'll tell you one thing. Anything we talk . . . in other words, this is one subject. Any subject we talk about, you can talk to me about. I know about it."

"You do not object to me when I say, 'That's the boss'? You are not mad at me when I say, 'I will. I am the boss'?"

Rizzo gave a short laugh. "See," he said, "them people . . . the money don't belong to Ricky. The hundred and fifty thousand belonged to him. Well, now we talk about the two hundred thousand. It don't belong to Ricky. It don't belong to Bill, Jerry, Evelyn, Maurice, Jacques, you name 'em. It don't belong. It belongs to the people where the thing came from. And they want their money. Now, I'm the person who's supposed to give them their money. Now, I guaranteed Ricky and Bill and the others, and you guaranteed—"

"Yes, I guaranteed them and—"

"Lemme tell you this. This is important. When I had the conversation with Ricky, I says, 'I'm not interested in your money. I'm interested in this money that you loaned. Because of this particular item.' And I says, 'I'm not gonna go. I'm no collection man for you, to collect your money.' I said, 'You do what the fuck you want with your money. Let your son collect it, your wife, whoever's around.' So, when he called up Maurice, he said, 'Look, do you wanna collect my money? If they got it, you get my money, too.' I says, 'All right, but my money comes first, the two hundred thousand, I gotta get, to pay off whatever I have to pay off, and then after the two hundred thousand, the next hundred and fifty thousand, on the end, that's your money. Then you get your money.' So, then he says, 'All right.' So, I says, 'How much does Fred owe?' And he says, 'Three hundred and fifty grand.' I says, 'Okay.' Then, this was before Bill was here. That's why I got very upset. 'Cause Bill says, 'I met Maurice, Ense and Fred at the Bayerischer Hof and Maurice says he's got no money comin'.' So, I says, 'Bill, why didn't you pick up a chair and break Maurice's head when you know your life is on the stake over there for this money? There's too much involved. How the fuck does this guy get off sayin' you have no money? Go call immediately. Call up Evelyn and let Evelyn get in touch with Ricky because she goes to see him every week. And you stay. You stay in Germany till you resolve it.' The next time he came in, into New York, and he almost got a heart attack because I started hollerin' at him. I says, 'You went there. You've got to resolve this thing.' Billy says, 'Right. Ricky's comin' out. He's comin' out 'cause his brother's sick and he'll be in Philadelphia.' He says, 'I swear, Evelyn didn't call up Maurice. Maurice did this on his own.' I says, 'All right, Maurice did this on his own.' He says, 'Look out for your own welfare. Let's call up Maurice.' So we called up Maurice. I says, 'Leave the money at Benjamin's. The money they have comin' and the money I have comin'. Let Benjamin or his associates collect this money, too.' "

Ense heard it all, and, with a slight tremor in his voice, he tried to turn Rizzo back to the question of whether the Coca-Cola Bottling Company of Los Angeles "is okay or not okay."

"Ense," Rizzo said, "you're off the train of thought I'm talkin' about. I'm talkin' about the money that Fred owes. Fred owes money. He bought some property in Spain or France or somethin'. And the property was gonna be sold for houses. This is the story they tell me. The money was gonna be placed in a bank, see—"

"Stop! Stop!" Ense shouted. "The story is true." He elaborated. As Rizzo knew, Barg was a very important man with a big company whose main offices were in Switzerland. In order to make his position stronger, "he put this merchandise in envelopes and the notary makes a stamp on it, and the check, 'I have checked this. This is okay.' So, nobody could check this merchandise because nobody was interested because nobody would sell this merchandise. It was only security." The merchandise was then put in a bank for safekeeping. Then Ricky and Jerry and Benjamin started demanding money.

"I know. I know all that," Rizzo said. "And Jerry was supposed to go with you or with Fred to Switzerland to open his account."

"Right," Ense agreed.

"But he never did."

"That's right."

"I know all this," Rizzo said. "You tell me, Ense, what has transpired as of now? It's about a year now. What has transpired? The deal that you was gonna do with Jerry, I want you to do with me now."

"Okay, okay, okay," Ense agreed with alacrity. "Now, let me tell you—"

"Let me finish this first," Rizzo said. "I don't expect him to come up with the three hundred and fifty thousand at one time."

"I know, I know, I know."

"It's very improbable. But I want to set up somethin', have some of this money before I go back. Set up an account. This way, I go to these people and they say, 'Vincent, did you do it? Did you set it up? Did you? We're gonna get our money?' I say, 'Yeah, I set it up. Your money's bein' returned.' "

Ense explained Rizzo's demand to Barg in German, telling him, "This is something we must do." He turned back to Rizzo and started through his explanation to Barg. "What I said to Freddie was, now you are only responsible to the people which supplied the merchandise a year ago, and they want to know—"

"They want their money," Rizzo said tersely.

"What price?" Ense asked. "How many marks for you each month that you can say when you go back?"

"The same as he was gonna do with Jerry," Rizzo said. "He says, October fifteenth. He called up. He says somethin' about, 'Do you have the money?' I think it was thirty-five or forty thousand dollars. He says, 'Yeah, I have the money.' Then it came to a hundred and twenty-five thousand. He says, 'Oh, I'll have that much money.' This is what they tell me over there. I don't know, 'cause this is the first time I spoke to him."

Ense spoke in rapid German to Barg, turned back to Rizzo and told him it would not be difficult to open an account into which money would be deposited every month to clear up the debt. Then he returned to an old refrain, insisting that he must know whether the merchandise was good or bad.

Rizzo was running out of patience about that. "Now," he said, "it's immaterial whether it's good or bad. Lemme tell you why. Suppose it isn't good. Whatever you need, I can get you, so what's the difference?"

But Ense was not satisfied with Rizzo's assurance. He continued to worry that point for several minutes. And then suddenly there was something new (and the listeners two rooms away stared at each other in bewilderment, trying to make sense of it, wondering how much more was going to come out before this meeting ended). "Maurice," he said, "gave merchandise to his Italian friends in Milano."

"Sure," Rizzo said. "But he gave them bills of exchange. Remember them? From the nuns and the saints of the Bush and all that."

"Yes, I have heard," Ense said. "This bills of exchange. Wait a minute. Rosario. Rosario. Something like that."

"Right."

"I said to Ricky, 'Ricky, I am a German. I'm not an Italian, but I know the Italians much better than you. You come from the States. Are you so sure that the people in Italy you can trust them? I must tell you something about the Italian people of Europe.'"

"But you can trust Maurice," Rizzo said.

"Absolutely," Ense agreed. "But he is a fool, this Maurice. He is very, very stupid. He makes mistakes a lot in a lot of places, but he is absolutely true and a man you can trust. He is French. But I never trust Italian people. I never trust them."

"What about me?" Rizzo asked softly.

Ense either did not hear that or decided not to pick up on it. "I was there in the wartime," he said. "I was in Italy two years. I know them so good. I speak their language a little bit. I don't like their language, only when they are singing. I don't trust them. I can't stand those people. When they open their mouths, they lie. And they have stories. They are very, very beautiful and very, very nice, but you can never finish a deal on this thing or that. They always look for a way to get you. And they get you."

"Why?" Rizzo asked blandly.

"Because we cannot do it. I mean, you and I are different. You are a stranger. You cannot do anything. And this is what I said to Ricky in London. 'You check and we take our half and bring it to Italy. We don't know what has happened there.' Believe me, I know him. I was in the car of Dr. Ledl. You cannot imagine the situation there. And I saw he's not a doctor, really. He's in prison now."

Rizzo barked a laugh.

"Yes," Ense said, "believe me, in prison. You know that he had only three fingers? He lost three fingers. And in Germany, the people say, 'Well, when you don't trust someone, you cannot give him your hand because you lose your fingers.' You must count your fingers."

"Ense," Rizzo interrupted sharply, "now, I'm serious."

But Ense would not be interrupted. He had started a story and he was intent on finishing it. "You know what he said to me? You cannot give him your hand. You cannot trust him because you'll lose your fingers. And so, Ense, that's me, has no fingers. And I said, 'Well, you must count them before you give your hand.' And now, I think two months ago, in the newspaper—what is it, he kills animals. His profession is a butcher. He makes meat."

"Yeah," Rizzo laughed. "A rabbi."

"Yes?" Ense asked uncertainly.

"A rabbi," Rizzo repeated.

"That is his profession," Ense agreed. "Not a doctor."

"Well," Rizzo said, "a doctor in prison is a rabbi."

"Oh," Ense said. "And this was the man Ricky sent to me. Maurice was in Rome. I was in Rome."

"I was there, too," Rizzo said matter-of-factly.

"Yes?" Ense was startled.

"If you know me," Rizzo said. "I was sitting in the other half of the Excelsior. I was watching all of you."

"Yes?"

"Yeah," Rizzo said, and he laughed. "They told me, 'Do you want to meet him?' I says, 'I don't want to meet him. I just want my money. What do I want to meet anybody for?' You know what I mean, Fred? I don't want to meet anybody. I came over here to get my money and I want to make more money. I mean, we have nothing else in common, just to make money over here."

Something in the way Rizzo said that obviously upset Ense. He searched for something new, asked, "Do you know Tony?"

"Tony? I hear he's a nice guy."

"Very nice. He's a very nice guy. The only thing I'm very sad is that Jerry told you so many lies."

"Jerry," Rizzo said, an edge to his voice, "is a son of a bitch. You know what a son of a bitch is?"

"I know," Ense said.

"That's what he is. And when I saw his father, I told his father that."

"But," Ense said, "Ricky is responsible for—"

"Yeah, he says, 'I'm responsible for my son.' I says, 'All right, your son's out of it. Push him out. If you wanna be responsible for your son, you stay responsible, that's all.'"

"That's right," Ense said. There was a long pause before he finally said, "Okay, what can we do that we must—"

"I'll tell you what we gotta do," Rizzo said. "We gotta make some kind of agreement."

"Yes."

"Between Fred and myself."

Barg apparently understood that, because he suddenly spoke in his hesitant English, "If we could postpone—"

"We'll do it tomorrow," Rizzo said.

"I won't be here," Barg said.

"He has to go to Frankfurt tomorrow," Ense explained. "But tomorrow, after five o'clock, I come to the hotel and we prepare something and when Fred comes back from Frankfurt, then we discuss it between us and we reach an agreement. All right?"

"Yeah."

If they were about to reach an agreement on this old outstanding matter, perhaps, Barg suggested, Rizzo might like to discuss the possibility of doing additional business with them. "It would be very easy to make a deal," Ense interjected, "when we get treasury notes."

"I got 'em," Rizzo said. "Now, I got two kinds. I got the ones that are hot. Then the cold. Take the cold or the ones that are hot. They're cheap, very cheap."

"Yes, but you must know something," Ense said. "When I go to the bank in Germany or in Berlin or in France or in Italy, they do the same thing. They only check whether it is good or not. They look on the list; if it is not there, then it's okay."

"How much can you get rid of?" Rizzo asked.

"Half a million dollars," Ense said. "But not in one piece."

"What's the least you could pay at the beginning?" Rizzo asked. "I don't know what arrangements you had with Ricky, but—"

"We cannot do that to him," Ense protested. "You come and you stay—well, you don't have to stay any longer than eight to ten days, then you get the money. You stay a week, and you take the first money. You take the first."

"What arrangements did you have with Ricky?" Rizzo said. "I mean, those arrangements are one thing. With me, it's another thing. There's the cost of the thing. The original cost of it, the expense of bringin' it over here. And then, how do you want to pay?"

"How much cost to bring it here, or in Brussels?" Ense asked.

"I gave the man twenty-five hundred dollars for bringing it over here," Rizzo said. "He brings it over in fifties. He brings it in one hundreds. He brings it in tens. And I promised him some money. I'd pay all his expenses. And he had five thousand comin'."

"Yes," Ense said.

"Of course, the cost of the thing, the cost will run between twenty-two and twenty-five percent. Right now, we're gettin' thirty percent, which is seventy percent left over."

"I see," Ense said. "That would be one hundred percent. Of course, we get the money. And we have only one partner more in the operation."

"Then you take care of my aunt," Rizzo laughed. "You know what I mean?"

"Certainly, certainly, certainly."

"All right," Rizzo said. "The first one I'll be givin' you will be one hundred twenty days, then ninety days, eighty days, right down the line."

"All right," Ense said. "Then, this merchandise is very fresh?"

"Yeah, oh yeah."

"You'll get the money in eight days. You'll stay with me and take the money."

"Yeah, good. I'm gonna give you a name now. And that's the fellow who will be bringing whatever it is. He'll be working to bring somethin' over here. And then we'll give him your number, because—"

"*Nein! Nein!*" Ense shouted in alarm. "I show you something. That's why I'm always so in a bad mood when somebody comes from the States and I have an appointment with Ricky and Jerry. This, the second part of this is a five mark. It's in his hands and I said to him, 'When you send me somebody, give him the other part of this.' No, never. Everybody I ask, 'No, I don't have it.' This is so easy. This is so easy. I tell you the truth. Yesterday, when Fred said to me, 'Well, somebody from the States that call, well, I don't know who they sent.' I said to him, 'Well, I am in so bad position in Germany here after what happened in Brussels, I cannot call the man and say, "Hello, my friend, how are you?" That is impossible for you.' If you send somebody, I must be sure."

"That he's a friend."

"Yes."

"Don't worry about it."

"When you send somebody," Ense said, "give him this when you send him. Then he's okay."

"Now, the telephone number I'm gonna tell him to call when he gets here will be Fred's number."

"Yes," Ense said. "Only Fred's number."

"Where will you be?"

"I don't know."

"If he's comin' here, you'll have to go very fast."

"Sure," Ense said, "because it costs a lot of money, of course."

"No," Rizzo said. "You see, he comes in here Friday, he stays one week."

"Sure."

"Next Friday, Saturday night, the man's on the plane."

"Yes."

"The deal."

"Yes."

"You see him Sunday morning."

"Yes."

"By Monday, you go to the bank."

"Six days. Good."

"You know what I mean?"

"And if it is possible," Ense said, "call the office of Fred and only say a friend comes. A friend comes on Monday, or Friday, whatever. Then we are informed that somebody comes."

"Yeah," Rizzo said. "Well, what I'll do is even better than that. When the man is gonna come, he'll call you up when he gets here. But if I call you, call the office and say, 'Callin' for Vincent'—you know, when you're callin' collect for Vincent—you'll say he isn't here. That means that somebody's comin'. You know what I mean?"

"That's all right," Ense agreed.

"Oh," Rizzo said, "another thing."

"Yes?"

"The amount. The first amount I'm gonna send down here is fifty thousand."

"Okay."

"You know why?"

"This way, everybody's satisfied," Ense said.

"That's right. That's it, all right."

"Okay," Ense said.

"No bullshit," Rizzo said. "Then the next is a hundred, then a hundred five times."

"Okay, okay," Ense said. "But make it clear to the people over there, I don't think we have more possibilities to do this here more than four times."

"Okay."

"Four times. I think then you are finished."

"You can do it as long as you want," Rizzo said. "What's the most you want at one time?"

"Fifty to a hundred," Ense said.

"Now," Rizzo said, "when the man comes, you take care of him."

"Sure," Ense agreed.

"I'm just gonna send him over here with that and I'll give him the hotel. As a matter of fact, he'll stay at the Bayerischer Hof, and that's it. As far as anything else, you take care of it."

"You know," Ense said, "when I did the deal with Ricky, the

first deal, he didn't know me and he gave me the treasury bills in my hand and I said to him, 'Okay, Ricky, I go to Brussels and I call you from Brussels.' I went to Brussels and then I called him. He was in the Bayerischer Hof, and I said, 'Ricky, it takes seven or eight days.' And then he made the biggest mistake. He came to Brussels and he said, 'I come to the same hotel you are.' And then he came to the same hotel and one of the Belgian people saw Ricky the whole time in the lobby of this hotel. He saw Ricky with me and he said to the bank, 'I saw this American guy. He was in the same hotel and he was always in the same suit.' He only had one suit with him."

"He must have come from England," Rizzo said.

"It was not necessary," Ense complained. "A big mistake."

"Forget it," Rizzo said. "See, whatever you want, like you mentioned, you want the thing, you have to tell me exactly what you want."

"I can always do something with note paper," Ense said.

"Well," Rizzo said, "if you want a loan, I can get a loan for you. But you have to tell me exactly what you want."

Ense repeated that to Barg, who said in his slow, effortful English, "I think we must discuss this very good. You see, I am make very much mistake. I don't know the business. I must speak to a German friend of mine. He was in the States, Christmas, because his daughter, she works there, she has a job in New York. He told me . . . what is the famous hotel in New York?"

"I dunno," Rizzo said. "The Plaza?"

"No," Barg said.

"The Waldorf-Astoria?"

"No, no, no. It was, uh . . ."

"The Pierre?"

"No."

"In New York City?"

"In New York City, yes," Barg said.

"The Hilton?"

"No."

"The Barclay?"

"No. It was a very good hotel." And then Barg went into a long story about how his friend had made an appointment to meet his daughter for lunch at a hotel restaurant, had waited in the restaurant nearly an hour for her to appear. He was still waiting when a waiter came to him and said that a young lady was sitting outside in the lobby. Barg's friend asked the waiter to show her to the table. "I'm sorry," the waiter said, "it's only for men, a special restaurant only for men."

"The interesting thing is," Ense said when Barg finished his narrative, "she could give you a New York information. You need something, she is of the consideration. I know her name. I have her telephone number. It is easy to make an appointment with somebody of your people and her in New York."

"Yeah," Rizzo said, "as long as it's small, very, very small."

"Okay," Ense said. "Then I may phone you?"

"You want me to get together with you and then we'll find a place for settin' up some kind of schedule for payin' back this money," Rizzo said. "I wanna know how much money I'm gettin' now. I wanna go back Friday, Saturday."

"Okay," Ense said. "You get the hundred tomorrow."

"All right," Rizzo said.

There was the sound of paper rustling. "Now," Ense said, "that we have the papers, we must have a name."

"It's Vincent," Rizzo said.

"Wincent," Ense said.

"Vincent," Rizzo said a little more distinctly.

"Wincent," Ense repeated.

"Vince."

"Wince," Ense agreed.

"Vince."

"Wince."

"V . . ."

"Wee-i-n-c—" Ense said.

"V . . ." Rizzo said sharply.

"Wee . . . Wee . . ." Ense said.

"V as in Victor."

"Yes," Ense said, "Wee as in Wictor, i-n-c . . . Wincent."

"Shit," Rizzo said.

"Okay," Ense said. "And now, I must go now." But, suddenly he remembered something else, something he wanted to clear up, a final thing that might, at last, put Rizzo on the defensive. He had cashed a check for Heshy Lebensfeld, but when he had deposited it in his bank, the check had been returned; it had bounced.

"Okay," Rizzo said without much interest, "give it to me so I can put it in his mouth when I see him. You know what I did to the fink? How much money was it for? Four hundred fifty?"

"Everything is clear," Ense said. "And now I must go. I meet you tomorrow after five o'clock."

"Five o'clock sharp, or five-thirty?" Rizzo asked.

"No, no, a little after," Ense said.

"You know one thing, Ense?"

"What?"

"You don't talk like a German. When you say five o'clock, do you mean five o'clock, or six?"

"It is impossible to make it quite sure for five," Ense said apologetically, "because it's rush hour."

"All right," Rizzo said, "so make it for six."

"Okay," Ense agreed, "six o'clock sharp."

"That's why my friend . . ." Rizzo began.

"What?"

"When he calls up your office, he says, 'I can speak to a German,' 'cause he's a German. He said, 'He was tellin' me about ten, eleven.' He says, 'You gotta be precise. It's either ten o'clock or eleven.' "

"If you are at a hotel downtown, it is easy," Ense explained.

"Yeah," Rizzo said, "I figured this was good. This is away from everybody. I don't want to go down there."

"You must stay in the Palace?"

"Why not? Take a chance for a change."

"Oh, it's very good here, very, very good."

"All right," Rizzo said, "look. . . ."

"Wincent," Ense said, and there was the sound of chairs moving, bodies rising, "I must go now. Wincent, I am glad to meet you."

"Yeah," Rizzo said. "Get you tomorrow."

"Tomorrow."

"Okay."

"So long, Wince."

8

• • • • • • • • • • • • • •

*T*here was silence then, for as long as it took to draw the first deep, exhausted breaths, to wipe away the sweat that had dripped for ninety minutes, for someone to move soundlessly across the carpeted floor, open the door a crack and watch as Rizzo escorted Ense and Barg down the corridor to the elevator, got into the elevator with them, disappeared behind the closing doors. A sign was given. Klaus Peter raced for the telephone, dialed, began a babble of rapid, frantic German.

Coffey dashed for the door, sprinted down the corridor, up two flights of stairs to his room on the fifth floor, perched tensely on the edge of the bed, reached for the phone. He halted, his hand in mid-air. He had to calm himself, had to order the impressions, ideas, hunches that filled his mind, that overflowed so he could barely contain them. He knew then that his intuition had been right that night when Rizzo and Crespino conversed so intently in the freezing rain, had been more right than he could have imagined. He no longer had to worry about the warnings of Hogan and the others. He had stumbled onto something so big he was not sure he could truly grasp it all. But what he knew without question was that he had found gold.

Sitting there, staring at the phone, staring at the scribbled notes he had made, he tried to make some sense of it all, tried to make himself understand at least enough of it so that when he made that call across the ocean, he would be able to report with some accuracy.

He read over the notes. There were all those names. There was Rizzo, of course, and the two Germans, Alfred Barg and Winfried Ense. Coffey had not yet gotten a look at them, had no idea what they looked like, could not describe them. There was somebody named Ricky whose last name might be Jacobs, though of that he was not completely certain since the name Jacobs had been mentioned only once, very near the beginning of that conversation. There was Ricky's son, Jerry, whom Rizzo thought was a son of a bitch, and a woman named Evelyn, who was probably Ricky's wife. It was more than likely that all of them were from California and that Ricky had been and might still be in prison. There was Billy Benjamin, the Philadelphia forger and dealer in stolen and counterfeit securities and money. There was Heshy Lebensfeld, though whether he had played any part in all of this except to give Ense a worthless check for $450, Coffey had no idea. There were those unnamed people in New York, and probably elsewhere in the United States, whom Rizzo said he represented and whose money he was in Munich to collect. Coffey was sure that among those unnamed people was Marty de Lorenzo. There was a Frenchman named Maurice, who was stupid and who made mistakes but was a man to be trusted. There was somebody named Tony, who had been in London and who, everyone agreed, was a nice guy. There was an Italian named Dr. Amato who was in Milan. There was a Dr. Ledl, who was not really a doctor but a butcher; who was probably German, since that was the language he spoke; who had contacts in the Vatican and who was in prison somewhere for some unnamed crime. There was Jacques Suesans from Amsterdam. There were the nuns of the Bush and something or somebody called Rosario. There were people in the Vatican who were working with Ledl and others, who wanted counterfeit securities, though whether they were clerics or laymen was uncertain. Whatever they were, that they were in the Vatican was almost unbelievable. And there were certainly a lot of others whose names had not been mentioned.

How much money was involved? There was no way Coffey could calculate that, but it certainly ran way up in the millions. There had been references several times to $900,000, and that was only one deal. There had been talk of $100,000 here and another $100,000 there, and several hundred thousand someplace else. There was no way of putting a figure on the counterfeits that had been discussed. There had been at least three stolen United States Treasury certificates that Ricky had given Ense, who had cashed one of them in Brussels. There was a lot of stolen stock, most particularly shares of Coca-Cola Bottling Company of Los Angeles. There were counterfeit securities that were supposed to have gone, may actually have gone, might still be going, to the Vatican. There was merchandise—it was impossible to say whether from the Vatican package or another—that had been recovered in Rome. There seemed to be so many stock deals—stocks that were stolen or counterfeit, deals already consummated or in the process—that it was impossible to keep track of them. And from the references to hundreds, fifties, twenties and tens, it seemed likely there was also something in the works about counterfeit money.

There was the money owed to Rizzo and his people in New York that he had come to Munich to collect from Barg and Ense—$200,000 due Rizzo and another $150,000 due Ricky. There was apparently money owing on the sale of the treasury certificate, and perhaps Ricky and Jerry had cheated Rizzo of his share. There was at least $25,000 that had been turned over to Jerry during a trip to Munich, probably part payment from Barg, and Jerry had not paid Rizzo his portion. There was an unspecified amount due on an Italian deal, which might or might not relate to the Vatican. There was obviously a lot more money that was owed, or soon would be, on a number of other securities deals, all of which seemed to originate with Rizzo. An agreement was being drawn between Rizzo, Barg and Ense to provide a means for the Germans to pay what they owed and to set up a bank account for Rizzo into which payments would be made regularly.

And, without doubt, there were things that would come to light only after a close and intense scrutiny of the transcript of that conversation, though there were probably things in it that would remain cloudy and indecipherable until the investigation had gone a lot further.

Coffey took a deep breath, picked up the phone, asked for the overseas operator and put in a call to Inspector Vitrano. It was evening in New York by then, but Coffey knew that nobody in the district attorney's office kept regular hours. Vitrano would certainly be at his desk and this could not wait.

"Inspector Vitrano," he said when the connection was finally made, "this is Joe Coffey, calling from Munich. Are you sitting down?"

"Why?"

"Well, hold on to your hat. You're not going to believe this." The story began to pour out of Coffey as he tried to get it all in at one breath.

"Wait," Vitrano shouted before Coffey had spoken a dozen

words. "You just sit there. I want to get Ron Goldstock in here to listen to this, and I want to put the whole thing on tape. Get it organized in your mind and then call me back in half an hour. We'll have everything set by then."

An hour later, Coffey went through it slowly, trying to omit nothing, trying to give not just the facts but the feel of those moments, trying, too, to add his impressions and intuitions, and his knowledge of people and things when he had that. Vitrano and Goldstock listened intently. The recapitulation was complete enough so that when Coffey finished they had a few questions to ask. "Good work, Joe," Vitrano said.

"Where do we go with it now?" Coffey asked.

"You sit on Rizzo until he leaves," Vitrano said. "Ron and I will get to the Strike Force. There's no way they're not going to want to come in on this with us now."

Within moments after Coffey hung up, Goldstock was on the telephone to Dan Hollman, head of the Strike Force in New York. Did Hollman remember that conversation they'd had a few weeks before, when they had given Hollman a tip and he'd turned them down, saying he wasn't interested?

Hollman remembered. He still felt the same way about it.

Well, Goldstock said, something new had just come up, something so hot, so unbelievable, so vast that the district attorney's office could not possibly handle it alone. In fact, it went far beyond Hogan's jurisdiction, maybe even beyond the jurisdiction of the Organized Crime Strike Force.

Hollman began to show a little interest. What was Goldstock talking about?

Goldstock would not tell him over the phone. If Hollman came to Leonard Street first thing in the morning, he'd find out.

The next morning, Hollman and his assistant, William Aronwald, appeared. Goldstock and Vitrano led them into a conference room. Vitrano started the tape of Coffey's report. Hollman and Aronwald leaned forward, listening, straining, began to look at each other and at Goldstock and Vitrano.

Coffey was later told: "We didn't even get halfway through that tape before one of them reached over and turned the machine off.

They were practically jumping through the hoops. They said, 'We'll buy it. We're in.' They reached for the checkbooks and they said, 'What do you need? How much do you want? You need cars? You got them. You need money? Just tell us how much and it's yours. You need men? We'll assign them. Whatever you need, you've got it. We're in this together now. We work together from now on, share everything.' "

If Coffey had been shocked and fascinated by the references to the Vatican, for the moment he was almost alone. The federal agency seemed uninterested. Two other things had sold the Strike Force so quickly that morning, had made Hollman, Aronwald and the Justice Department so eager to join forces with the district attorney's office that they were willing to pay any price, go to any lengths. One was the mention of Coca-Cola Bottling Company of Los Angeles. The rapidly escalating trade in stolen and counterfeit securities had become a major preoccupation of the department and the FBI. While no one was certain just how vast it was, a Congressional subcommittee estimated that there were more than $50 billion worth of such securities loose around the world and that figure was growing all the time. What was certain was that it had become a potential peril to the economic well-being of corporations and of nations, that it had become a major element in the empire of organized crime and that efforts to stop it had, at best, achieved only minor success. Of some concern had been the stock of Coca-Cola Bottling Company of Los Angeles. A large block of those securities had disappeared from the United States mail somewhere between Los Angeles and New York in the fall of 1970, and had turned up later in Panama and then in various parts of Europe. Wherever the stock had turned up, there were indications that it had been a cornerstone in huge swindles, though just who had been doing the swindling and how successful they had been was not known. Though a few of those shares had been recovered along the way, most were still missing. So, it appeared to Hollman and Aronwald that a key might well lie in that conversation in the Palace Hotel in Munich.

The other attraction for the feds was the mention of one name— Ricky Jacobs. For a considerable time, he had been at the center of that ever-widening investigation into the hot securities racket.

Born in Philadelphia in 1917, or 1918, or 1919—the date depended on whom he was giving it to at the time—Manuel Richard Jacobs, a short, fat man with an open, winning expression and an ingenuous manner that seemed to inspire confidence and trust, was one of the most accomplished American swindlers and confidence men of the time. He had early developed a passion for gambling and even as a teen-ager was running card games, usually crooked ones, in his native city, and supplementing his income through robberies and burglaries. By the time he was thirty, he realized that the climate in Philadelphia did not completely suit him and that he ought to seek his fortune somewhere else, preferably far away, especially since the Philadelphia police were very anxious then to ask him some embarrassing questions about several burglaries. He packed his belongings and with his first wife, Evelyn (who divorced him a few years later, at which time he promptly married another woman named Evelyn), and their small son, Jerry Marc, headed for the sunshine of Southern California. No sooner had he settled down, though, than the Santa Monica police took him in to ask him about a string of burglaries there, and while his answers did not fully satisfy them, the charges were eventually dismissed.

It did not take long for Jacobs to become a ubiquitous figure in the Los Angeles "sporting" world. His name began to appear regularly on the police blotters for gambling and bookmaking. At the same time, he was making a lot of important friends, in both the underworld and the upperworld, and was being invited into some of the better homes in Beverly Hills and into some of the best clubs.

The name Ricky Jacobs first brushed the edges of public awareness in 1965, when the scandal at the Friar's Club in Beverly Hills erupted. Jacobs, along with several close friends, including John Roselli (one of the leaders of the Los Angeles syndicate, and the man who had been recruited together with Chicago's Sam Giancana by the federal government to develop a plan to assassinate Cuba's Fidel Castro), had taken fellow members of the Friar's Club—Hollywood celebrities, sports figures and prominent businessmen—for more than half a million dollars by rigging supposedly friendly card games. They had concealed mirrors in the ceiling, had positioned spotters to peer through peepholes strategically bored over card tables and flash signals electronically to Jacobs, Roselli and others.

Even after those disclosures, even after Jacobs was convicted three years later on federal conspiracy charges growing out of that scandal and sentenced to four years in prison, even after the revelations that he had bought supposedly secret federal-grand-jury transcripts, there were still plenty of people in Los Angeles who refused to believe that Ricky Jacobs could really have done anything reprehensible. He was, they said, so disarming, so mild-mannered, such a gentleman that it all had to be some kind of mistake. Jacobs managed for some time to keep the prison gates from closing behind him through a series of other complicated legal maneuvers that kept putting his surrender to serve his term off into the future. Meanwhile, there were more than a few prominent people who continued to open their homes to him and continued to sit in on card games he arranged at other houses in Beverly Hills, which he rented for just that purpose. These people refused to believe that the games could be crooked no matter how much they lost, refused to believe that they had as much chance of winning in a Jacobs-run poker game as a swimmer has of surviving in a tank filled with hungry sharks.

By then, though, Jacobs was much more than just a crooked gambler with a winning manner. He had emerged as one of the major American dealers, first on the West Coast and soon around the country and across the world, of stolen and counterfeit securities. He had learned all the angles and he knew everyone. Through his friend John Roselli, he had met, become close to and was working with the leaders of the syndicate, Miami's Dominic Mantell, Detroit's Joe Zerilli and a lot of others, and he had developed a series of contacts and outlets in Europe, Asia and Latin America. There were rumors that he was on friendly terms with several high officials in the American government. When there were securities to be dealt, Ricky Jacobs had become the man to see.

Even with prison hanging over him after his conviction in 1968, Jacobs continued to ply these waters as though he had nothing to fear from the law. And even after he finally went to a minimum-security prison in California early in July 1971, his dealing did not end. His wife, Evelyn, carried messages and orders to and from him on her weekly visits, and somehow he managed to persuade the prison authorities on several occasions to give him furloughs because of family problems (a sick brother in Philadelphia, for instance, to whose side he had to rush). And there was, too, his son, Jerry Marc, who served as his proxy when it was impossible for him to deal personally and directly.

By early 1972, the Justice Department and the FBI were sure

that Ricky Jacobs was the man behind several million dollars' worth of stolen and counterfeit blue-chip American corporate and government securities that had been turning up all over the United States and around the world. The trouble was, they could not prove it, could not find the evidence, had only suspicions. So, when his name came up so often in that conversation in Munich between Rizzo, Barg and Ense—came up in conjunction with both stolen treasury bills and Coca-Cola Bottling Company stock—it looked as though that evidence might at last be found.

9

• • • • • • • • • • • • •

*I*n Munich, all Coffey knew was that Hollman and Aronwald had listened with such fascination and excitement to the tape he had made that they had bought their way into his case, and already the first steps were being taken to merge the investigations by Hogan's office and the FBI. But he had his own concerns during those days. There was no assurance that Rizzo's only reason for making the trip was to meet with Ense and Barg, and so Coffey had to stay until Rizzo left in case something else occurred. And there was a mountain of reports and documents to be interpreted with the aid of the Munich police; possibly they could help clear away some of the mystery and confusion that so overwhelmed him at the moment.

He had plenty of time for all that. Rizzo did little of any interest. He stayed close to the hotel the day after the meeting, wandering through the neighborhood window-shopping, observing the construction at the nearby site of the forthcoming summer Olympic games. By five-thirty, he was back in his room, waiting for the arrival of Ense. The German called a few minutes later. Rizzo, assuming he was in the lobby, told him to get on the elevator and come up to the room. But Ense was not in the hotel. He was, he said, at the Excelsior. He had been delayed by several urgent appointments and it would be impossible for him to keep the date that afternoon. But he wanted to assure the American that everything was progressing as Rizzo desired. Barg was still in Frankfurt, but one of the things he was doing there was trying to arrange for some letters of credit so that when he returned the following morning, they could all go to the bank, open an account for Rizzo and settle matters to everyone's satisfaction. Rizzo should just be patient. Ense would call him about noon with word of the final plans.

Indeed, at noon the next day, Thursday, Ense called as he had promised, and asked Rizzo to meet him at four o'clock at Barg's office at Tengstrasse 38.

Rizzo trusted the Germans no more than they trusted him. He decided to put a little extra pressure on them to make certain they were not giving him the runaround. He placed an overseas call to William Benjamin in Philadelphia within minutes after Ense had rung off. "Bill," he said when he reached Benjamin, "there's somethin' you've got to do."

"Anything you say, Vince," Benjamin replied.

He told Benjamin of the pending meeting at Barg's office. "I want you to call them fifteen minutes before I get there," he said. "You tell them they'd better do the right thing and give me the money they owe. You tell them I've gotta get at least fifty thousand dollars, that it'd be better if they gave me a hundred grand to take back to New York right away or there's gonna be trouble all over. You tell them they'd better get it right away even if they have to borrow it. You tell them I've got to make some notes good and I want that money. And you tell them that I'm only an errand boy and there are guys behind me who don't like to be put off. Understand?"

"Don't worry, Vince," Benjamin assured him. "I'll do just like you say."

At precisely four o'clock that afternoon, Rizzo walked into Barg's office. (The surveillance team of German detectives could only wait outside in the street in frustration.) Ense and Barg were waiting. It became apparent to Rizzo with the first words that the two were, indeed, trying to stall, trying to find a way to avoid paying up. Both Ense and Barg would later say that they had tried to explain to Rizzo that there was no way they could possibly come up with the amount of money Rizzo was demanding at that moment. They simply did not have it and had no way of getting it on short notice. Rizzo was enraged. His voice rose, became harsh and threatening, and the threats he uttered, Barg and Ense were convinced, were no idle ones. They were not sure that Rizzo would not turn to physical violence against them if they did not find some way to placate him.

They played their one remaining card. Barg told Rizzo that arrangements had been made to set up a bank account in his name in Munich, and the following day they would go to the bank and complete the transaction. Rizzo had heard too many empty promises already. He wanted more than the word of Barg and Ense. With

Rizzo standing over him and watching, Barg dictated a letter that Ense translated into English, a secretary typed and Barg signed:

Dear Mister Rizzo,

Referring to our last meeting, we herewith confirm, that the following sums agreed upon will be deposeded [*sic*] next week in your account Nr. 3745 at the "Otto Dierks & Co." Bank. This is to say that DM 10,000—will be deposeded [*sic*] in cash and SFR. 46,000—in obligations of FINAG.

The remainder will be payed [*sic*] on a percentage basis on the sale of the real estate in BEL AIR.

Details will be negotiated in a separate contract, showing the possibilities of a write-off for the purposes of taxes in France and questions concerning your problem of taxes in the United States.

Yours sincerely,
INTERPROMOTIONS LTD.
Alfred Barg [signature]

The next afternoon, the formalities were taken care of, the account for Rizzo opened at the Otto Dierks Bank, the deposit made. Outside the bank, the three men talked briefly, then went their separate ways, Rizzo back to the Palace Hotel for dinner and a quiet evening. Within twenty-four hours, on Saturday afternoon, he was on his Lufthansa flight heading back to New York.

He did not know it, but when he got off that plane at Kennedy Airport, FBI agents and detectives from Hogan's office were waiting. From that moment on, he would be tracked, and he would rarely be out of the sight or the hearing of his pursuers.

Coffey stayed on in Munich for another day to finish his own business—the cementing of contacts and friendships with Klaus Peter and the other German cops, reviewing with them the events of the previous week and steeping himself in the papers they fed him, and the theories they exchanged with him, trying to learn all he could about the international market in hot securities.

He could not have picked a better place to gain that education. Munich was the center of the pond into which were tossed the pebbles—stolen and counterfeit securities from all over the world, but most importantly from the United States—that spread in ever-widening circles across the Continent. If there was a center to this center, it was in the newly renovated Regina Hotel on Max-imilianplatz, an establishment not quite on the level of the super-deluxe Palace or Bayerischer Hof, but no seedy fleabag, either. According to the Munich police, more than a million dollars' worth of hot securities were likely to be stashed in rooms at the Regina at any one time. The cops were not only sure of that, they were also sure they knew exactly who had control of those securities, who was spreading them out to a waiting throng of customers across Europe. It was a combine of German swindlers and Americans who had once served in the military stationed in Germany or who were frequent travelers in and out of Munich.

And they knew just how the ring operated. They could explain to Coffey the discernible pattern of the illegal securities market, from the source of supply to the uses to which the ultimate custom-ers put the merchandise. For all its secrecy, duplicity and illegality, the business is governed no less than any other by the classical eco-nomic dictates of supply and demand. There is, of course, almost no limit to the potential supply of those ornately engraved pieces of parchment, their value guaranteed by the might and stability of corporations and governments, the binding obligations to share-holders and creditors, which are among the foundations of Western capitalism. The securities can be counterfeited, providing a major font for those who deal in them. But counterfeits are only one source. There are the real ones, too. They rest in the vaults of banks and brokerage houses, in safes in private homes, in the pouches of messengers carrying them through the streets from one place to another, in registered parcels sent through the mails, in the sealed rooms of official printers and engravers, in the repositories of pen-sion funds, in a hundred other places. Theoretically, they ought to be safe. But in fact they are prey to thieves, some in the pay of the organized underworld, some free-lancers hoping to make a killing for themselves, some dishonest employees of the firms that hold them. All have developed the means to break the supposedly un-breakable security systems, to make away with what they want al-most at will. Even the pension funds are not secure. Avaricious trustees are sometimes willing to sell what they hold to friends in organized syndicates and then replace them with syndicate-supplied counterfeits, confident that the theft will never be discovered so long as the funds continue to collect their dividends and no one tries to sell the stocks, either the real ones or the counterfeits.

If the sources of supply are legion, the demand through other than legitimate channels is insatiable. For the certificates are bought at a discount and sold for close to their face value if the holder acts before the theft has been discovered and the securities can be listed on the hot sheets distributed to banks and brokers around the world. And even after they have been listed, they will have a considerable value, though not as great, perhaps, as when they are fresh. Shady brokers can still market them to unwary customers or to those who have a special use for the paper that does not depend on whether they are on the hot sheet. They can be used as collateral for bank loans. They can be used to inflate a corporate balance sheet; listed as assets, they make the corporation look a lot healthier and so may enable it to win contracts, float debentures, attract new investors, broaden lines of credit and so on. The uses are endless and those who swim in these waters are constantly finding new ripples, and so the demand constantly swells.

For those in the middle—those like de Lorenzo and Rizzo and their associates in the United States and their sometime partners in Munich, like Ense or the Regina ring, those who hold the stocks and so control the distribution—the potential for profit is mind boggling. The securities cost them almost nothing if their own people have come up with them, at most twenty-five percent of the market value if they buy them from free-lancers. But they can sell them for whatever the market will bear, fifty percent or more of the going price. And they can rent them out to those who need them for only a limited time for some special purpose, at a third of the market price, then reclaim them at the end of the lease and rent them again, and again, and again.

In Munich, the Regina group was a major mover of those securities. Winfried Ense was not part of that organization. He operated on a more elevated stratum—his hangouts the Bayerischer Hof and the Excelsior, his friends men of considerable standing. But, despite his guise of respectability, Ense was not completely unknown to the German police. At forty-seven, the son of a prosperous and respected physician in prewar Berlin, he had lived since the end of the war, having served with the German army in Italy, in that shadowy gray area along the borders between legality and illegality. Except for an arrest for smuggling right after the war, he had moved in that shifting world with some impunity, had gone his way with little official notice. He maintained a surface of probity and standing as the owner of two small but apparently fairly profitable concerns—F. Bobinger, of Munich, an importer of sanitary equipment from Italy, and Winfried Ense House of Confections, a lingerie and textile house in Sindelfingen. It was only later, when Ense came to the attention of the authorities, that they began to suspect that those two companies were no more than covers for his real business.

The German police had taken their first close look into his affairs when he had a friend cash a stolen $100,000 United States Treasury bill in Brussels for Ricky Jacobs. They interrogated him several times and twice searched his house for evidence, which they did not find. Though he escaped them with only the temporary loss of his passport, the episode was enough to make him the subject of considerable official interest, and the closer the police looked at him and his affairs, the more they became convinced that Winfried Ense was actually a rather accomplished swindler and dealer in stolen securities, a funnel through which those securities were spreading throughout Europe on a loftier and grander plane than the one occupied by the Regina group. The Munich police in particular were watching him, trying, though without much success, to trap him and bring him to trial.

The conversation in the Palace Hotel was, for them, vital, for it was the first solid evidence they had tying Ense to the securities racket. It also put a light for the first time on Alfred Barg.

Until then, except for his excessive drinking, Barg's image had been that of the prototypical hardworking German businessman and entrepreneur, always on the verge of a major success and while often falling just a little short, still an honest man, a good family man. He was thirty-eight when this new and darker side of him was suddenly revealed, and it seemed a shocking revelation, for his fortunes were on the rise as never before. He was doing well enough to own an extensive home in a wooded estate area on the outskirts of Munich, to drive a big Mercedes sedan, to dress in custom-tailored clothes. He owned a large and profitable warehouse in Offenburg that was used by a number of foreign companies to store merchandise they planned to market in the Federal Republic. More important for his career, he was managing director for German affairs of Interpromotions, Ltd., and of its parent company, Finag Akhiengeselschaft of Rathausgasse/Glarus, Switzerland. With $20 million in assets, a president, Jules Landolt, who was district governor of Glarus, and an attorney who had been attorney general of Switzerland, Finag was a rapidly growing industrial and investment firm whose interests and holdings were expanding across Europe. One of its wholly owned subsidiaries, Ferienstadt Bel Air, of which Barg was a major officer, as he was of other Finag subsidiaries, owned more than a million and a half acres of land, near Montpellier in southern France, on which it was building more than five thousand expensive vacation homes, some for sale and others for rent. One of Barg's functions through Interpromotions was to find and negotiate with suppliers, contractors and others on the Bel Air project.

The more Coffey learned in those days in Munich about Barg, his background and his position, the more confused he became as to why a man with such credentials and such promise of even greater success would ever get mixed up with a swindler like Ense, and, through Ense, Rizzo. Just what had driven Barg into the stolen securities market? Coffey turned to Peter and his German hosts for help, but they were just as bewildered. Ense they could understand, and so, too, the gang that operated out of the Regina Hotel. But Barg was something else. It would take months and more digging before the explanation came to the surface.

Coffey, during his ten days in Munich, learned enough about the international market in stolen and counterfeit securities to know that, when he boarded his Pan American flight for the return to New York, he'd been given a searching glimpse into a world he had hardly realized existed, and a world in which, over the next years, he would come to move with increasing confidence and knowledge, would come to know and understand as well as any man and better than most.

Part Three

. . . .

TAPS AND BUGS

1 0

. . . .

When he had departed for Munich, his wife and children had been the only ones to see him off. Now, on his return, a limousine was waiting for Coffey at the airport, to speed him without delay into Manhattan, to the eagerly awaiting FBI agents, Strike Force attorneys and his friends in the district attorney's office. For the next two days, with only a few hours out for a reunion with his family, he answered a thousand questions, went over again and again in excruciating detail all that had taken place in Munich, his reading of those events, the interpretation of the German authorities. What he reported began to give a direction to what until then had been essentially an amorphous and unfocused investigation.

Now, after Munich and the Palace Hotel, the skin was being peeled away and they were seeing the core and its magnitude. They were being given a look into the multi-billion-dollar trade in stolen and counterfeit securities, were seeing how it spread across oceans and around the world, were learning that languages and borders were no barriers to those who traveled through that world. It was huge enough and dangerous enough—physically dangerous and economically perilous—to have united the Manhattan district attorney's office and the Justice Department in an all-out campaign to stop it.

Indeed, the FBI had thrown its arsenal into the hunt, its vast store of men, equipment and money. What Hogan had wanted to do and could not was now being done. The FBI computers were whirling away, developing patterns, spewing out information, crosschecking, cataloguing. In a dozen cities across the country, agents were taking that information, developing new leads, feeding what they learned back into the computer banks. Attorneys went to court seeking the right to wiretap any and all suspicious phones, including those at William Benjamin's home and office in Philadelphia, at the

Columbia Civic League Club, at Rizzo's home and at his L and S Coffee Shop. (When investigators discovered that the phone at the coffee shop was about to be cut off for nonpayment of the outstanding bill, they paid the bill and arranged with the telephone company for the order to be quashed and a notice sent to Rizzo explaining that the threatened termination of service had been a mistake.)

A major breakthrough had grown from Coffey's hunch and from the work he and others in Hogan's office had been doing, and now there seemed little the FBI was not willing to do to make certain the investigations melded and that cooperation was total. An agent was offered, to work with Coffey as a partner, and Coffey was asked if he had any particular agent he preferred. He did. A few years before, he had worked on another joint investigation with Richard Tamarro, an agent about his own age and physical size. But in many ways, they were antithetical. Coffey had grown up on the streets of New York, was intuitive, willing to act on hunches and bend or break the rules if he had to. Tamarro was Rhode Island born and bred, a strait-laced FBI agent in the mold stamped out by J. Edgar Hoover, a mold from which it had never occurred to him to deviate. But he was a superb researcher, at home with papers, able to read reports and make sense out of obscurities, able to take a plethora of information and turn it into a coherent memorandum. And he was willing to bow in the field to the street-wise Coffey. "He wasn't too sharp when it came to street knowledge," Coffey says, "but then that's true of most FBI guys who haven't grown up in a big city. When it came to taking papers and a Dictaphone and a computer and the rest of the office-type stuff and putting things together, though, he was very competent, very sharp. In that area, he was able to generate a hell of a lot. I liked Tamarro and we worked pretty well together. But, really, the reason I asked for him, the reason we actually got in touch with him ourselves when they offered us an agent, was because we knew him and we figured we might as well have somebody we knew as some eightball they might hand us who'd fuck everything up. We figured we could probably handle Tamarro, at least to some extent."

Making all the arrangements for the future of the investigation took days, and it was the middle of the week following his return from Munich before Coffey could get back where he wanted to be—in the field and into the middle of the accelerating chase. He showed up as soon as he could at the Stuyvesant Town plant, eager to go over the logs, read transcripts, listen to the tapes, find out what had gone on while he was away. The other detectives were waiting for him. When he came through the door, the first thing he saw were photographs of himself taped to the walls, all labeled with messages: God Is Back! Jesus Has Returned!

He could laugh at that, recognizing the levity in it, knowing that he was a hard taskmaster, a ballbreaker, who constantly demanded work and more work from those working with and under him. But there was something he could not laugh at. The logs for the time he had been gone were empty, the tapes blank.

"What gives?" he demanded.

"Nothing," somebody said. "You were off in Europe with Rizzo, Joe, having a good time with the frauleins. What could have been going on?"

Coffey could hardly believe what he was being told. "What do you mean, what could have been going on?" he said. "You bastards have been goofing off, that's what. You've been having a big party all the time I was away, that's what's been going on. Do you guys realize you could have screwed up this whole investigation? Rizzo's not the only one who uses that phone. Tortora uses it. Jerry de Lorenzo uses it. Tartaglia uses it, and so do a lot of other wise guys. But you decided, screw that. Do you realize that Rizzo could have called in from an outside phone in Munich and because you decided to have a party and fuck off, we'll never know it?" He turned to one of the detectives, a veteran of years on Hogan's staff, who had been charged with running the plant in Coffey's absence. "I want to talk to you," Coffey said. "I'm going to take you out to dinner tonight. Let's go down to Mulberry Street and have Italian."

The restaurant was a favorite of the detectives, and when they entered, they were welcomed warmly, given a table in the rear where they could have a little privacy. Coffey ordered martinis for both of them, and when they had finished, ordered another round. They chatted casually about inconsequentials over their drinks and through dinner. Coffey waited until steaming cups of coffee were poured and placed in front of them. Then he leaned back, stared hard at the other detective, said, "Hey, fuck-up, I want you to tell me exactly what you did while I was gone."

The older detective looked at him and grinned. "Screw you, Joe," he said. "You're not my boss. So what's the big deal?"

Coffey glared. "No?" he said. "Well, I'll tell you exactly what you did. You didn't do one damn thing. You sat around on your ass and you told those other guys, 'Fuck him, he's only a detective like the rest of us. He's not here anyway. He's over in Germany having a good time. How's he ever going to find out?' You fed them all that shit and they listened. Well, you're older, you're more experienced, they listened to you. You're the guy who was supposed to keep things going while I was away. That was your responsibility. And you fucked it up. So, I'm going to tell you what I'm going to do. I'm going to lock you up."

"What are you going to lock me up for?" the older detective said, aghast.

"I'm going to lock you up for nonfeasance. How's that for a start?"

"Jesus, Joe."

"Don't Jesus me, you bastard. You could have blown this whole case."

It went on for ten, fifteen more minutes, Coffey growing angrier, his voice more determined and convincing, cowing his companion. But the rage and the threats had their effect on both of them. Coffey rid himself of the frustration and fury that had been building since he had first walked into the plant. By the time they left the restaurant, they had come to terms, declared a temporary truce. The older detective would go back to work, would shape up. And for the moment, Coffey would watch, see how things developed, do nothing untoward. "Actually," Coffey says, "from then on he worked as hard as anybody, so maybe it all turned out for the best. But, I was really pissed off that day and I wasn't going to let anything like that happen again."

He would never know what, if anything, had been lost because he had been gone. He was, though, always certain that there was something, perhaps even something vital. Now that he was back, he was determined there would be no future lapses. He instilled his own passion into the others, not least because, with the entrance into the hunt of the FBI, the reality of his hunch was confirmed and everyone began to see potential gain for himself. "This was turning into the biggest thing the office had had in twenty-five years and they knew it," Coffey said. "And they knew that they would be able to heap glory on themselves if they did it right. There'd be promotions and all the rest. Everybody got to thinking that, so there wasn't any more goofing off after that."

Once more the tapes began to roll, once more the monitors began to emit the sound of voices confident that nobody was listening. Torrents poured forth. Evidence of crimes of every sort mounted higher and higher.

Vincent Tortora answered the phone. It was Izzy Marion calling from Las Vegas. "Popo," he said, "I got somethin' I'd like you to do for me."

"Name it," Tortora said.

"There's a guy over in Jersey, name of Capasso. You know him?"

"I heard of him."

"Owns seven, eight garbage trucks over in Lodi."

"Yeah."

"I want you to mess up those trucks."

"How bad?"

"Just the transmissions. You know, whatever you can do. I don't want nothin' done to Capasso or his people personally. Just the trucks, that's all."

"I got you," Tortora said. "I got to meet some people over in Belleville tomorrow. I'll talk to 'em. They'll do anythin' I ask. They owe me a million favors as it is."

"Whatever it costs," Marion said, "you let me know. It will be fair because it's good people involved."

"Okay," Tortora said. "Before I do anythin', I'll call you back at the salon and let you know what it's gonna cost."

The next day, detectives and FBI agents followed Tortora to Belleville, N. J., saw him meet with several New Jersey hoodlums, though they did not hear what was said. A few days later, Capasso's garbage trucks were immobilized.

What was behind it became clear within a week, when Marion called Tortora to tell him that he was on his way to Syracuse. Marion had been trying to muscle his way into a New Jersey company called Scientific Incineration Devices, Inc., which had developed some products along the guidelines laid down by the Environmental Protection

Agency to reduce toxic odors and pollutants during the disposal of waste. The company was trying to market those devices throughout the northeast. One of SID's directors was Frank Capasso and apparently he had been resisting Marion's efforts to become a partner. The attack on Capasso's trucks was designed to change his mind and demonstrate that Marion could be a very valuable partner.

It apparently worked. When Marion arrived in Syracuse and checked into the Holiday Inn, he was not alone. With him were Ray Neal, a major syndicate figure in Oregon and the Pacific Northwest, and Michael Riccardelli, a director and leading figure of Scientific Incineration Devices. On the hotel register, Marion identified himself as a sales representative for the company.

Marion, Neal and Riccardelli were in Syracuse for three days, with a side trip one evening down the New York Thruway to Utica. Watching their every move were two of Hogan's detectives, who had rushed upstate as soon as Marion's travel plans were known, and several FBI agents attached to the Syracuse office of the bureau. Those three days were a time of constant meetings. Marion, Neal and Riccardelli went into conference with nearly every major figure in organized crime in upstate New York. They met with elected officials of Syracuse, and after those meetings, Marion was heard to boast, "We sold them an incinerator." They had a long dinner session with Utica's mayor Michael Caruso, and when dinner was over, they went on to visit with the man who controlled all the bookmaking in central New York. And throughout those days, they were in constant contact with Sergeant Jack Dinaro of the Syracuse Police Department and head of that department's Patrolmen's Benevolent Association. Several times a day, he called Marion at the Holiday Inn and Marion called him.

It was during those days that the FBI came perilously close to blowing the investigation. As Coffey explains it, "We don't operate the way they do. We prefer to stay undercover as long as we can. We don't come out in the open until we absolutely have to, and we never interview people until we've made our case. Their philosophy is that if they come right out up front and flash those magic credentials, they're going to get information, people are just going to open up and spill everything at the sight of those wallets flashing open in front of them. But by doing that, they can wreck the whole operation, which they nearly did in Syracuse and a half a dozen other times."

Near the end of Marion's stay, two local FBI agents approached the desk clerk at the Holiday Inn, flashed their credentials and asked to see the telephone records for Marion's room. The desk clerk produced the records. He also did something else. He called Sergeant Dinaro at Syracuse police headquarters and told him of the appearance of the FBI agents. Dinaro passed the word on to Marion. Marion must have made some kind of connection, become convinced that one of the numbers he had been calling was tapped and that was what had put the FBI on to him in Syracuse. He rushed from his room to a pay phone, dialed long-distance.

In Jimmy's Lounge in New York, the phone rang. In the Stuyvesant Town plant, the tape recorder began to spin, the monitor to give out the sound of Marion's voice. Coffey, standing nearby, heard it all.

"Is Popo there?"

"Just a minute. Popo, phone for you."

"Yeah?"

"Popo?"

"Yeah."

"You know who this is?"

"Yeah. I recognize the voice."

"Don't say my name."

"What? Why?"

"Just listen to me. I'll give you a number. You go to another phone and call me right back. I got to talk to you."

"You can talk," Tortora said. "This is my safe phone. There ain't nothin' to worry about."

"Listen to me, Popo, and do like I tell you. I'm tellin' you, take a walk, go to a public phone, anyplace, and call me back."

"You nuts?" Tortora said. "We can talk now. Nothin's wrong here."

"I won't talk now. I want you to do like I say. I'll explain then."

For more than ten minutes they argued. Realizing that Marion was adamant, Tortora finally agreed. A hundred feet from where he stood in Jimmy's Lounge, out on the street corner, there was a public phone. It would have taken Tortora thirty seconds to get to it and make the call. But Tortora was so certain his phone was secure he would not make that hundred-foot walk. He merely waited five minutes, then picked up his own phone and dialed the number in Syracuse that Marion had given him.

"Okay, Izzy," he said.

"You on another phone?" Marion demanded.

"Sure, just like you said. I'm callin' from outside."

(In the plant a block and a half away, Coffey and the other detectives stared at the monitor and at each other in disbelief, could barely hear what was being said as they erupted with laughter.)

"Okay," Marion said.

"So, what's the big deal?" Tortora asked.

"I think your phone's tapped."

"You nuts or somethin'," Tortora said. "How could it be tapped? We're payin' off enough guys. We're checkin' all the time. So, if it was tapped, we'd sure as hell know."

"Yeah?" Marion said. "Well, Jack just tipped me. The feds have been askin' some questions. They was here lookin' up the phone records for my room. One of the numbers they got to come up with is yours."

"So what?" Tortora said. "You been callin' a lot of places, right?"

"Yeah."

"So, what are you worried about? What makes you think they'd figure there was somethin' special about this one?"

"I just got a hunch."

"Forget it."

"Yeah? Well, tell me, how'd they'd know I was here?"

"Who knows? A dozen ways. It don't mean nothin'. Forget it. Look, you comin' down?"

"Yeah. Soon as we finish up here. I'll call you when we get in."

It had been a near thing. For a long time afterward, Coffey worried that Tortora might begin to have some second thoughts and if he did, the phone in Jimmy's Lounge that had been paying such high dividends in so many areas, and all the other tapped phones, as well, might suddenly go silent. He waited. And then he began to breathe easier. Neither Tortora nor Rizzo nor any of the others who used all those phones so often and so openly grew suspicious until it was far too late. Even Marion's fears were calmed; within another day he was back on that line, speaking as freely as ever.

But Coffey did not forget. He went back to the office in a rage. "I told the boss that the FBI was a bunch of fuck-ups who were going to blow this whole investigation unless he did something. We had a meeting and we sat down with the feds and we said, 'This has got to stop unless you want this thing to collapse right around your feet.' Well, they agreed to play it cool, and except for one or two other times down the road when they went back to their old tricks, they did just that. So, no harm was done, but it sure could have been."

Their business in upstate New York finished, Marion and Neal boarded a flight on a Sunday afternoon in late March for LaGuardia Airport. Coffey, other detectives and FBI agents were waiting for them when they landed. But it was dusk on Sunday and traffic into the city from Long Island was very heavy. By the time they crossed the Triborough Bridge into Manhattan, they had lost sight of the car containing Marion and Neal. There was one hope of picking them up again. Marion had told Tortora he would call once he was in the city. Coffey raced back to the Stuyvesant Town plant, hung anxiously over the monitor for the next few hours waiting for that call. It finally came late in the evening. He and Neal, Marion informed Tortora, were in rooms 706-07 at the Delmonico Hotel on Park Avenue.

There was a rush to Leonard Street. Orders for wiretaps and bugs were drafted, a judge was roused to sign them, and then it was back into the cars to speed uptown to the hotel. The Delmonico's manager, Charles Gray, was informed just who the guests were in rooms 706-07. When he heard that, when he saw the official wiretap and bugging orders, he offered to do anything he could to help, assigned the detectives a room just down the hall from Marion. It quickly filled with Hogan's men, FBI agents and technicians lugging in their load of listening devices. Then they could only wait and hope that Marion and Neal would leave so they could gain access and install the taps, plant the bugs.

The wait was a short one. Within an hour, Marion and Neal left, got into a cab in front of the hotel and headed for the Separate Tables, a restaurant on Third Avenue favored by people well placed in the entertainment world, politics and the rackets. Close behind Marion and Neal were cars filled with FBI agents. Their job: observe what was going on and, more important, let Coffey and the technicians at the Delmonico know if and when either Marion or Neal left the restaurant and started back. Other agents and detectives were stationed downstairs in the hotel lobby to keep watch just in case either managed to slip past those observing the restaurant.

The technicians moved in. The phones were tapped. A sophisticated bug, far superior and more sensitive than the one provided by the CIA in Munich, was planted. The technicians returned to Coffey's room, did a check on the bug. Something was wrong. The tap was working fine, but the bug was picking up nothing. They would have to return to the suite and try to figure out what was wrong. They needed time.

Coffey got in touch with the FBI agents watching the Separate Tables. "Everything okay?"

"Everything's fine. No sweat."

"They're still there, inside?"

"Nice and cozy. A couple of people are with them."

"Who? You recognize them?"

"One of them's Popo Tortora. A couple of other guys we don't know, two dames."

"Okay. Let us know if they move."

"Don't worry. We've got them staked out. Nobody's going to get past us."

Assured, Coffey sent the technicians on their return mission. They went over the installation, slowly and carefully, made a few repairs on what seemed like possible trouble points, returned to their room and went through the tests once more. Something was still not right. The bug refused to function. They would have to get back into Marion's suite once more, and it was growing late.

Coffey reached the FBI surveillance team again. "Are they still there?"

"Sure. We told you we'd let you know if they move."

"You're positive?"

"Yes."

"Because we're having some trouble here. We need more time."

"Don't worry. We're sitting on them. Nobody's left the place. If somebody does, we'll let you know."

Coffey took a deep breath, nodded to the technicians. "It's still clear. One more time. Only, for Chrissake, get it right this time."

The two wiremen, both dressed in shabby work clothes, moved down the hall one more time, picked the lock on the door of the suite one more time, pulled the door open and started in. Ray Neal was sitting on the bed. He was naked. Next to him was a forty-five-caliber pistol. Marion might still be at the Separate Tables, but somehow Neal had managed to leave without being spotted, had managed to return to the Delmonico, pass through the lobby, ride up the elevator and get into his suite without being observed by any of the watchers. He looked up at the sound of the door opening, saw two men standing in the doorway, one holding a set of lock picks. He stared at them in surprise for only a moment, then leaped from the bed and rushed for them. They slammed the door in his face. He grabbed the inside knob and tried to pull it open. They held the outside knob tightly to keep it closed. The tug-of-war went on and on, the wiremen holding tightly from the outside, Neal pulling and shouting from the inside. It was a stalemate that could not last. Neal's grip relaxed. The wiremen let go, turned and started to race down the corridor, seeking escape.

Behind them, they heard a door open. They glanced back. Neal was coming out the door, still without any clothes but now holding on to his forty-five, waving it and shouting. They turned a corner. They were trapped. They had come against a cul-de-sac and there was no way to turn. Neal came around the corner. He saw them, stared, raised his pistol and started to aim. Suddenly he stopped. It was as though he had just realized that he was standing in a public hallway in a hotel, holding a pistol, completely naked. He spun, raced back toward his room.

Coffey and the other detective who had remained with him heard the commotion but had no idea what was happening . . . until Neal called the front desk. Through the wiretap they heard him say that two guys had been trying to break into his room and he had chased them down the corridor, had them trapped. He demanded that the cops be called immediately.

That worried Coffey. Gray was gone for the evening. Nobody else on duty except the switchboard operator knew what was going on. The precinct cops would soon be on the scene, and they would be joined by the burglary squad and by units from all over midtown and the east side; the hotel was about to become the arena for a massive manhunt, certainly a room search on the seventh floor. Coffey was sure of that. Not long ago, the Pierre Hotel had been the scene of a major jewel robbery. The thieves had not yet been caught and there was some fear that another major hotel burglary or robbery was going to take place at any time. The police had been alerted for any sign of a repetition at other luxury midtown hotels. If the cops entered the room during their search, they would certainly have Neal with them to identify the men who had broken into his room. They would not only spot and identify the two wiremen but they would also see the electronic hardware and then the game would be over. Neal and Marion would have been warned. The whole investigation might then be set back.

Coffey rushed out into the hall, grabbed the two wiremen and pulled them back into the room. Even through the sealed windows, they could hear the sirens of the police cars pulling up in front of the hotel, could see through the windows the flashing lights of at least twenty radio cars jamming the streets, could see scores of cops and detectives pouring into the hotel. The room phone rang. It was the switchboard operator. The cops, she said, were just coming through the door. What should she do?

Coffey had a sudden inspiration. One of the wiremen, Pete Di-Castol, was about fifty years old, but with his gray hair and seamed face, he looked a lot older. Coffey told the woman on the switchboard to tell the cops that DiCastol was an old man who rented the room on a permanent basis and lived there with his grown son. Then the electronic gear was shoved under the beds and into the closet. The second wireman and Coffey's partner hid in the closet as well, the door locked behind them. The room was straightened. DiCastol got undressed and climbed into bed. Coffey stripped, jumped into the shower and turned the water on.

There was a pounding on the door. Coffey turned off the shower, wrapped a towel around his middle, went to the door. DiCastol sat up in bed, looking as though he had just awakened. Coffey opened the door a crack. "Yes?"

"There's been a report of a burglary on this floor," a cop in uniform said, "a couple of rooms away. Have you heard or seen anything suspicious?"

Coffey shook his head. Neal stood just behind the cop, trying to peer into the room, seeing only the shape of DiCastol in bed, not his face. Other cops filled the hall. "No, we haven't, officer," Coffey said. "There's just my father and me in here. He went to bed a while ago and I've been in the shower. We haven't heard a thing."

The cop looked around the room from the doorway. He did not enter. He could see nothing out of the ordinary, only an older man in bed, half awake, and a younger man, obviously young enough to be the son, standing just inside the room, a towel wrapped around his middle, obviously just out of the shower. "Okay," the cop said. "If you do happen to hear anything suspicious, call downstairs. We'll be here for a while."

It was some time before the hotel finally quieted and the cops left, having found nothing despite their search. The situation was still tenuous, though. The bug in Neal and Marion's room still needed to be repaired. The problems would have to be corrected before Marion returned or the project would turn out to be useless. Some means had to be found to get Neal away from the hotel long enough for the wiremen to get back to that room and do what had to be done. Coffey pulled a two-way radio out from under the bed, called Robert Nicholson, a sergeant in Hogan's office who was down on the street, and asked him to come up to the room.

"Look," he said when Nicholson came through the door, "we've got to get that guy out. Why don't you go knock on his door and tell him you're from the burglary squad and you want him to go down to the station with you and go over some mug shots to see if he can pick out the two guys? That way, you can keep him away while we find out what's wrong with the bug."

"I've got a better idea," Nicholson said. "He could go through the mug shots in less than an hour. So, what I'll do is this. I'll take him around to the bars in midtown, tell him we've got an idea the guys may be hanging out in one of them and we want to see if he can spot them. That way, you can have as long as you need. We'll find some way to keep Marion away, too. I'll call you every half-hour or so and you can let me know how you're doing."

Nicholson did just what he said. And this time it took the technicians only a few minutes to trace the trouble and get the bug working. Then it was wait and see what came through.

But what came through that bug was hardly worth the trouble. In the early hours of the morning, both Neal and Marion had returned to the suite. Neal told Marion the story of the evening's excitement. Marion played tough guy, informing Neal that he should have shot the two burglars where they stood instead of worrying about the fact that he didn't have any clothes on.

The wiretap, however, did pay off. Marion phoned his partner in Scientific Incineration Devices, Mike Riccardelli. "I want you to call up Gabe Piermonte in Boston on Monday," he ordered. "You know who he is. He's the deputy mayor up there. You tell him you're with Izzy Marion. He can do a lot for us up in Boston with the incinerators."

And Marion took another step along the path he had first trod more than a month before, a path that had its twistings toward Munich and the Palace Hotel. He talked to Vincent Rizzo.

"The guy in L.A. is duckin' me," he said. "I want your okay to get heavy with him."

"Okay," Rizzo said. "You got it."

"I want to go in and crack him up."

"Okay," Rizzo said.

"You think maybe he's gonna yell cop?"

"I dunno," Rizzo said. "He might."

"Then maybe we ought to send somebody else in to give him a whack first, so he don't recognize me right away."

"If you want."

"What do we do if we still don't get satisfaction?" Marion asked.

"We go the ultimate," Rizzo said.

The satisfaction that Rizzo demanded was not forthcoming. Marion contacted a friend in Las Vegas, a thug named William Robertazzi, ordered him to pay a call on the recalcitrant debtor in Los Angeles. "Find that guy," Marion said, "and tell him the next visit won't be a friendly one."

(Coffey was by then convinced that the debtor had to be Jerry Marc Jacobs; convinced, too, that the debt grew from money Ense and Barg had paid Jacobs and which he had not turned over to Rizzo. On the first point, he was right. On the second, and for one of the few times in this investigation, he was wrong. The money was the price Rizzo was demanding for $100,000 worth of United States Treasury "E" bonds that Rizzo had given to Jerry Jacobs to sell and which had been seized in Canada from an associate of Jacobs before the sale could be consummated. Rizzo had informed Jacobs that as far as he was concerned, he didn't care what had happened to the bonds after Jacobs had taken possession of them. That was Jacobs's problem, and it was Jacobs's responsibility to pay Rizzo the agreed price of $25,000. Jacobs maintained that since the bonds had been lost, everybody was out his profits and so Rizzo could really expect nothing. That was not acceptable to Rizzo and he had let Jacobs know during a confrontation in a bar in Arcadia, California, when he slapped the younger man around, that if he didn't get his money, Jerry Jacobs would be a very sorry young man.)

Acting on Marion's instructions, Robertazzi hurried to Los Angeles, met Jerry Jacobs at a Rexall Drug Store on La Cienega Boulevard. He dismissed Jacobs's explanations, grabbed him by the collar, lifted him off the ground, nearly strangling him, and shouted, loud enough for other customers in the store to stare with alarm and back away, "I don't want to hear none of that crap. I come here to get the twenty-five grand you owe and I ain't leavin' until I get it. You understand? Don't think you can run away, because you can't. No matter where you go, we'll find you. So, you better get the dough, or else."

Jacobs gasped that he didn't have the money with him and there was no way he could get it. Robertazzi dragged him into a phone booth, dialed a long-distance number, said something, then shoved the phone against Jacobs's ear. Izzy Marion was on the other end. "I'm a friend of Vince Rizzo," Marion said, "and I'm the guy who sent the guy you're with to collect what you owe. Now, I want you to understand somethin'. You think the guy you're with is bad? Well, I'm mean and rotten, and if you don't come up with it, somethin' is gonna happen to you. I don't want to hear no more bullshit. I want that dough, and I want it quick." Marion hung up. Robertazzi yanked Jacobs out of the booth, slammed him against a nearby wall, told him that nobody was kidding around, that it was pay up or push up daisies.

Despite the beatings and the threats, Jacobs continued to hold to his position that no money was owed to Rizzo, continued to refuse to pay. And so Izzy Marion took the next step, as Rizzo had dictated. He got in touch with his police friend in Syracuse, Sergeant Jack Dinaro, and asked if Dinaro could get him "an unregistered thing."

Dinaro returned Marion's call, to the suite at the Delmonico, told him he had made a trip to Buffalo to pick up "the unregistered thing" and would send it out to Marion in Las Vegas within a week with one of his cops, James V. Quatrone.

"Okay," Marion said. "Only, tell him not to carry it in his coat because they'll pick it up that way. Tell him to put it in his suitcase."

"I'll do that," Dinaro said. "By the way, he's going to Vegas with his wife."

"Okay," Marion said. "I'll make arrangements for Mr. and Mrs.

Quatrone to stay at Caesar's Palace as long as they want."

"Well," Dinaro said, "they'll be flying out under the name of del Popolo. Mr. and Mrs. G. del Popolo."

That put the authorities in a quandary. They did not want to do anything that might tip those they were after until they were ready to make their move, and they were not ready for that. Yet they could not stand idly by, knowing that a murder was being planned, that the weapon was about to be delivered to the potential killer.

Hogan's detectives and FBI agents gathered to decide what course to follow. They would move slowly, carefully, it was agreed, allow Quatrone to travel unmolested to Las Vegas, though watched all the way. What they would not let him do was deliver the gun to Marion. The Las Vegas police would be notified at the last minute and, supposedly operating on a tip from an informant, would move in and arrest both Marion and Quatrone just as the gun was being passed. That way they would both prevent a murder and avoid compromising the larger picture.

"Then the FBI screwed it up again," Coffey says. "We sent two of our guys to Las Vegas to be there when Quatrone got off the plane and get word to the locals. The FBI, which was spending money like it was water, decided to be frugal for a change. Instead of sending some agents who knew what the score was and what we were doing and why, somebody like Dick Tamarro, they wired out to the FBI office in Chicago and told them that a guy traveling under the name of del Popolo was coming through on a plane from Syracuse to Las Vegas that's going to be stopping in Chicago and he's got a gun in his suitcase. What do the agents in Chicago care? It's not their case. So what do they do? They move."

The FBI's Chicago office obtained a search warrant permitting them to go through "del Popolo's" luggage. When the flight arrived at O'Hare International Airport, FBI agents and sky marshals were waiting. They took Quatrone into a private office, brought in his suitcase, found the gun, and confronted him with it.

Faced with the presence of that pistol and the hard eyes of the FBI and the sky marshals, Quatrone tried to find an explanation. His name, he said, was not really del Popolo. He was traveling under the name, he said, because he had bought his tickets through a contact at a discount and they were made out in that name. His real name was James Quatrone and he was a Syracuse cop. The reason he was carrying the gun, a twenty-five-caliber Beretta automatic, was not because he'd wanted to carry it but because his police sergeant, Jack Dinaro, had ordered him to. When he got to Las Vegas, he was supposed to contact a friend of Dinaro's named Izzy Marion, give him the gun and in exchange receive special privileges and favors during his stay in the gambling center. As far as Quatrone was concerned, the FBI and the sky marshals could keep the gun. He didn't want any part of it any longer and he certainly had no further use for it.

Quatrone was released. He resumed his trip to Las Vegas, where he had a pleasant stay. Jerry Marc Jacobs's life was spared. But Izzy Marion's suspicions were aroused once more. When his own phones were tapped a week later, as a result of this episode, the taps proved useless. All conversations, both from his home phone and the ones at the salon, were circumspect. Marion was observed often using pay phones.

As for Jack Dinaro and James Quatrone, the story and the evidence to support it were turned over to the Syracuse district attorney. He elected not to prosecute either man. Neither Dinaro nor Quatrone was ever indicted or even arrested. Dinaro retired from the police force a while later on a full pension. Quatrone remained on the force and was, soon after, promoted to sergeant.

1 1

● ● ● ● ● ● ● ● ● ● ● ● ●

A stranger stumbling into the dingy secret basement room in Stuyvesant Town in the spring of 1972 and remaining an hour would have gone away with an education in the workings of organized crime. The tape recorders and monitors and other electronic devices were rarely silent. Rizzo or Tortora or somebody else always seemed to be on the phone. If Izzy Marion in Las Vegas had communicated his own suspicions that somebody might be listening in, they ignored him and continued to discuss their business with absolute confidence.

Jimmy Heimerle and Freddy Mayo, the syndicate travel agents, were kept very busy during those months. Hardly a day passed when they were not given orders to dip into their bottomless barrel of airline tickets and credit cards, run them through their stolen validating machines and book flights to Florida and California, to Hawaii and Tokyo, to Hong Kong and Buenos Aires, to London and Munich. If one thing was certain it was that those trips were being made neither as vacations nor for sight-seeing. Knowing Rizzo, Tortora and the others, and now armed with all that had been uncovered since this investigation had begun, Coffey and Dick Tamarro and the others in the district attorney's office and the FBI could easily speculate about the purpose of these trips. The movement of narcotics seemed a sure thing, and so, too, did the movement of stolen and counterfeit securities. But speculation, even conviction, was not absolute knowledge, and the only way to get that was to move in at a crucial moment and make an arrest. That they did not want to do. It would tip their hand before they were ready, before they had unraveled all the threads and found all the answers.

So, they let most of those trips take place undisturbed, though those who made them had company. And every once in a while, when they were sure it would not hurt anything, they passed the word to the airlines that somebody was flying for free, then sat back and listened with no little pleasure to the results.

"Popo, listen," a frantic caller cried over the phone early one evening from Miami. "Everybody got pinched with those things."

"Who?" Tortora demanded.

"The two kids."

"You're kidding me."

"They're pinched."

"Oh, my God," Tortora said. "When did it happen?"

"Today."

"Yeah, yeah. How come? How'd it happen?"

"Possession of stolen property."

"Where are they? In Florida?"

"Yeah. The two kids are in Florida. The other ones, they let them go because he's a bondsman and he bought them from a guy in the Bronx. Now, Popo, how the fuck am I gonna get home?"

Rizzo's loansharking business was flourishing. The conversations over the phone confirmed that. He had money out all over the city and was reaping an interest of ten percent and more each week, and most who owed him money paid without a complaint. Rizzo's customers had learned long before that when a Rizzo collector showed up, excuses were not accepted—only money.

John Calamarus, though, was having a little trouble. His Blue Seas restaurant on Third Avenue was not doing well. He was into Rizzo for several thousand dollars and he couldn't make his payments. When Patty Marino called in to tell Rizzo that, Rizzo told him to reach into the till and grab whatever was there. He had already done that, Marino said. The problem was, there was only $17 in the cash register.

"Take it," Rizzo ordered, "and tell Calamarus he's got to come up with another three hundred right away. Tell him he is taking advantage and we can't be good no more."

But Calamarus had no way to come up with any more money. Rizzo ordered Marino to camp out in the restaurant, sit behind the cash register and pocket everything that came in. It was still not enough to satisfy Rizzo. Calamarus was taken to the dark place and given a lesson in what happened to those who failed to meet Rizzo's demands, then was sent back to work at the Blue Seas, no longer for himself but thereafter for the new and secret owner, Vincent Rizzo.

Calls like those were incriminating enough, and proof enough of felonies, so that judges had no hesitation in regularly renewing the applications for continuance of the taps. And what came over the phones was logged, transcribed, filed, put through the computers and correlated. When the time came, it would be presented to grand juries and to courts.

But those calls were, for the most part, about side issues. What the investigators thirsted to hear was more about the flow of hot securities in and out of the United States, about the transaction in the Vatican that had been mentioned for the first time by Winfried Ense in Munich, about all the other deals that lay at the real center of this hunt. But the Vatican was never mentioned, and conversations about securities were inevitably guarded and elliptical so that those who heard them had to have some prior knowledge, had to know how to strip away the covering.

Thus, Rizzo called William Benjamin in Philadelphia—collect, as were all his long-distance calls—and asked for a sample. It did not have to be an original, he said.

A day later, he called collect again, apologized for not calling earlier and asked, "How'd you make out with that thing? All right?"

"I'm going to get a hold of him today," Benjamin replied.

"Right," Rizzo said. "But those papers are all right?"

"As far as I'm concerned, he hasn't even started. But he says don't worry about it. I'll have to bug him."

Rizzo called Marty de Lorenzo and said he needed to collect "some mortgage money." Uncle Marty said he understood the problem and as soon as he heard from Salli he would be down to see Rizzo.

(Coffey, Tamarro and the others who were listening understood that Rizzo and de Lorenzo were talking about Sam Salli, a syndicate leader in Buffalo and notorious as a major source of counterfeit money. Thus, Rizzo's "mortgage money" had to be counterfeit bills.)

Marty de Lorenzo showed up at Jimmy's Lounge one afternoon, availed himself of that telephone and made three calls, to George Adamo, Joe Verrone and Tobias "Teddy" Cohen. According to an informant, the three were de Lorenzo's partners in the theft and distribution of more than $4.5 million in treasury notes. But unless someone knew that, there were few clues in those conversations. They were filled with "You know what I mean" and "You know what I'm tryin' to say" and "As soon as I get word, I'll call you" and a number of elliptical references.

It became so frustrating that it seemed the only way to penetrate the cover and get to the center was to put somebody inside Jimmy's Lounge. The man chosen for the job was an undercover detective named Jimmy Rodriguez. Putting on old work clothes, Rodriguez dropped into the bar, ordered a drink, sat around for hours. He repeated this performance daily until he became a regular, was accepted as one of the standard fixtures—if not one of Rizzo's people, still only a harmless neighborhood wino. Rodriguez was good at his job, managed to pick up odd bits that filled in corners of the growing picture as those habitués of the bar were soon talking easily around him, though rarely directly to him. And he observed meetings in the back room of Jimmy's Lounge between Rizzo, de Lorenzo and many other important syndicate leaders. But the back room was off limits. He could see those conferences but he could never get close enough to hear what was being said.

If Rodriguez was picking up some important hints, nevertheless there was considerable concern for his safety. If his true identity was revealed, there was no doubt what his fate would be. Jimmy's Lounge was not Ponte's. It did not have the kind of clientele that might serve as a shield against violence and give him time to escape. Indeed, there had already been a demonstration of what could happen to unwelcome outsiders who happened into Jimmy's Lounge, and that unwelcome outsider was not even an undercover cop.

Late in March, a Puerto Rican named Jose Brocero wandered in off the street, went up to the bar and ordered a glass of beer. Rizzo strode across the room, shoved him away from the bar, spinning him around. "Get out of here, you fuckin' spic," he ordered. "We don't serve spics in this place."

Brocero gave him an argument, insisting that he had a right to have a beer anyplace he wanted as long as he had the money to pay. Rizzo turned, picked up a pool cue, went after Brocero, left him on the floor in a pool of blood. Brocero was dragged out of the bar and dumped into a nearby hallway.

It was later that evening that Rizzo, during a casual phone conversation, mentioned that there had been a little trouble in the bar earlier, that he had personally taken care of it. The detectives in the Stuyvesant Town plant got worried, made an anonymous phone call to the local precinct. All the first cops to reach Jimmy's Lounge discovered was a broken window, though nobody in the place seemed to know how that had happened. But at six-thirty the next morning, one of the precinct cops accidentally came upon Brocero in that dark hallway where he had been deposited. One look convinced him that he had found a murder victim. He summoned an ambulance to take the body away. When the medics arrived, however, they discovered that Brocero was not dead, though he was just barely alive. He had a fractured leg, several fractures of the skull, cuts and bruises all over his body; his body temperature was down to 84° and he was in a coma. It was several days before he regained consciousness and was able to talk to the cops. But he would say only that he had been attacked from behind on a street corner by a group of men he did not know and could not identify. Though Coffey and the others in Hogan's office were certain they knew precisely what had happened, they had no way then of persuading Brocero to tell it to them or a grand jury.

What had happened to Brocero, then, hovered like a grim shadow over Jimmy Rodriguez all the time he was in the bar. That and the fact that he was developing only a little more information than was coming over the wiretaps seemed to necessitate another kind of infiltration. Remembering the success of the electronic surveillance in Munich, and successes in other places in other cases, Assistant District Attorney Goldstock went back to court to obtain an order that would permit the planting of a bug in that back room of Jimmy's Lounge.

The order came down, and now it was necessary to gain entry. That was not easy. The bar was open seven days a week, on six of those days from ten in the morning until four the next morning and sometimes even later. When it was closed, there were always people wandering the nearby streets. Given that, there was just one time when it might be possible to get inside. Jimmy's Lounge closed early Sunday night; by two or three in the morning, it was dark and empty and the streets, too, were usually deserted.

The judge handed down the order for the legal bug on a Monday. It was good for thirty days, and the time clock began to run the moment it was signed. Coffey fretted. Six of those thirty days would pass before they could get into the bar and plant the bug. Sunday night came. Two trucks were borrowed from Consolidated Edison Company. The detectives, the expert who would pick the locks to open the doors, and the wiremen all dressed in Con Ed uniforms. They waited until nearly three in the morning to make sure that everything was deserted, that there was no chance of discovery. They drove the trucks to the front of the bar, parked, opened a manhole, set up barricades and lights, pretended to be servicing the gas and electric lines beneath the street. The pickman went to work on the lock.

For two hours he worked, shielded from the view of any chance passersby by the bulk of the Con Ed trucks and the barricades. He struggled. He could not master the locks. They were different from any he had ever worked on before. No matter how delicately and expertly he inserted his picks and tried to maneuver them, he had no success. The locks refused to yield.

Coffey grew more nervous. At any moment, somebody might show up, somebody they did not want to meet. The sky in the east was starting to grow light. "For Chrissakes," he said several times, "can't you move it? Time's running out."

"Don't worry," the pickman kept assuring him. "I'm the best. If anybody can pick this lock, I'm the guy. I just need a little more time and I'll have it."

But time was something they didn't have. "Look," Coffey said finally, "if you can't do it, say so. If you can't do it right now, let's call the whole thing off and we'll get the feds to get us one of their guys."

That made the pickman furious. All he needed was a couple of more minutes and they'd be in. Coffey watched him, knew he would never succeed without a stick of dynamite. "Let's pack up and get out of here," he said. "All we can do is try again next week."

The pickman argued, began to shout. Coffey was in no mood to listen. He gave orders. The equipment was packed back into the trucks. Jimmy's Lounge was left as pristine as it had been when they arrived.

A week later, they were back, this time with one Con Ed truck. Coffey was once more in command, and with him were Detective Larry Mullins and a couple of others from Hogan's office, two wiremen and a pickman lent to them by the FBI. "He turns up," Coffey remembers, "like he'd seen too many commando movies. He was dressed all in black—black clothes, black watch cap, black gloves, even his face was colored with black stuff. But he was the best. We didn't know it then, but he was the guy from the White House Plumbers, the guy who picked the lock of Daniel Ellsberg's psychiatrist's office."

Once more, they enacted the charade in front of Jimmy's Lounge. The barricades and work lights were put up, the manhole cover was opened, the detectives in their Con Ed uniforms clambered down and pretended to work, climbed out and lounged against the barriers and the walls of nearby buildings, drinking coffee as though on a break.

The pickman, fading into the night in his black uniform, went to his task. He had something Coffey had never seen before, a pickgun—an instrument that was placed against the lock, the trigger fired gently, the picks inserted into the lock to catch and work the inner mechanism. In order to conceal what he was about, the pickman placed the gun against the lock, then turned so that his back was to the door and he was working the pickgun with his hands behind him. If anyone caught a glimpse, it would look as if he were merely leaning idly against the door.

Just as he started to work, Coffey saw trouble approaching. Ruthie was walking her dogs. "She was the neighborhood punchboard," he says. "I knew her back when I was in uniform working the ninth precinct. Ruthie used to give us low-level information on street narcotics, things like that. But, the thing about her was that she had a hundred dogs. If you went into her apartment, you needed a gas mask because of the stink. The first time I met her, I was introduced by another cop, and she took us up to that apartment to give us a little information. We got in there and the first thing she did was close the door and take off the doorknob. I looked at her and I thought, What the hell is she doing that for? Maybe she's afraid of junkies breaking in. Well, that's her business. She gave us the information we were interested in and then we got ready to leave. 'Ruthie, where's the knob for the door?' She looked at us and she said, 'You're cops. You find it.' We said, 'Ruthie, we've got to get out of here.' She said, 'Hey, you're sharp guys, you find the knob and you can get out of here.' It took us half an hour before we found it. She was a real cuckoo clock. Now, this night, we were standing there, pretending we were Con Ed guys on a coffee break, watching the pickman fiddling with the lock, when I saw Ruthie coming along the street with her dogs, right at us."

Coffey turned to the other cops and said, "You're not going to believe what's coming down the street," and quickly told them. Ruthie walked directly up to him, surrounding him with the yapping dogs. He was momentarily trapped. She stared into his face. It was obvious she did not recognize him. She let go of the skein of leashes, reached out and grabbed his crotch, squeezing. He slapped her hand away. She laughed. She looked around, noticed the pickman, leaning against the front door of Jimmy's Lounge. She grinned, walked toward him, reached out and grabbed him by the balls, squeezed hard. He let out a scream of pain. The pickgun with all its delicate picks flew from his hand, out of the lock, the picks scattering across the sidewalk. "Get this fucking broad away from me," he hollered in pain, trying to fend her off, to twist away from her.

Coffey gestured to one of the cops. "Grab her," he ordered. "Get her out of here. Go buy her a cup of coffee, anything, but get her away from here fast."

Ruthie was removed, laughing loudly, the pack of dogs racing on ahead. When she was down the street, the pickman gathered his equipment and went back to work. Within moments, he had the door open. Coffey and the wiremen rushed into Jimmy's Lounge, racing to the back room, planting the bug. Coffey looked around, saw the pickman lying on the floor under the bar. He had removed the locks from the door, was working on them with a file and a tiny flashlight. In the twenty minutes it took to plant the bug, check it and make sure it was working, the pickman made a set of duplicate keys to the locks, handed the keys to Coffey, replaced the locks in the door and disappeared into the night.

It was close to five-thirty on a freezing Monday morning in April by the time they had sealed the doors of the bar, making sure that everything was as it had been so that nobody would suspect they had been there, had packed up the barricades, lights and other paraphernalia and stowed everything in the rear of the Con Ed truck. Coffey switched on the ignition. Nothing happened. He swore under his breath, tried again. The motor coughed feebly and died. He tried several more times, but the engine refused to start. The battery was dead. And by then the first of the early morning pedestrians were beginning to appear, glancing at them curiously.

Coffey looked at Larry Mullins on the seat beside him. "The damn thing's dead," he said. "I know what we'll do. My car's parked a couple of blocks away. You sit behind the wheel and I'll go get it and then we'll jump the battery." Coffey was back within minutes, his old Volvo parked beside the Con Ed truck, the hood raised. He took jump cables from his trunk, tossed them to Mullins. "Okay," he said, "hook them to the battery and I'll try to start this thing."

Coffey got behind the wheel of the truck, ready to try the starter once Mullins had made the connections. Mullins attached the cables to the truck's battery, ran them to the Volvo. He clamped on a terminal. As he fastened the second cable, the battery exploded, metal and acid flying everywhere. He'd attached them to the wrong terminals. Mullins was lucky; he had been leaning away from the engine compartment of the car as he was affixing the cables and so was uninjured.

But now they were stranded. The truck and the Volvo were disabled. "We knew we couldn't call the local precinct," Coffey says. "So we did what we should have done in the first place. We called Con Ed and they came and towed the truck and my car away. But all the time we were waiting for them, more and more people were out on the streets and we were sitting there out in the open. I kept wondering whether Rizzo or Popo or one of the barmaids would show up and make us. Fortunately, they didn't, and we got away from there without anybody the wiser. But it was a near thing."

Coffey did not go home. He went directly to the plant. He wanted to be there the moment the bar opened, to hear the first voices come over the bug.

The two barmaids, Loraine and Tootsie, entered Jimmy's Lounge. Their voices were clear, precise, every word distinct. Coffey and the other detectives in the plant nodded with satisfaction. And then the music started. The jukebox began to play, its volume turned up as loud as it would go. All that day and all that night, through every day and night, the jukebox blared. "They played the same goddamn tunes over and over again until we knew them by heart, until we were practically dancing in the plant. That's all we ever got over the bug, just that damn music. Except one time, and maybe that one time made it all worthwhile."

There had been a retirement party several blocks away for one of the local precinct detectives. When the party broke up that evening, a few of the plainclothes cops from the precinct wandered into Jimmy's Lounge for a nightcap. As usual, Jimmy Rodriguez was at the bar, drinking, listening, observing, enacting his role of the neighborhood idler. One of the detectives from the precinct knew Rodriguez. When he saw him at the bar as he came through the doors, he froze. It took him only seconds to understand what was going on. He continued into the bar, nodded as he reached the undercover cop, said, "Hello, Jimmy," and went on down the bar and across the room to a table where Vincent Rizzo sat. "Vinnie," he said, "you know who that little guy at the bar is?"

Rizzo shrugged. "Shit," he said, "he's just one of the locals. He's in here all the time."

"That's how much you know," the detective said. "His name happens to be Jimmy Rodriguez and he's an undercover cop from the D.A.'s squad."

For once the jukebox was not spewing out its deafening din. And so, a block and a half away, those words came through the monitors and into the ears of the listening detectives. Coffey jumped out of his chair, shouted at Les Frank, one of the other detectives, "Les, get into that fucking bar as fast as you can and get Jimmy out of there. Right this minute. He's blown. You know what Rizzo's likely to do."

Frank raced out of the Stuyvesant Town basement, across the street and into the bar. Rodriguez was still there, talking to the bartender, playing with his half-empty glass of whiskey. Jimmy's Lounge was silent. Rizzo was standing beside his table, staring at Rodriguez. Frank edged up to the undercover man. "Jimmy," he whispered, "get the fuck out of here."

Rodriguez grinned, shook his head, "No, man," he said, "I'm havin' a good time. I'm stayin' right where I am."

"Jimmy," Frank said urgently, "you don't understand. You're blown. Get the fuck out of here."

"No, man," Rodriguez repeated, "I'm stayin'." He had not understood what Frank was trying to tell him and nothing Frank said seemed to penetrate.

Frank hurried out of the bar and back to the plant, told Coffey, "Jimmy won't leave."

"I know," Coffey said. "We heard it over the bug."

"What are we going to do?"

"You're going back there," Coffey said, "and you're going to get him out. I don't care how you do it. I don't give a fuck if you have to drag him out by the neck, you just get him out of there, right now. They know who he is."

Frank raced back, tried again to get Rodriguez to leave. Rodriguez still would not listen. And Rizzo was watching. It was obvious to Frank that the only thing that was restraining Rizzo from going after Rodriguez was the presence of the precinct detectives. If Rodriguez was still there when they left, Rodriguez would not leave alive.

Frank grabbed Rodriguez by the arm. "No more shit, Jimmy," he said. "I'm taking you out of here." He hauled Rodriguez away from the bar, ignoring his protests, pushed him out to the street and led him back to the plant.

That was all anyone ever got out of the bug that had been planted with such difficulty in Jimmy's Lounge. But nobody ever doubted that it had been worth the trouble. It had, after all, saved a cop's life.

1 2

• • • • • • • • • • • • •

*T*here was never a doubt that the success of the investigation would ultimately hinge on turning somebody. Coffey's hunch had begun it, but it had been only an intuition that had panned out. The wiretaps and the bugs had provided details and evidence and given direction, but much of what had come over them was cloudy and enigmatic. The computers and the tedious paperwork and physical surveillance had turned up links and patterns. But it was not enough. If they were ever to know all the trails, understand them well enough to follow them to their endings and so amass the evidence that would stand up in court, they would have to turn somebody on the inside. It would not be de Lorenzo or Rizzo or Tortora or anybody high up in the conspiracy. No matter what, there was no hope that any of them would talk, reluctantly or willingly. The first turning would have to be someone near the bottom, trapped so tightly in a net that he had no hope of escape or exculpation. Faced with the certainty of long years in prison, he would be given the choice: take the fall or become an informer and perhaps go free or even enter the federal witness program and begin a new life under the aegis of the government. He would obviously have to be a weak link taken at the moment of his utmost peril, someone whose fear of prison was so great that it outweighed his fear of the deadly revenge of Rizzo and the syndicate. That first turning was the essential one, for even if the pigeon could give little himself, he would surely lead them to others ever higher in the chain until all the pieces would come together.

As the investigators listened to those taps, as they observed those in Rizzo's circle, as they pieced together the computer print-outs, the target seemed apparent: Freddy Mayo. "All you had to do was take one look at him, listen to him whine about his troubles over the phone, look at his yellow sheet," Coffey says, "and you knew that prison wasn't in his plans for a life-style." In the years between 1969 and 1972 alone, the forty-one-year-old Mayo had been arrested eleven times, almost all as a result of his dealings in stolen and forged credit cards and airline tickets. He was under indictment, was awaiting trial, and he was terrified at the thought that he would be convicted and sent away. Mayo would certainly crumble if he were picked up once more, and especially if the bust were for something even more serious than possession of stolen and counterfeit instruments and theft of service—something like narcotics. By himself, Mayo might be minor, but he would be the first card in the house of cards, would start the inevitable fall.

They would watch and pick their moment, and in the spring of 1972 they were in no hurry, were content to pile up what they could from the taps and bugs and other sources, hoping to at least make a start down every major avenue. Then the moment picked them.

Near the end of April, Rizzo answered the phone in Jimmy's Lounge and heard a voice with a British accent ask, "Vincent?"

"When did you get in?" Rizzo asked. "We've been trying to get a hold of you all day."

"Noon," the Englishman said. "Is there any news yet?"

"Not yet," Rizzo said. "Benjamin had to go back to Philly a little while ago. He'll be back tomorrow. We ought to know somethin' then, maybe the next day. But we gotta meet. You come down here tomorrow and we'll get together."

The next morning, soon after Rizzo arrived at Jimmy's Lounge, Marty de Lorenzo drove up, got out of his car, went inside, joined Rizzo in the back room. A few minutes later, Benjamin turned up, followed almost immediately by a nattily dressed, slim, elderly little man. The four huddled in that back room. What they said was drowned out by the blaring jukebox.

The conference lasted about an hour. The little man was the first to leave, hailing a cab outside the bar and heading toward midtown Manhattan. Across the street, Coffey and Tamarro were waiting in Coffey's car, which had been repaired. They tailed the little man to the Diplomat Hotel. A glance at the guest register produced the identification: Tony Grant of 2 Sherwood Court, London, England.

The name meant nothing. Coffey and Tamarro decided it must be a phony, but, to be sure, they asked Interpol whether the international police agency had any information about an Englishman named Tony Grant.

The reply came back the next day. Tony Grant, Interpol said, was a name often used by a sixty-two-year-old native of Liverpool whose true name was Hyman Grant. He had several other aliases, including Hyman Clebanoff. At times he claimed to be a self-employed jeweler, and he was, as it happened, very familiar with precious gems. He also represented himself as a master tailor, and it was apparent from the care he took with his dress that he knew a lot about good clothing. But his main occupation was as a swindler, confidence man and forger who operated on an international scale. He was known to authorities throughout the civilized world and had a criminal record dating back to 1934. It would be impossible to recount all the deals with stolen and counterfeit securities and currency that Grant had worked, Interpol reported, and while in recent years, centering his operations out of Argentina, he had managed to avoid arrest, he was wanted by Portuguese authorities for swindling a gullible couple out of a horde of valuable jewels with payment of $20,000 in counterfeit United States currency.

As Coffey read that dossier, he had a gnawing sense that he had come across Tony Grant before. The name Grant meant nothing to him; it was the first name, Tony, and the combination of Tony and England, Tony as an Englishman. But the connection kept eluding him the harder he tried to establish it. He put it aside, went on to other things and then, in an idle moment, a certain conversation came back to him. He rushed to Leonard Street, dug up the transcript of Rizzo's meeting with Ense and Barg in Munich.

ENSE: Well, the first time when I met Benjamin before, in London ... before we started this deal ...

RIZZO: You mean with Ricky and Tony?

ENSE: Yes. Tony, Ricky, Benjamin, some people else, I don't know them, Maurice and me. The first man I met there was called Dr. Ledl. And this guy was a friend of Ricky.

RIZZO: Right.

ENSE: And couldn't speak to Ricky because Ricky doesn't speak any German and he doesn't speak any English. And Ricky said to me, "Please ask him what does he want. What does he want for his friends in Rome?" So, I learned they had a deal in Rome, this deal would be made with his people in the Vatican, and Dr. Ledl said, "Okay, I need this merchandise." . . . Tony, Jerry and Dr. Ledl and Maurice and me, and two . . . other German people . . . I sent them by car to Rome. . . .

Could this be that same Tony? Coffey's intuition said he was, and if that was so, then maybe what he was doing in New York had something to do with that still-mysterious deal in the Vatican, and even with other deals with Benjamin, Ricky Jacobs, with the Germans, with Rizzo, and even with things they knew nothing about. What was certain was that Grant was in New York about something big, perhaps something on an international scale. Otherwise there would have been no reason for Marty de Lorenzo to have been present at that morning meeting in Jimmy's Lounge.

They would stick to Grant and see where he would lead them. But in Tony Grant they were dealing with a man who had been in the game a long time, a man who rarely took chances unless the payoff was more than worth the risk, and even then only with caution. No sooner had Coffey and Tamarro placed him in the Diplomat Hotel than he moved to another hotel, shifted residences constantly every few days, never staying in one place long enough for a tap or a bug to be planted until, in early May, he paused, checked into the Commodore Hotel and remained.

Events started to accelerate in what at first seemed unconnected directions. Rizzo called Sam Salli, the Buffalo Mafioso who was a prime supplier of counterfeit currency, turning it out with his own printers and engravers as well as importing it from Canada.

"Sam," Rizzo said, "I'm callin' for Uncle Marty."

"Yeah," Salli said.

"We need some merchandise."

"Sure," Salli said. "How much?"

"Two packages," Rizzo said. "One for eighty, one for six hundred."

"You got 'em," Salli said. "The usual price, one for ten."

"No argument," Rizzo said. "Only they got to be good."

"All my stuff is good," Salli said. "You know that."

"Not the last batch," Rizzo said. "I had somebody take a look. He said all they was good for was to wipe your ass. Uncle Marty was very upset. This has got to be good."

"Believe me," Salli said, "I'll get you the best. I'll even deliver it personal."

"How soon? We need the merchandise fast."

"A couple of days," Salli said. "I'll let you know when I'm comin' down."

For those familiar with Sam Salli, there was little mystery in that conversation. Rizzo wanted two packages of counterfeit money, one for $80,000, the other for $600,000. He had no objection to paying Salli's asking price of ten percent of the face value, or $68,000.

A few days later, Salli made the trip into New York from Buffalo, met Rizzo in a room at the Hotel Piccadilly in the Times Square area. The exchange was made, out of sight and hearing of Rizzo's trackers. Though they knew what was going on in that hotel room, and though they knew that the briefcase Rizzo carried away with him contained $680,000 in counterfeit bills, they made no move to intercept him and seize that money. It was more important to find out what those bills were going to be used for.

What that transaction did accomplish, however, was to bring new forces into the chase. The Secret Service, charged not merely with protecting the President and other high government officials but also with protecting United States currency and investigating any suspicion of counterfeiting, was notified. Its resources and agents joined those of the FBI and the Manhattan district attorney.

While he was awaiting Salli's arrival, Rizzo had some orders for Freddy Mayo and Jimmy Heimerle, though when he gave them there was no hint that there was a connection. He told the two travel agents to book flights to San Francisco and to Miami, using their stolen credit cards, airline tickets and validating machines (it was just another example of Rizzo's willingness to take unnecessary risks if he could save a penny in the process). There were to be two reservations to San Francisco and three to Miami, separated by several days.

And then the seemingly unrelated elements began to merge. Mayo and Heimerle themselves boarded the plane for San Francisco. They were going, it was learned later, as couriers for de Lorenzo and Rizzo and they were carrying with them a package of $600,000 in counterfeit bills. When they arrived in San Francisco, they immediately got in touch with two of the city's leading mobsters, Joseph Calise and William Mizono, who picked them up and escorted them to the Mark Hopkins Hotel. A Japanese businessman was waiting for them in a suite. The counterfeit package was turned over to him. The next day, the businessman was on his way back to the Far East, to spread those bills around on the black markets in Tokyo and Hong Kong.

Mayo had hardly returned from that mission to the West Coast before he was off again, this time heading south to Miami. With him were Rizzo and the Englishman, Tony Grant. And with them, concealed in a suitcase, was $80,000 in counterfeit money. They went directly from the airport to the Deauville Hotel in Miami Beach. Grant checked into a room on a high floor overlooking the ocean. Rizzo and Mayo checked into another a few floors below.

They had been tailed all the way by two of Hogan's detectives, joined in Miami by local FBI agents and Secret Service men. But everything was happening too fast. There was no time to get a court order and plant bugs and tap phones. They could only wait and watch from the lobby, and wonder what was happening in those rooms on the floors above. Even from that isolation, though, the little they saw led them to strongly suspect that narcotics were involved. They would learn the details months later.

That afternoon, a South American walked into the Deauville, stopped at the desk, asked for Mr. Grant's room, spoke briefly over the house phone before riding up in the elevator. He was an Argentinian named Carlos Canonico, a stranger to Rizzo and Mayo but not to Grant. Canonico was a close associate of Adolf Soboski, another Argentinian Grant had come to know very well during his frequent trips to and from Buenos Aires and especially during his residence there in the late 1960s. Soboski just happened to be the biggest South American source for cocaine, and anyone who wanted to import large quantities of the drug into the United States had to deal with him.

Canonico was in Grant's room for fifteen or twenty minutes, then Grant took him down the few floors to meet Rizzo. The introductions made, Canonico reached into his pocket and pulled out a package of Marlboros, dropped it on the bed. Rizzo retrieved it, tore it open. It was filled with a white powder. Rizzo sniffed the powder, then handed the pack carefully to Mayo and ordered him to sample it and give his opinion.

Mayo took a taste tentatively. "Well," he said, from limited experience, for narcotics were not his thing, "it tastes like cocaine to me."

"It is," Canonico said. "It is pure."

Rizzo was satisfied. He opened the suitcase and took out the package of $80,000 in counterfeit money and tossed it to Canonico. It was payment for one kilogram of pure cocaine. The arrangements had been made by Grant with Soboski. For Rizzo, this was a bargain. Perhaps Soboski, and Canonico, could distribute those counterfeits in Latin America and elsewhere for close to their face value. But Rizzo had paid Salli only $8,000 for them, while a kilo of pure cocaine was going on the New York market for $66,000. And that hardly touched its true value, for that kilo could be cut twelve times before it was finally sold on the street; thus nearly $850,000 could be realized from the sale of that single kilo of cocaine.

Rizzo, however, did not deal in small things, like a single kilo of narcotics, and so what was happening in that hotel room at the Deauville in Miami Beach was merely a sampling session, an opening to bigger things. Rizzo was about to make a major move into the cocaine market. If he was satisfied with the quality of the merchandise Canonico showed him, then he was prepared to use Soboski as his source for some very large shipments. And he was satisfied.

Before Canonico left the room, arrangements had been made for the immediate purchase of eight more kilos of pure cocaine, to be paid for partly in counterfeit money and partly in real bills, and to be delivered in New York within ten days. And a second and larger deal was set in motion, one that, because of its size, would take longer to complete and would require some intricate logistics. Rizzo ordered from Soboski eighty-two kilos of pure cocaine. Street value: about $70 million.

If the aroma of narcotics was now fragrant, still those on the outside, the investigators, got only the scent, knew none of the details. But they were convinced a major delivery was imminent. Why else would Grant remain at the Deauville while Rizzo and Mayo returned to New York? Why else would Rizzo call Grant every day asking for news?

Then, as the week was drawing to a close, the phone rang in

Jimmy's Lounge. It was Grant calling from Miami Beach. Contact had been made, he told Rizzo, and so he and his South American friends were about to drive north and would like to meet Rizzo on Saturday to bring things to a satisfactory conclusion.

Saturday morning, Hogan's men were ready. If they did not yet know where the meeting would take place, they were sure it would not be hard to find out. Coffey parked his car across the street from Rizzo's home and waited, prepared to tail him wherever he went and then get word to Sergeant Bob Nicholson and the other detectives. Patty Marino drove up in Rizzo's Mercedes. Rizzo appeared, got in beside Marino, and the Mercedes started north. Coffey moved after it, keeping a block behind. It took him only a few minutes to realize that Rizzo was wary, was on the alert for a tail. The Mercedes made sharp turns, squared blocks, veered in and out of traffic lanes. Coffey could see Rizzo's head turning, watching through the rear window to see if they had a tail, if they had shaken it. At that moment, he was glad he was alone; two men in a car would have been a sure sign to Rizzo that he was being followed.

The Mercedes accelerated, screeched around a corner into Thirty-first Street. As Coffey turned the corner, he saw the Mercedes come to a sudden stop at the end of the block. He braked, pulled into an empty space at the curb a few hundred feet behind. Rizzo got out of his car and started to walk slowly back along the block. Coffey slumped down behind the wheel, trying to make himself invisible while still being able to peer over it. Rizzo kept walking toward him, getting closer. About twenty-five feet from Coffey's car, he stopped, stared at it, squinting to peer through the front window. Coffey slumped lower. Rizzo saw no one. Apparently reassured, he turned and headed back to the Mercedes, got in and the car started up. Coffey waited until it had turned the corner before starting his own car and taking off in pursuit. He spotted the Mercedes again heading north and kept pace with it.

The Mercedes finally pulled into the parking lot at the Americana Hotel on Seventh Avenue. Marino took the parking stub and he and Rizzo went into the hotel. Coffey followed. From a phone in the lobby, he called the waiting Nicholson and within fifteen minutes the hotel lobby was filled with Hogan's detectives.

Rizzo and Marino had been the first to arrive. They went into the French Quarter restaurant off the lobby and took a large table. They did not have long to wait. Tony Grant appeared, accompanied by two Argentinians, Raul Crotti and Andres Puchet, agents for Adolf Soboski. There were greetings, introductions, the ordering of lunch. There was some intense conversation. No detective was close enough to overhear; most were in the lobby, a few at other tables around the restaurant, watching. They saw only one thing that seemed significant: Crotti took a piece of cardboard from his pocket, a parking stub, and handed it surreptitiously to Marino, who shoved it into his own pocket.

The lunch went on and on. Coffey started to grow concerned. The hotel had so many exits that it might be possible for somebody to slip away unnoticed. He went to Nicholson. "Look, Bob," he said, "I'm going to go and sit on the Mercedes, just in case."

He went to the parking lot, got into his own car and waited. Suddenly, Rizzo appeared, alone, got into the Mercedes and drove off. Coffey had no time to alert those still watching the table in the Americana; he had to move with Rizzo, and Rizzo took him on a weaving, twisting, circuitous half-hour ride downtown, to Fourteenth Street and Third Avenue—to the Blue Seas restaurant. Rizzo parked and went inside. Coffey parked across the street, rushed to a pay phone. He called Dick Tamarro at home, told him what was happening, and Tamarro said he would be there as soon as he could. Then Coffey called the Americana. "I had made no arrangements to let them know I would be calling," he said, "but Bob Nicholson is a pretty sharp guy. He's got a brother who's a doctor, so I had the hotel page a Dr. Nicholson. He picked up the phone and I told him the story. I said when the rest of them leave, in case you lose them, they're probably coming here, to the Blue Seas."

A half-hour later, Tamarro now with him in the car, Coffey saw a cab arrive at the Blue Seas. Grant, Crotti, Puchet and Marino got out and went inside. A little while later, Nicholson and the other detectives appeared. "We lost them," Nicholson said. "Did they show?"

"Yeah," Coffey said. "They're all inside."

Should they move in? "We wanted to go in there and find out what was going on," Coffey says. "With the South Americans, we knew they must be dealing big in narcotics. But we couldn't do it. We couldn't afford to make a move that would blow the whole thing. We had to lay back, watch, pick up what we could and add it to everything else."

They would learn later that what they had been watching were the details of the delivery of the eight kilos of cocaine and the payment for it. The money, in real bills and counterfeits, had been stashed at the Blue Seas and Crotti and Puchet had made the cab trip there to pick it up and deliver it later to Soboski. The cocaine was in the trunk of a rented car that Crotti had parked at the Americana, the parking stub for which he had handed to Marino. Sometime that evening, Marino returned to the hotel, picked up the car, managed to elude his trackers as he drove away with the cocaine.

While Marino was weaving through Manhattan traffic that Saturday night with his load of cocaine, Grant was back in his room at the Commodore, making a phone call. He reached Freddy Mayo and asked if Mayo could get him a ticket on a Braniff flight leaving for Buenos Aires the next morning. Over one of the taps, the listeners heard Mayo confirm the order and say that the ticket would be delivered to Grant before he left for the airport.

The district attorney's office was immediately informed and Inspector Vitrano sent out a hurried call for Coffey. "Joe," he said when Coffey arrived, "pack your bags. You're leaving for Argentina in the morning." The trip to Munich in February had shattered forever the ancient code; no longer would there be any hesitation about sending a New York cop out of the country on a case.

But Coffey did not want to go to South America. It was not that he spoke no Spanish; his lack of German had not hindered him in Munich. It was that something else was happening that might necessitate another sudden trip to Europe.

Rizzo had been growing increasingly perturbed about the behavior of his German friends over the previous several weeks. When Heshy Lebensfeld told him that he was on his way back to Europe, Rizzo had asked him to stop in Munich, see Alfred Barg and "ask him how much money did he put in my account in the Otto Dierks and Company Bank. And, Harry," he had added, "have him give you the deposit slip for what he put in."

But Barg had deposited no money after that initial payment into Rizzo's account, and Rizzo wanted to know why. Several times, he ordered William Benjamin to call Barg in Munich, tell him to stop playing around and do what he agreed to do or something unpleasant was likely to happen to him. Benjamin reported back that he had tried several times, had been unable to reach Barg; the German was always someplace else—one day in France, another out of the office, never near a telephone. "I can't get through," Benjamin complained. "Now there's only one thing has to be . . . Someone has to go out and lay the law down and make a procedure which has to be followed every week, and if they don't do it then you gotta take action about it, 'cause I'm fed up with the bullshit, every fuckin' day I'm makin' telephone calls."

There was obviously only one person who could lay down the law and be heeded, and that was Vincent Rizzo himself. Rizzo began to give indications that he was about to do just that. And then he indicated that he was going to bring in even bigger guns to force the issue. He called Marty de Lorenzo and urged him to accompany him to Germany, saying that maybe de Lorenzo's presence, and his position, would make the difference and get them what was coming to them.

Thus, Coffey was convinced that at any moment Rizzo and de Lorenzo would be on their way to Munich. If they were to go, then he wanted to go with them. That was a side of the case, or cases, with which he was now expert, and he had established a rapport with his German counterparts that would take someone else time to pick up.

Vitrano and Goldstock agreed. Coffey should wait, prepare himself for that flight to Munich. But somebody had to tail Grant to Argentina. If he was involved in major narcotics, they wanted to know about it. "Send Jimmy Rodriguez," Coffey said. "When it comes to undercover work, there's nobody better. And he speaks Spanish."

On the morning of Mother's Day, 1972, Rodriguez and Larry Mullins were in their seats on a Braniff flight to Argentina, just down the aisle from Tony Grant. In Buenos Aires, they were met by local agents of the Bureau of Narcotics and Dangerous Drugs. (With the indications that a major narcotics deal was in the works, that federal agency had also been brought into the hunt.) Rodriguez and Mullins were in Buenos Aires for a week, working closely with the BNDD agents. They received only minimal assistance from Argentine authorities. They followed Grant everywhere, and he was a busy man indeed—meeting regularly with people they could not identify, and seeing Adolf Soboski very often. But there were few clues as to what those gatherings were about.

It was only a little later that they learned the details. Grant and Soboski were making the arrangements for the purchase of those eighty-two kilos of cocaine and setting up the means to get them into the United States. They found a way. Soboski purchased a house trailer, secreted it in the jungle along the border between Paraguay and Chile. With the connivance of the former head of the Chilean narcotics enforcement bureau, the cocaine was smuggled across the border into Paraguay and then hidden inside the trailer. The intention was for the trailer to make an innocent journey up through South and Central America and cross unmolested into the southern United States.

Those secret arrangements made, Grant returned to New York. Rodriguez and Mullins, uncertain as to what, if anything, they had actually witnessed or learned, followed on the same plane.

Coffey was not there to greet them. He was in Munich. Two days after Grant had left New York for Buenos Aires, Rizzo called Lufthansa and made reservations for himself and de Lorenzo on a flight to Germany scheduled to leave the following day.

The instant those plans were known, Coffey, pausing only long enough to pack his suitcase, was on his way. This time, he had company: Mario Trapani, the detective he had worked with undercover at Ponte's restaurant. The FBI had been asked to send Dick Tamarro along, too, since Tamarro was the agent most deeply involved and so most knowledgeable. But the FBI, like the New York police before Coffey's initial trip, had an inviolate policy of refusing to send its agents outside the country. They relied instead on the agents in place—those assigned to embassies and missions overseas—even though they might know nothing about the investigation. Permission for Tamarro to go along was denied.

The Munich police, Coffey's friends now, were waiting, and this time there was no need to persuade them of anything. Rizzo and de Lorenzo were booked into the Bayerischer Hof Hotel. The phones in their suite were tapped; in the bedroom a bug was planted in the lamp on the table between their beds.

Within minutes after they arrived, Rizzo called Barg and Ense, demanded that they appear at the hotel immediately, told them there were things that had to be settled and he would brook no more delays. Rizzo's tone was enough to win prompt acquiescence.

Coffey and the German detectives gathered around the monitors in their room down the hall, expecting a replay of the scene at the Palace Hotel in February with, perhaps, more revelations. They got nothing. The bug had been planted in the bedroom; the conversations took place in the living room.

But Barg, Ense, Rizzo and de Lorenzo did not stay in the suite long. Using all his charm, Barg insisted that they be his guests for dinner at the Excelsior Hotel. Barg was nervous, shaking, terrified. Through that dinner, Rizzo rarely smiled and generally behaved in such a manner as to give Barg good reason for his terror. De Lorenzo merely sat and ate and looked on, smiling benignly, nodding now and again. But his presence added weight to Rizzo's demands.

During that dinner, Heshy Lebensfeld suddenly appeared, saw them, joined them for coffee, and then took de Lorenzo off with him, leaving Barg, Ense and Rizzo alone. Barg had a suggestion. Perhaps Rizzo would agree to drive with them out to Barg's home in Gruenwald, a Munich suburb, meet his family and, in the privacy of his study, try to find a solution to their problems.

The hour in his own study was hardly a pleasant or reassuring time for Alfred Barg, nor for his friend, Winfried Ense. Rizzo told them bluntly that he had run out of patience. He would tolerate no more delays in settling accounts. Why, he demanded, had Barg put only a few deutsche marks into the account that had been opened in early March? Why had Barg not made the payments he had agreed to make? Now, Rizzo said, he had brought with him a very important man, the man they had had dinner with. This was a man who enjoyed his own home and surroundings, who would travel long distances only in cases of extreme need. And this was the man to whom the money was owed. The only thing that would save Barg and Ense from more trouble than they could possibly imagine was the immediate payment of the $350,000 that was long overdue.

Barg stammered that unfortunately he was not in a position to pay that kind of money then. Perhaps Rizzo would accept some valuable jewelry he had in his safe as part payment?

Rizzo refused. He was not interested in jewels. He was interested in money. Period.

Barg had another proposal. Perhaps Rizzo and de Lorenzo would accept a binding letter that would guarantee them a share in the profits of the Bel Air vacation homes project in Montpellier? Since the homes were just then being built and only the first ones had been sold, it might be a little time before the profits would begin to flow. But, from the projections that had been made and from all indications, Bel Air was going to be an extremely profitable venture and the Rizzo-de Lorenzo share would earn them at least $1 million within the next five years. And to demonstrate his good faith, Barg offered 14,000 deutsche marks (about $6,000) to pay for their expenses on this trip to Germany and for their trouble.

If the offer was legitimate and prospects as real as Barg said they were, and the papers he showed Rizzo seemed to indicate that, this counterproposal was enticing, indeed; especially since there seemed little hope of wringing $350,000 in cash out of Barg and Ense at that moment. Rizzo, however, did not commit himself immediately. He said he would discuss the proposition with de Lorenzo and get back to Barg with an answer. But Rizzo's reaction was enough to convince Barg that he had won at least a temporary reprieve. He and Ense drove Rizzo back to Munich, took him to a favorite café for a nightcap and then dropped him off at the Bayerischer Hof.

When Rizzo put Barg's offer to de Lorenzo, Uncle Marty bought it. The next morning, both appeared at Barg's office on the third floor of Tengstrasse 38, and when they departed it was with a contract, in the form of a letter, cutting them in on the profits of Bel Air. It must have seemed a satisfactory solution to everyone at the moment, for over the next few days, Rizzo and de Lorenzo did little but enjoy themselves, taking in the sights, the restaurants, the night life.

And Coffey stewed. It was all happening in secret, out of his sight and hearing. Nothing was coming over the bug except those late-night reflections by de Lorenzo. Further, something important was about to take place in New York. During one of his regular calls to Vitrano, he learned that Hogan's office had received a tip from an informant, and the tip had been confirmed by a guarded telephone conversation overheard in the Stuyvesant Town plant, that Mayo and Grant were about to take part in a large narcotics exchange. On Saturday, May 20, they intended to drive to Philadelphia, pick up a shipment from Benjamin and carry it back to New York. The decision had been made to intercept them. Trapped with narcotics, Mayo would certainly turn, and with luck they might also be able to turn Grant, and that might open more doors than they dared speculate about. Coffey was not about to miss that. He told Trapani to stay in Munich, keep watch over Rizzo and de Lorenzo just in case they did something else, while he made the first available flight home.

Reaching New York late on Friday, Coffey rushed to Leonard Street, spent the rest of that night and most of the next day going over the plans for the bust.

Early Saturday morning, Mayo and Grant set out for Philadelphia, met Benjamin, turned and started back for New York. They were tailed all the way, word of their movements radioed back regularly. When they turned off the New Jersey Turnpike to take the Goethals Bridge to Staten Island, Coffey and the other detectives made their move. In two unmarked cars, they sped to Staten Island, intercepted Mayo and Grant on the expressway crossing the island. Mayo turned the car off the expressway onto the Staten Island streets, desperately trying to lose them. The two unmarked cars stayed with him, came up on him on a narrow dark street, forced his car over. The detectives leaped out of their cars, surrounded their target, threw open the doors and ordered Mayo and Grant out.

Mayo took one look at the threatening men around his car, was convinced they were hijackers come to seize the narcotics he had supposedly picked up in Philadelphia and then kill him and Grant. He started to whimper, to shake uncontrollably. He began to plead. He was so terrified, he wet his pants, a dark wet stain spreading across the front and down his legs. When the shields were flashed at him and he was told he was under arrest, he started to laugh with hysterical relief. All the time, Grant merely stood to one side, silently, calmly, stoically, ready to accept his fate without a murmur.

Mayo and Grant were searched and handcuffed. No narcotics were found on them. The car was searched thoroughly. Still no narcotics. The pickup in Philadelphia had been aborted, Benjamin telling them he had heard there might be some trouble and so the delivery was being called off for the time being. Still, the evidence that had come from the wiretap and from the informant's tip was enough to permit an arrest on charges of narcotics conspiracy. The two were put in separate cars and driven to Leonard Street, kept apart and questioned.

Coffey and another detective went to work on Mayo, sure this weak link would collapse without any sweat on their part. They were right. Faced now with the certainty of long years in prison, Mayo buckled, leaped eagerly at the idea that he might be able to make a deal, might even, if he told all he knew, find shelter in the federal protected witness program and so be able to disappear beyond Rizzo's reach.

In an unbroken monologue, he spilled all he knew about the stolen and counterfeit airline tickets and credit cards. He talked about his trip to San Francisco with Heimerle, his meeting with Calise and Mizono and the passing of the counterfeit bills to the Japanese businessman at the Mark Hopkins. He talked about his trip with Rizzo and Grant to Miami, the session at the Deauville with Canonico, the deals that Rizzo had made for the importing of cocaine from Soboski in South America. He talked about Heimerle, Patty Marino—about everything and everyone he knew. But when the questioning turned to Europe, to Munich and Rome, to securities, Mayo could only shake his head. "I don't know nothin' about that," he said. "I wasn't part of that and they didn't tell me nothin' about that. All I did was fix the tickets and get the flights."

So, even though Mayo provided solid evidence in a dozen areas, he still left an essential area empty. But, as they had thought, he was that essential first card in the stack. It was time to turn to Grant, to put pressure on him, for there was no doubt that he knew much more than Mayo about many things. Grant was lodged in the Tombs, and every day Larry Mullins or another of Hogan's detectives went to see him, to try to persuade or force him to talk. But Tony Grant was no Freddy Mayo. He had been in prison often enough to have lost his fear of bars and cells. He had no answers to any of the questions. He offered only a knowing smile. For Grant was sure he had nothing to worry about. He had done enough for Rizzo to be sure he would not languish in the Tombs or go to prison, that Rizzo would supply whatever he needed. He was sure he could depend on Vincent Rizzo.

But Rizzo did not appear. Rizzo sent no one to see him. Rizzo sent no lawyer to defend him. Doubt began to seep through Grant. He sent a message from his jail cell. He was a chain-smoker and was suffering without his cigarettes. Would Rizzo please send him some.

Grant waited. There was no reply. He sent out another message, this time a demand that Rizzo send him a carton of cigarettes. Rizzo did not reply.

More days passed and the realization gradually reached Grant that he had been abandoned. He sent out a different message. He would, he told the authorities at the Tombs, like to see some cops.

This was the hoped-for break. Mullins dashed to the Tombs, took custody of Grant, hustled him back to Leonard Street, ushered him into an office where Coffey and Assistant D.A. Ron Goldstock were waiting.

"You wanted to see us?" Coffey said.

Grant looked at him, at Mullins, at Goldstock. "Have you got a cigarette?" he asked. Coffey took out a pack, handed him one, held out a match. Grant inhaled deeply. He smoked it down to a minute butt, in rapid puffs, as though convinced there would never be another. When only ash remained, he looked at Coffey. Coffey shook a second cigarette from the pack, held the match while Grant lit it, then handed the pack to Grant.

"You wanted to see us?" Coffey said again.

Grant was in no hurry. He inhaled his cigarette, relishing the taste, examined the glowing butt, inspected the room and his interrogators. At last, he said, "Do you know Vincent Rizzo?"

"We know him."

Grant made a sour face. "That man," he said, "is a cheap son of a bitch. I've never known anyone so cheap. Do you know, I asked him for some cigarettes and he was too cheap to send them. He never even had the decency to send a reply. And after all I've done for that man."

"Is that right?" Coffey said. He looked at Goldstock and Mullins. They kept their faces emotionless, struggled to conceal the excitement that was building.

"Oh, yes," Grant said. "Believe me, I've done plenty for him. I can help you. I can give you Rizzo."

"Is that so?" Coffey said. "How?"

"I can tell you whatever you want to know," Grant said. "Just ask me."

"About what?"

"About everything," Grant said. "I was in on most of it, and what I wasn't in on, I know about. I know you know about drugs.

That's why you were waiting for Mayo and me when we came back from Philadelphia. But do you know about Soboski? Do you know about the trailer that's waiting in Paraguay? I can give you the details."

"What about Soboski?"

Grant spelled it out for them—how he had negotiated on Rizzo's behalf with Soboski for the purchase of eighty-two kilos of cocaine, and arranged for its shipment into the United States concealed in a house trailer.

(That information was immediately passed on to the Bureau of Narcotics and Dangerous Drugs. Acting on it, BNDD agents in South America sped to the jungle along the border between Chile and Paraguay, came upon the trailer precisely where Grant had said it would be. But when they searched it, they found nothing. A message was flashed to New York that the tip must be wrong, the trailer was clean. Hogan's office flashed a return message: the tip was correct; the cocaine was hidden in the trailer; if necessary, the trailer should be torn apart. The BNDD agents took the trailer to pieces. Concealed within its walls were the eighty-two kilos of pure cocaine. Within weeks, Soboski, arriving in the United States on a visit, was in custody, charged and then given the choice of spending most of the rest of his life in an American prison or becoming an informant. He decided to talk, and so turned from major supplier of illegal narcotics to the American market to major supplier of information about the intercontinental drug traffic.)

"What else?" Coffey asked.

"I'm sure you know about the deal in Panama," Grant said, "the thing with Shinwell and Ricky Jacobs and the rest. I wasn't part of that, but I learned about it and I can fill you in. And the deal in the Vatican? You must know about that. I'm sure, though, you don't know everything. But I know enough about what Rizzo and Ricky Jacobs and that Austrian, Dr. Ledl, were trying to do. I can tell you. Gentlemen, just ask me and I'll tell you everything I know about Mr. Vincent Rizzo. It will be my pleasure to give him to you. But, please, just one thing in return. I would like you to keep me supplied with cigarettes."

So, Grant turned—not, like Mayo, to save himself, but to gain satisfaction. Rizzo was going to discover that his refusal to meet Tony Grant's simple request would cost him a lot more than the price of a pack, or even a carton, of cigarettes. With Grant's turning, major obstacles were cleared away and the road to the center was clearly marked. All along that road, with Grant as a guide, they would come upon others who, to save themselves or to gain a measure of their own revenge for slights and injury, would turn, too, and make the road smoother, wider, easier to navigate. The thousand strands began to come together; a picture began to emerge; the patterns, lines and connections began to take on an understandable shape.

Most of the events had happened long before Coffey or any investigator had had any awareness of them, had stumbled on the first clues. So, though it might all be history to Grant and the others who would provide the narrative, to those who listened, it had the fascination of immediacy and freshness, as though the events were being played out before them as they occurred.

Part Four

. . . .

COCA-COLA

1 3

• • • • • • • • • • • • • •

*I*f there was a single event that set in motion the story told by Grant and all the informants who came after him, it occurred on a hot afternoon in the late summer of 1970 at the Beverly Hills Hotel. Long before Coffey or any investigator became aware, Ricky Jacobs turned to his old Philadelphia friend, William Benjamin, and said, "I need tons of stock. I can use all you can get."

Though Jacobs and Benjamin had known each other well for years, they had gone their separate ways. For his securities, Jacobs relied mainly on West Coast sources—his friend and sometime partner, the syndicate bigshot John Roselli; small-time thieves who found themselves with paper they did not know what else to do with but turn over to Jacobs; others who had hot merchandise they knew he could market—and on syndicate leader Dominic Mantell and others in Florida. Though he had cultivated outlets all over the United States, customers who besieged him with demands for stock, he had more and more turned his attention to the international arena, particularly Europe and Latin America. There, the demand for American corporate and government securities, based as they were on the dollar (then still the world's premier currency, the standard against which all others were measured and so the rock on which rested the economic stability of the Western world), was increasing at an astronomical rate. There, it was possible to operate with greater latitude, shielded by distance, by the time lag between the theft, its discovery and the arrival abroad of the hot sheet, by the seemingly more relaxed checking procedures of officials in banks and brokerage houses. Thus, the potential for profit with less risk was enormous in Europe and Latin America. Jacobs's international dealings were growing at a rapid rate as he developed contacts throughout the world, certain that he was the equal of the most accomplished and sophisticated confidence men anywhere. But as this empire grew, Jacobs had need for additional sources of supply. His bid to Benjamin, then, was an opening to the powers in the East, with whom he had rarely dealt before.

Benjamin was the right man to bring them together, as Jacobs well knew. He was a vital link in the eastern operation, in that chain that led from the acquisition of stolen and counterfeit securities to their ultimate disposition. He was middleman for the rulers of the eastern syndicate, and especially for Vincent Rizzo, who was becoming known within the clandestine securities business as the man who ran the syndicate's operation. Rizzo and his associates had the means to amass limitless quantities of securities. But their existence within the heart of the Italian-dominated organized underworld made them essentially narrow and provincial, suspicious of outsiders they had not done business with over the years and could not control. Thus, they had never developed the contacts, outlets and means to broaden the distribution of their securities. For that, they relied on men like Benjamin who had been in the rackets for decades, knew everyone across the broad spectrum, and were not circumscribed in their dealings by Mafia traditions. They knew Benjamin was able to turn up the dealers who had the expertise, who knew how to move hot paper at great profit to themselves and the organization. And they trusted Benjamin to make the best arrangements and never hold out or try to cheat them. He was trusted because he seemed to know his place in the organization's scheme, did not aspire to positions he could never attain and was willing to obey orders. But, then, Benjamin, like so many others, was terrified of Rizzo and what Rizzo was capable of doing if crossed, and so he rarely questioned Rizzo's dictates (like registering Rizzo's Mercedes in his own name in Pennsylvania yet never getting a ride in it unless invited). Still, he was certain that Rizzo would protect him when necessary, would provide him with regular employment and a good living moving stocks and doing other errands. And those were no small things. By the time he met with Ricky Jacobs, he had handled scores of stock deals involving millions of dollars.

Even while doing Rizzo's bidding without murmur, somewhere deep inside Benjamin a resentment stirred. He might never voice it to Rizzo or anyone else in the syndicate, but to close friends he sometimes let those feelings seep through. He once lamented to Tony

Grant: "Rizzo's a member of a family, and he can get whatever he wants. I can't be a part of a family, so I have to rely on what he wants to give me." To friends (and a long time later, when he was sure he had no other choice but to turn informant and become a protected witness, to authorities) he complained that Rizzo, de Lorenzo and the others were forever taking advantage of him. When a deal was going, he said, they almost always insisted that he put up some of the front money before they gave him the stocks to deal, and then when the sale had been made and he had been paid, demanded the bulk of the profits and left him only a pittance.

It was just such an arrangement that, in a convoluted way, led to his reunion with Ricky Jacobs. In June 1970, he was in Jimmy's Lounge with Rizzo, seeking a new supply of hot paper. Two of his better contacts, Los Angeles insurance brokers Paul King and Ted McGoey, had a profitable sideline dealing in stolen securities. No matter how much Benjamin gave them, they always insisted they could use more; they never quibbled about price, paid the moment they had made their sales and even cut Benjamin and his people in on a share of the profits. Now, Benjamin said, he was under considerable pressure from King to come up with some more good stuff. One of de Lorenzo's partners, Tobias "Teddy" Cohen, was in the bar at the time, overheard the conversation and mentioned that perhaps he could help out. He had just come into two valuable pieces of paper, a $100,000 Consolidated Intermediate Credit Bank bond and a $100,000 United States Treasury note. He expected to realize at least $50,000 from them. He would be willing to turn them over to Benjamin on payment of $15,000 in front money and would not press for the other $35,000 until King and McGoey had paid for the bonds. Of course, Cohen added, he would also expect a share of anything over the $50,000 that happened Benjamin's way.

Benjamin wanted those bonds. However, he explained to Cohen, he was a little short of ready cash.

That was too bad, Cohen said. While he had faith in Benjamin, based on past performance, still he had a hard-and-fast rule that he would never part with merchandise without cash up front.

Benjamin looked to Rizzo for help. Rizzo shook his head. But, then, Benjamin knew that it was only on very rare occasions that

Rizzo ever dipped into his own pocket to back a deal. Rizzo, however, had a suggestion. Benjamin ought to go to see Peter Raia and cut him in on a share of his profits in exchange for the $15,000 advance. Benjamin had better do it right away, Rizzo added, and Cohen nodded agreement, because Cohen would want an answer before the day was out, otherwise he would find another way to dispose of those bonds.

Had there been an alternative, Benjamin would never have gone to Raia. But there was no alternative and, besides, he read Rizzo's suggestion as an order. And so, with great reluctance, Benjamin made the trip uptown.

Then in his early forties, Peter Joseph Raia, who was also known as Peter Martell, Peter Martella, Joe Costanza, Jack Fassoulis and a lot of other names, was the owner of the J. Martello Shoe Concession at New York's Park Sheraton Hotel and of a Seventh Avenue dress house. But they were merely fronts. Over the preceding twenty years, Raia had been arrested fourteen times, for crimes ranging from using the mails to defraud, to armed robbery and assault with a deadly weapon. He had served five terms of from one to three years in federal and state prisons. He was a hulking, dangerous thug—six feet four inches tall and two hundred seventy pounds. The only thing he loved more than money was battering to near death anyone who displeased him. A reputed killer named Michael "The Animal" Affinito was always at his side to do his errands. It was whispered that he was high up in one of the New York crime families, was a trusted confidant of the bosses. He was not. At best, he was a Mafia hanger-on, used by Rizzo and de Lorenzo and others because he had certain jealously guarded contacts and sources of supply for various goods. Because of his value to them, they worked with him now and then, threw him an occasional profitable bone. On this occasion, Benjamin and Teddy Cohen's bonds were such a bone.

"Are you absolutely sure you can work the deal?" Raia demanded of Benjamin when the proposition was put to him.

"You know me," Benjamin said. "Would I try to con you? I'm a hundred percent sure."

"Okay," Raia said. "I'll get you the fifteen grand."

That night, Raia's money was put into Cohen's hands, the bonds into Benjamin's and by the next day, Benjamin was in Los Angeles turning them over to Paul King. True to his promise, Cohen waited patiently for his $35,000, certain that when King completed his end of the deal and paid Benjamin, he would get his due. But as time passed, Raia was not so patient. He called Benjamin daily, demanded news, demanded action, told Benjamin time was running out and if he didn't get his money soon, he might have to send Affinito down to Philadelphia to pay Benjamin a visit.

Benjamin was petrified. He tried to reach King, was told King was out of town. He went to Rizzo for protection, was told he had nothing to worry about so long as King made the sale and Raia got his money. Of course, if something went wrong, Benjamin would have to watch out for himself. After all, it was he who had borrowed the money from Raia.

Raia grew more strident in his demands, more threatening, and Benjamin more desperate. Then, three weeks after he had carried the bonds to the West Coast, King finally called. He apologized for the silence and the delay, but he and his wife had been in Las Vegas for a short vacation. However, he had some good news. He had been able to combine his pleasure with some business, had managed to cash the bonds for their full face value. Benjamin could pick up his share of the $200,000 anytime.

Cohen was informed. Raia was informed. Benjamin boarded a plane for Los Angeles. Raia appeared, took the seat next to him. With the payoff at hand, Raia had no intention of being on a different coast, of permitting Benjamin to wander around loose with all that money. Besides, he told Benjamin during the flight, this gave him a good reason to visit his sister who lived in Los Angeles and whom Raia had not seen in several years.

When they landed, they were met by an old friend of Benjamin's, Louis "Potatoes" Gittleman, a small-time gambler and bookmaker and, most recently, a courier for Rizzo and Benjamin, ferrying merchandise from California to New York and back again. Gittleman dropped Raia off at his sister's home, then drove Benjamin to the Sportsmen's Lodge on Ventura Boulevard. In the bar, Benjamin met King, had a drink with him, walked away with a heavy briefcase.

When Benjamin opened the door to his room, a suspicion was confirmed. Rizzo and Patty Marino were sitting on the bed. Though he had refused to put up any of the front money, had sent Benjamin to Raia for it, Rizzo was a full partner, had followed to Los Angeles to take possession of what was his and Cohen's. He relieved Benjamin of the briefcase, checked to make sure it contained all he expected, and then informed Benjamin that he was taking it back to New York. The splits would be made there.

Benjamin was in a terrible quandary. He was only a little less terrified of Raia than he was of Rizzo. What would Raia do to him when he learned that the only thing he was getting out of his flight to California was a visit with his sister? Benjamin pleaded with Rizzo. If he couldn't turn something over to the man, he said, Raia was very likely to make a lot of trouble. Rizzo knew what Raia was like. He laughed, opened the briefcase again, counted out $15,000, and told Benjamin to deliver it to Raia and say that Rizzo said he would get whatever else was coming to him when he got back to New York.

A few days later, Raia had his profits. Benjamin got enough to pay his expenses and keep him satisfied, but only a fraction of what should have come to him. He did not complain. His fortunes improved somewhat during this summer, as Rizzo kept dispatching him to King and McGoey in Los Angeles and to his contacts in other cities with more stocks and bonds. And there was one other thing to be grateful for: Raia was not involved in most of those deals.

Then, early in September, Raia had prime merchandise once more and Benjamin had no choice but to work with him. Some freelance thieves had made away with three $100,000 United States Treasury bills from the vaults of Manufacturers Hanover Trust Company in New York (it would be a considerable time before the bank discovered the loss). They had approached Raia and offered him the bills for $75,000. Raia was not about to put up that much money himself, especially since he did not have the outlets to market them. Remembering that Benjamin's man on the West Coast had sold bonds at full value not long before, Raia approached Rizzo and Benjamin, offered to cut them in as full partners in exchange for $25,000 each. It was too good a deal to turn down, but Rizzo never bought anything without bargaining first. He told Raia that he and Benjamin were interested, but not at Raia's price. The most they would kick in for the two-thirds Raia was willing to turn over to them was $20,000 each. If Raia wanted the deal to go through, wanted Benjamin's contacts, he'd either have to put up $35,000 himself or chisel the thieves down to $60,000. Raia managed to do just that, and late one night in early September, at the Crazy Horse Bar on Manhattan's Upper East Side, a fat envelope containing $60,000 was passed across a table in exchange for a thin one with three $100,000 treasury bills.

The next morning, Benjamin was on his way back to California. He checked into the Beverly Hills Hotel and called King, asked for a meeting. King went to the hotel, examined the bonds, sadly shook his head. They were beautiful, he told Benjamin. He would love to handle them. The thing was, he and McGoey were temporarily out of business. The federal government, he explained, had begun an investigation into the illegal securities business in Los Angeles and he was afraid they were getting close to his operation. Discretion dictated that he and McGoey do nothing but sell real estate until things cooled off. Still, King said, there was no reason for Benjamin to be concerned. One of their mutual friends had been after him for the last several months, trying to get his hands on good securities. Maybe if Benjamin called Ricky Jacobs, a deal could be struck.

And so, that late summer afternoon in 1970 at the Beverly Hills Hotel, Benjamin and Jacobs renewed acquaintance. When Jacobs departed he carried with him the three treasury bills and the assurance that this was only the beginning of a very profitable relationship, that Benjamin should return to New York and tell Rizzo and the others that with Ricky Jacobs as their guide and partner, they were about to discover the gold that lay across the oceans.

Jacobs knew exactly what to do with those bills. He flew to Munich, checked into the Bayerischer Hof Hotel and summoned Rudolf Schoppman, one of the prime movers of the ring that operated out of the Regina Hotel. When Schoppman examined the bills and waxed lyrical about their possibilities, Jacobs relaxed, certain it would be only a few days, perhaps even just hours, before he was on his way back to the United States flush with profits.

But for some unexplained reason, Schoppman dillied and dallied, kept telling Jacobs that he was on the verge of selling the bills at full price, that he needed just a little more time, that Jacobs should have patience. But as days passed with only Schoppman's constant assurances, Jacobs grew increasingly irritated, ran out of patience and finally told Schoppman he was out of the deal, that Jacobs was taking the bills to Switzerland, where he knew people who could move with dispatch and without excuses.

Schoppman had blown the deal for himself. What he did not want was to blow the possibility of future deals. He tried to convince Jacobs that he had done his best. Of course, he said, he understood why Jacobs had become impatient, understood why Jacobs had made this decision. But, to show there were no hard feelings on his part, and to save the American the expense and inconvenience of going to Switzerland, he would like to introduce Jacobs to a very prominent man in Munich who would be able to accomplish precisely what was desired, and with great speed and circumspection.

The man Schoppman sent to the Bayerischer Hof the following day was Winfried Ense. Jacobs and Ense took to each other immediately. For Jacobs, Ense appeared a far more promising partner than Schoppman. After all, Schoppman was not exactly an unknown to the authorities and Jacobs had long been concerned that just being in Schoppman's company in public places might arouse suspicion. Ense, however, still occupied a shadowy territory onto which official light had not yet been cast; he seemed on the surface the very model of probity and success. Ense examined the three treasury bills, expressed a cautious enthusiasm. He was, indeed, impressed with them, he said, but he would like to take a sample and do a little checking, see whether it was still clean and so could be sold openly or whether another way would have to be found.

Jacobs was dismayed. Was this to be a repetition of the Schoppman exercise, with delay and delay until time ran out?

Ense assured him it would be nothing of the kind. What he had in mind would take only a few hours, a day at most. Ense took the sample to the Bavarian Mortgage and Drafts Bank, showed it to an official with the request for an opinion on its authenticity, explaining that he had just met a rich American, a Mr. Jackson, who wanted to buy some jewelry and was offering the treasury bill as payment. The bank official looked closely at the bill, said it appeared to be legitimate, checked the hot sheet and found it was not listed. He told Ense the bill was obviously negotiable and the bank would certainly be willing to handle the sale if Ense desired. Ense said he was not sure he wanted to sell, that he might just decide to hold on to the bill. The same procedure was repeated, as a double-check, at the Otto Dierks Bank.

While Ense was very interested in disposing of the bill and receiving a commission, he had no intention of doing the trading personally, and certainly not in his native Munich, where it might be traced back to him. He proposed what seemed a safe alternative to Jacobs. Ense and a close friend, Dagobert Fayer, would take the three bills to Brussels, where Fayer had important corporate and financial connections. Once there, Fayer would make all the arrangements. Neither Ense nor Jacobs would appear publicly. When the bills had been sold, Ense would return to Munich with the money. The whole transaction should not take long if everything went without a hitch.

In Brussels, Fayer turned the three bills over for sale to a director he knew at the Belgian branch of Continental Illinois Trust Company. Though there was nothing suspicious about the securities, and they still had not appeared on the hot list, some European banks, and especially those with close links to the United States, had begun to grow a little apprehensive about accepting American paper without complete authentication. Fayer's friend said that before the sale could be consummated, he would have to send the treasury bills to Chicago to be checked. Fayer brought the news to Ense. Ense checked with Jacobs in Munich. Though not happy with the idea, Jacobs decided to go along. But, he told Ense, only one of the three bills was to be sent to Chicago; the other two were to be retained by Ense and Fayer so that if anything happened, they, at least, would not be lost and if Chicago approved the first, there was no reason why the other two could not be sold later without a check. And, he said, Fayer should emphasize the need for a quick response. Too much time had been lost already by Schoppman's antics.

The emphasis on the need for speed came not only from Jacobs. He was under mounting pressure from his new partners in New York. He was getting telephone calls nearly every day from Benjamin, Vincent Rizzo and Peter Raia, demanding action. He had not previously met Rizzo or Raia, but he knew of them and their penchants from Benjamin and he knew of Rizzo, as well, by reputation. If Jacobs was the hotshot he was reputed to be, he was told, why hadn't he moved the bills yet? Time was running out. Rizzo, Raia and Benjamin had $60,000 in this project and they wanted to earn their full profit on that investment. If they didn't they would hold Jacobs responsible.

To force the issue, Jacobs flew to Brussels, confronted Ense at the Hilton Hotel. Ense was distressed, not merely over the sudden appearance of Jacobs but over the fact that he arrived without luggage and with only the clothes he was wearing. Ense worried that if they were seen together, suspicions might be aroused. That did not concern Jacobs. He had made the trip to see that something happened and he had no intention of leaving without either the cash for the sale of the bills or the three bills themselves. Ense tried to soothe him, advising a little more patience. Jacobs said that Schoppman had given him the same advice and it had resulted in nothing. He had been patient long enough.

While Jacobs and Ense were arguing, the phone in Ense's room rang. It was Fayer. He had just heard from the Continental Bank. The treasury bill had been authenticated; it had been sold in Chicago, a certified check for $97,000 had been received and the money deposited in an account for Fayer. Further, the bank official told Fayer, if he wanted to sell the other two bills, the bank was prepared to do so immediately; there would be no delays and no further checking was necessary.

Jacobs decided not to press his luck. He told Ense and Fayer to forget about selling the other two bills, just to turn them back to him along with the $82,000 he had coming—Ense's commission on the sale was 40,000 deutsche marks, or about $15,000.

Ense handed back the treasury bills. Then Fayer explained it would be a few days yet before Jacobs could have the cash, since it would take that long for the certified check to clear and allow him to withdraw cash from his account.

Jacobs said he couldn't wait. He had to have the money then.

Fayer said in that case he would be willing to write a check for the amount due Jacobs on the account. By the time the check was cashed, the funds would be available.

Jacobs took Fayer's check, though he was less than pleased not to have cash, flew back to Munich, collected his belongings and then was on his way back to Los Angeles. Since he had been only partly successful and had taken longer than expected, hardly an auspicious beginning to the new partnership, he had little appetite for a personal settling of accounts with Rizzo and Raia. Instead, he sent the two bills and the Fayer check to New York in the care of courier Louis Gittleman, instructing Gittleman to explain that Jacobs was so busy he couldn't spare the time to fly east, knew Rizzo would understand and was sure Rizzo would send his cut back with Gittleman.

What Rizzo sent back was fury. He demanded that Jacobs appear in person or he'd send somebody out to bring Jacobs back. When Jacobs arrived in New York, Rizzo threw the check at him and, as he later told Ense, "I told him to stick it up his ass." If Jacobs knew what was good for him, Rizzo said, he'd get on the first plane back to Germany and turn that check into cash. In fact, just to make sure there were no slipups, Rizzo was going along on that trip.

Only days after he had departed, Jacobs was back in Munich, back at the Bayerischer Hof, Rizzo in an adjoining room. Rizzo relaxed, went sight-seeing, stayed out of sight. He was there for just one reason—to collect his money. Jacobs called Ense, explained that there had been a little difficulty about Fayer's check. Not that it had bounced, but only that the people in the United States did not like checks and would accept only cash.

Ense calmed him. There was nothing to be concerned about, he said. He understood the natural hesitation of Americans about checks in foreign currency. However, if cash was what was wanted, then they would simply convert the check into cash and all would be well.

In the morning, Ense and Jacobs flew to Frankfurt. While Jacobs waited outside in a cab, Ense went into Fayer's bank, cashed the check, turning it into deutsche marks. Back in the cab on the way to the airport, he handed the package of German currency to Jacobs. It had been a simple matter, he said; there had been no difficulty, it had taken only a little time and not much inconvenience, and now everyone was satisfied; good faith and trust had been restored and should lead to more and better deals in the future.

Rizzo was waiting for Jacobs at the Bayerischer Hof. He took the package, counted the bills to make sure that everything was there. He put the package in his suitcase, told Jacobs he was going home in the morning and taking the whole bundle with him. The delays, the failure to sell the other two treasury bills, which had just been added to the hot sheet and so now had a sharply reduced value, were Jacobs's fault. Jacobs had cost Rizzo and his partners plenty of money, and one thing Vincent Rizzo would not tolerate was to lose money. If Rizzo lost, everyone lost. Jacobs would not see one penny of what was in that package, not even to cover his expenses, unless he could con something out of Ense or his other German friends. Chalk it off to experience, Rizzo said. Maybe the next time Jacobs would know better than to play around with Rizzo's property.

It had not been a happy beginning to what Jacobs had hoped would be a long and lucrative relationship. He was not used to being treated the way Rizzo had treated him, yet he realized that as long as he needed the supplies that Rizzo controlled, he would have to work with the man. But in the future he intended to take some precautions to protect himself and perhaps even play it cool for a while until Rizzo needed him enough to come to him again and so restore the balance.

Jacobs was hardly through the door of his home in Los Angeles when the phone rang. When he hung up, he knew he would have to go to Rizzo once more and without delay. He urgently needed stocks, and not hundreds of thousands of dollars' worth, but millions.

Ever since that day at the Palace Hotel in Munich, the words that had passed between Rizzo, Ense and Barg had been indelibly etched in Coffey's mind. He had listened to the tape and read the transcript so many times that it had become part of him—he knew it by heart, had underscored the sections he did not understand, the questions he could not answer. He was determined that before this case ended, he would understand all of it.

As Grant's tale unfolded before him, he remembered the words spoken in Munich that past February. Rizzo had said to Ense, "When you cashed that bond. Ricky gave you three?"

Ense had replied, "Yes. You mean, the treasury bills?"

"Yes," Rizzo had said. "Why couldn't you cash the other two?"

Now Coffey understood the whole journey that had been taken by those treasury bills, understood who had supplied them, where they had gone, what had happened to them. He could write "solved" for the first time against one of the puzzles that had emerged that afternoon in Munich.

1 4

· · · · · · · · · · · · · ·

What Coffey was soon to realize, the deeper he dug and the more he learned, was that the treasury bill affair was not an isolated incident. There was an essential relationship among all the things Rizzo, Ense and Barg had talked about that afternoon in Munich, and things they had not mentioned, too. The treasury bills were basic to the whole picture, were the beginning from which so much else evolved. In this puzzle, each piece was integral, meshed with the others, grew from those that preceded and led inextricably to those that followed. Only by trying to make sense of their seemingly incomprehensible convolutions would he be able to decipher the greatest enigma of them all—the Vatican Connection.

And so, from the treasury bills he moved on, into what at first seemed unrelated, was certainly bewildering. He started down a road filled with stocks and bonds, with that Coca-Cola stock mentioned so often and with such concern in Munich, followed to Panama and beyond.

The call Ricky Jacobs received so soon after returning from Europe was from Miami. The caller was Dominic Mantell, second only to the powerful Santo Trafficante in the world of organized crime in Florida. "Ricky," he said, "we need merchandise, and we need it right away."

"How much do you need?" Jacobs asked.

"Millions," Mantell said. "All you can get. Only they have to be the best."

"I'll see what I can do," Jacobs said. "I'll get back to you as soon as I know something."

"I'm not kidding around, Ricky," Mantell said. "We got to have them right away."

What Mantell needed those millions of dollars' worth of securities for was nothing less than the economic rape of the Republic of Panama. The scheme had been under way for months, since midsummer of 1970. It had been conceived in the fertile brain of Ernest Shinwell, scapegrace son of one of England's most illustrious families—his father was Lord Emanuel Shinwell, who had served queen and country as Labour member of Parliament, as minister of defense, as foreign secretary, as peer of the realm. Ernest was the blot on the family escutcheon. Blessed with a politician's charm, the ability to convince with disarming sincerity, and an overweening self-confidence, he had parlayed those gifts not, as his father, into a successful public career, but rather into masterminding dozens of swindles and confidence games. Though he had been arrested several times, more often than not the Shinwell name had been enough to rescue him. But, in 1965, when he tried to sell thousands of shares of phony stock, the crime was considered no youthful prank—he was, by then, middle-aged—and the name no shield; he was tried, convicted at the Old Bailey and sentenced to three years in prison.

The time in prison gave Shinwell the opportunity to contemplate not the cost of his misdeeds but how to proceed on a grander scale. Free once more, his eyes turned across the Atlantic, to Central America, to Panama. He constructed the persona of a flourishing industrialist and financier and set up a host of corporations with himself as president or major officer.

In the summer of 1970, Shinwell, then fifty-two, arrived in Panama. Using his family name and reputation and his corporate empire as calling cards, he set about wooing prominent Panamanian lawyers, bankers, businessmen and government officials, spreading out before them a vision of economic development and progress, a vision he was prepared to turn into reality, with their help. He was persuasive, indeed. To the junta of General Omar Torrijos, he held out the possibility of turning Panama into a tourist mecca. He spread out detailed maps, meticulously drawn architectural renderings, profit projections and more (all worked out in concert with his silent partner, Dominic Mantell), and won from the junta license to build and operate on the mainland and on offshore islands five tourist centers, with hotels, facilities of all kinds, constructed around the centerpiece of palatial gambling casinos. That, of course, was what had convinced Mantell to throw his weight and power behind Shinwell when they were brought together by a mutual friend and Shinwell had described at least part of his plan. For Mantell had a long-held dream: he saw himself as master of a gambling empire in the Caribbean that would rival, if not surpass, the one Meyer Lansky had set up to loot Cuba in the years before the Castro revolution. Shinwell offered a way to make it possible.

But Shinwell's scheme encompassed more than a vision of a gambling haven. He intended gambling to be part of a whole new world of a flourishing Panama, he told his new Panamanian friends. He would found a bank, or buy an existing one. He would purchase vast tracts of land, develop them for modern industry and agriculture. He would establish a small airline to serve those holdings. And then he set about showing that this was not all empty and grandiose talk. As adviser on the financial aspects of his plan, he hired American David W. Slater, an expert in banking and international finance with a sterling reputation. He began negotiations with Roy Hammac, an American rancher and landowner. For $5.5 million, Shinwell would purchase three tracts totaling more than 200,000 acres of Hammac's vast holdings of Panamanian ranch and forest land. He discussed buying a fleet of planes with an aircraft dealer, who just happened to be on Mantell's payroll. Whenever anyone asked any questions about Shinwell's ability to handle so many ventures on such a large scale, especially since all there had been so far was talk, he glibly mentioned $5 million, or $7 million or $10 million or more at his disposal in safekeeping accounts in banks in Switzerland, flashed receipts reflecting $6 million in letters of credit on deposit at Credit Suisse in Switzerland, though he conveniently failed to mention that those letters of credit had been issued by his own Bahamian-based Zurich International Investment Corporation and were hardly worth the value of the paper.

By fall, with the preliminaries at an end, Shinwell began to come under pressure to demonstrate that he indeed was committed to his projects and to Panama by transferring some of those millions to Panamanian banks. Particularly insistent was Jose Antonio Perez Salamero, general manager of the Banco Exterior. He had established a close working relationship with Shinwell, had advanced him several hundred thousand dollars in credits, and, perhaps, aspired to a prominent position in the Shinwell empire, for his was the major bank Shinwell was talking about buying. Salamero sought help from

David Slater, and together they framed a message in Shinwell's name and sent it to Credit Suisse asking for the transfer of funds represented by those letters of credit to Banco Exterior. Credit Suisse did not reply.

Somewhat concerned, Slater went to Shinwell, was told there was nothing to worry about, the funds were on the way. They didn't arrive. Shinwell said he couldn't understand it; he and his companies had plenty of money in stock in Switzerland, and he showed Slater evidence of recent deposits of $7.5 million in securities of a fund called Multi-National Investment, and $15 million in notes issued by the kingdom of Greece in the name of McDonald Construction Company of Los Angeles, the proceeds available to him since members of his group controlled McDonald. What he did not tell Slater was that McDonald was under the sway of Mantell and others in the syndicate.

If he had all that money at his command, Slater said, then it ought to be a simple matter to deposit some of it in Panama, and so allay the doubts of Salamero and others. In fact, Slater strongly advised him to do so without delay.

Shinwell went to Miami, to Mantell. They had, he said, operated on talk up to then; now they had to show that it was something more. They needed to deposit some stock, probably a couple of million dollars' worth, with Salamero. It didn't have to be the best, he said, since Salamero was in with them (something David Slater later came to believe strongly; the pressure for deposits from Salamero, he felt, was intended as a protection in case of future questions). Once Salamero had the stock on deposit, Shinwell said, he was prepared to open up major lines of credit. That would permit the land deal with Roy Hammac to go through, would enable construction on the casinos to begin, would smooth over any misunderstandings with important Panamanians. And most important, it would entrench Shinwell so deeply in Panama that when and if any irregularities were discovered, it would be too late; the banks and everyone else would have the choice of either incurring such devastating losses that it might be years, if ever, before they and the country recovered, or covering up and going along for the long ride with Shinwell, and Mantell, in the hope that eventually the situation would right itself.

Blinded by his dream of a gambling empire that Shinwell would build for him, and out of which he would shove Shinwell once it had come to fruition, Mantell said he knew just the man who could fill the order. He would call his friend in Los Angeles, Ricky Jacobs.

So, the order came from Mantell, and Jacobs knew that he would have to look to the East once more, to Benjamin, Rizzo and Raia. He could not have called at a more propitious moment. They were sitting on some very valuable paper.

Over the preceding months, there had been a series of thefts of registered mail. In every case, the stolen parcels contained securities on their way from banks and brokerage houses around the country to their counterparts in New York. A group of thieves, predominantly black, employed in the cargo areas of the airports in New York, had been watching for those parcels. The leaders had come to an arrangement with Peter Raia; they would steal the parcels and he would pay them a fraction of their worth. A few weeks prior to the call from Jacobs, in mid-October, a pouch containing several registered letters on their way from Security Pacific Bank in Los Angeles to banks in New York had disappeared, though it would be several months before any of the banks realized it. In those envelopes were securities worth more than $2 million, including 31,000 shares of Coca-Cola Bottling Company of Los Angeles common stock in batches of 10-, 50-, 100- and 1,000-share certificates; and 7,100 shares of Occidental Petroleum Company common and 6,000 shares of Norton Simon, Inc., common, all in 100-share certificates. All were in such solid street names as Bear Sterns Company, Gooss and Company, Nadart and Company and others. This was just what Jacobs needed to fill Mantell's order.

Raia crammed the securities into a suitcase and, together with his muscleman, Mike Affinito, and Benjamin, flew out to California to meet Jacobs at the Beverly Hills Hotel. Jacobs looked over the cache, offered Raia a $5,000 downpayment on the spot and a guarantee of five percent of the market value of the shares, or about $100,000, as soon as he had completed his own arrangements and been paid. Raia accepted, turned over the stocks and flew back to New York.

Then those stocks began the first leg of what would turn out to be a long, difficult and complicated journey. Ricky Jacobs handed the suitcase to his son, Jerry Marc, and put him on a plane for New York while he got on another one for Panama City. From New York, Jerry Marc Jacobs flew on to Miami, met Mantell and then went on with him to join up with Ricky Jacobs at the El Panama Hotel. There they were met by Shinwell and his close associate, John Westcott. The securities were examined. They were, indeed, satisfactory, just what was needed. Even Salamero agreed to that when he looked at them the next day. His qualms vanished and he told Shinwell that Banco Exterior was now prepared to open a $500,000 line of credit for the Shinwell group with the pledge of those stocks as security.

Mantell went back to Miami, carrying with him Shinwell's assurance that it would only be a matter of weeks or months before the ground was broken for the first of the five casinos. Ricky and Jerry Jacobs stayed on at the El Panama. Ricky was not about to depart until he had in his pocket a share of that $500,000 now available to Shinwell, enough to satisfy Raia and give him a handsome profit, as well.

But Ernest Shinwell had no intention of paying Jacobs for those stocks, at least not yet. He kept delaying, telling Jacobs that Salamero was working to set up the line of credit but there were still more details to be worked out and it would be some days until the funds were available. It was only a matter of time; there was nothing to worry about. Why didn't they go home, go about their other business? As soon as the money was available, Shinwell would get it to them. Besides, he had something else he would very much like Jacobs to do for him when he returned home. He would like Jacobs to put together another package of securities, as large as possible, to feed to Salamero. The more stock they put into the Banco Exterior, the more credit Salamero would make available to them; and the deeper the Panamanian got involved in the plot, the less chance he would have to back away no matter what second thoughts he had.

Still, Shinwell's delays and evasions were making Ricky Jacobs a trifle nervous. He talked to Mantell, who allayed his fears, telling him that if he himself was willing to trust Shinwell, then certainly Jacobs ought to have nothing to worry about, and so Jacobs ought to go home and do what Shinwell asked.

What nobody yet understood—certainly not Mantell or Jacobs—was that Shinwell was committed to nothing but the swindle. He had never had any intention, not at the beginning and not since, of carrying forward those enticing and grandiose visions. They were all merely ploys, the means for Shinwell to swindle Salamero and his Banco Exterior out of as much as possible, to con Roy Hammac out of his land, to dupe even Mantell and Jacobs. The evidence might be there, and growing, but Shinwell was blessed with the ability to make people trust him, to accept his delays. His excuses were so convincing that not even the other swindlers doubted him.

So, Jacobs went home, and by early December he was able to inform Mantell and Shinwell that he had put together another sterling package of securities. One of his longtime suppliers had just put into his expert hands a bundle worth perhaps $10 million or more, which had been lifted from a registered-mail shipment bound from Union Trust Company in Saint Louis to Merrill, Lynch, Pierce, Fenner and Smith in New York. Among the securities were IBM, Beneficial Finance Corporation, National Aviation Corporation, General Portland Cement, Capital Holding Company, Unishops, American Hospital Supply, California Computer Products and others. But, Jacobs said, he had no desire to make a return trip to Panama. If Mantell and Shinwell were interested, they should send their own trusted people to California to examine the securities and, if they liked what they saw, carry them back to Miami and then to Central America.

Mantell and Shinwell agreed. Mantell dispatched Herbert Creekmore, a sometime aircraft dealer in Central America who had been one of those Shinwell had talked with about his proposed airline and a smuggler of currency, securities and other merchandise for Mantell in and out of Latin America. (Within a few years, Creekmore, cornered and facing a long jail sentence, would turn government informant, testify before Senate committees and at trials, and eventually disappear into the protected witness program to begin a new life.) Shinwell sent one of his British associates. James Rogers. They met Jacobs in their room at the Century Plaza Hotel, looked over a sampling of $3 million worth of those new securities, which Jacobs dumped on a bed for them. Creekmore told Jacobs they looked pretty good to him, that he would report to Mantell and perhaps the deal could be concluded in the morning.

But Rogers was getting cold feet. He and Creekmore went down to the bar and Rogers started to drink heavily. He began to talk, telling Creekmore he had not realized the scope of Shinwell's swindle when he first got involved, was becoming afraid of the consequences, and not just from the law, as the realization of its magnitude and ramifications began to seep in. He wanted out. He was going back to Miami.

That was enough for Creekmore. He was not prepared to follow through if Shinwell's own man was going to run off at the mouth in a public place and had become so frightened he was ready to turn and flee. Creekmore decided to forget the whole thing, tell Jacobs there had been a hitch that meant aborting this deal, and then head for Miami and report to Mantell.

Jacobs was furious and told Mantell that it had been a waste of his time putting together the package. Mantell said that he was not happy, either, but at least Jacobs had the stock and could probably deal it elsewhere at a good profit. And Mantell told Shinwell that if he ever got his hands on Rogers it would be the last anyone ever saw of the man. Shinwell replied that he was of the same mind. But at the moment there were other things to be concerned with.

In Panama itself, David Slater had begun to have some doubts. At the start, Slater thought he had been put on to an enormously profitable venture and was dealing with a man of reputation and probity, a man whose name stood for something honorable. By late in the fall, however, Slater began to realize that his value to Shinwell was not in the advice he could give but in his character, in his reputation. More and more, Shinwell was dealing behind his back.

Still, Slater held his suspicions to himself, or voiced them in the most careful and veiled terms only to his closest friends, until Roy Hammac came to him for advice. After months of delay and hedging, Hammac's negotiations with Shinwell seemed about to be sealed, with Shinwell upping the agreed payment for the land to $6 million with $500,000 in cash and the balance in securities. Hammac was a little concerned about those securities Shinwell was proposing to throw into the deal. If he signed over the land, he asked Slater, could Shinwell really come up with the stock? Did he own it? What kind was it? Slater's advice: see Salamero and put the questions to him, ask to see the securities, and then use his own financial channels to discover how valid those securities were and whether Shinwell actually did own them.

When Shinwell learned of Slater's discussion with Hammac, he was furious. How dare Slater try to screw up the pending deal? "From now on," he said, "the only advice you'll give is the advice I tell you to give." It was not long before Slater was giving Shinwell no advice at all.

Doubt is contagious. By the turn of the year, the infection was everywhere. In New York, Raia and Rizzo, impatient for the $95,000 owed them on the stocks, were after Jacobs for the payment, warning that it had better not turn into a repetition of the treasury bill affair in Germany. In Los Angeles, Jacobs, haunted by just those fears, was constantly on the telephone to Shinwell, demanding immediate payment or the return of the stock. In Miami, Mantell was rapidly running out of patience, was asking in increasingly strident tones when he was going to see something concrete. In Panama, even Salamero was starting to shift ground. He had thrown Banco Exterior behind Shinwell and was concerned not merely about the safety of the bank but about his own safety and future as well. He kept looking at those stocks Shinwell had turned over to him. In light of the questions about the validity and ownership put to him by Hammac, he was growing worried that others might start to ask some embarrassing questions, too. He decided to take a step that would cover himself yet, in light of Panama's banking laws that stringently protect the identity of depositors, would not do damage to Shinwell.

Early in 1971, Salamero composed a careful letter to the Security Pacific Bank in Los Angeles, the transfer agent for the shares Shinwell had deposited with him. He wrote that very recently a large number of shares of Coca-Cola Bottling Company of Los Angeles, Occidental Petroleum and Norton Simon, in the street names of Bear Sterns, Nadart, Gooss and others "were deposited in our security boxes, as guarantee of the depositors for some transactions made with us." After listing the certificate numbers, Salamero added, "We would appreciate your confirmation at your earliest convenience of the authenticity of the above mentioned firms as authorized holders of these shares, in your records. Please also state whether there are any limitations as to free sale and availability. Please note that the above mentioned shares have been deposited in our Bank as a guarantee for the financial transactions given to depositors."

Security Pacific Bank at last discovered that the stocks it had sent by registered mail to banks in New York in October had somehow found their way into the vaults of Banco Exterior in Panama. A message was immediately sent to Salamero. The stocks were stolen and could not be sold or used for any purpose; they should be returned promptly along with particulars as to how Banco Exterior had come by them and who had placed them in the bank.

Salamero had taken a calculated risk and he was not about to go any further. He took his time about replying, then wrote back that while he knew the name of the depositor, a European and a client of his bank, and the name of the person, a North American, who had given the stocks to the bank's client, he had no intention of supplying either name to Security Pacific or anyone else. Security Pacific appealed for help, but Salamero rebuffed the overtures of the American mission to Panama, American investigators and other foreigners. Even when Inspector Robert Pinzon of Panama's Department of Investigation was brought in, Salamero continued to stonewall. Without a court order, he said, he would be violating Panama's banking code if he revealed anything, and if, somehow, a court order were obtained, he would merely turn it over to his attorney and together they would decide whether to obey it. He would, however, tell Pinzon and the Americans that Banco Exterior was actually barely involved in the situation. His client, he said (refuting what he had originally written to Security Pacific), had simply deposited the stocks with the bank without any guarantees whatsoever, without intending or attempting to receive any money on them, and the bank had only held the shares for safekeeping.

The Americans were stymied. There was little they could do to compel Salamero to reveal what he knew, and the United States mission to Panama realized that all too well. In a classified report to the State Department, officials of the mission said, "The Embassy was in no position to request a court order in this case and . . . a Secret Service agent should *not* be sent to Panama to investigate this case without the consent of Panamanian authorities. Further, any attempt to develop information in this case that smelled of an investigation should not be made."

The stalemate lasted until midspring. Suddenly, Salamero had his last word for the Americans. As far as he was concerned, he said, the matter had become moot. The bank's client had been told that the stocks were stolen and so, in February, he had retrieved them and returned them to the American who had originally supplied them to him. Banco Exterior and Salamero had no further interest in the matter and nothing more to say.

In that final word to the Americans, Salamero, of course, did not go into the details of his final transactions with his client. Once he received the initial response from Security Pacific, he summoned Shinwell and, in a rage, ordered him to remove the stolen securities from Banco Exterior. Shinwell replied that he would be only too happy to do just that, especially as he was under increasing pressure from Jacobs, and from Mantell, to whom Jacobs had appealed for help, either to pay up or return the stocks.

Not so fast, Salamero said. Shinwell had taken his bank for a lot of money and Salamero had no intention of being left with a depleted treasury and, perhaps, of being made the scapegoat for the Shinwell adventure. Shinwell would have to find some way to make good, and until he could come up with some securities to replace the Coca-Cola, Occidental Petroleum and Norton Simon, Salamero would just hold on to them.

The threads of his scheme rapidly unraveling, Shinwell tried to repair the fabric while there was still time. Once more he rushed to Miami, somehow managed to convince Mantell that the scheme was still alive, that Salamero was still with them, was merely holding back because he had been frightened by the revelations from Security Pacific and the investigation resulting from that ill-advised letter to that bank. But, Shinwell said, Salamero's stake was so high and his involvement so deep, he would certainly continue to play along if he received something as a substitute for the stolen securities, something not on a hot list, untraceable. Then the casino building program would begin and the whole plan would be on the way to fruition. Both Shinwell and Mantell knew that the one man who could supply what would satisfy Salamero was Ricky Jacobs, and Jacobs might be very happy to do just that if he knew he would get the original stock back and finally make a profit on the deal.

The proposal was put to Jacobs. With resignation, he agreed to see what he could do. It took him only a few days to find what he considered a suitable substitute, more than $10 million worth of stock certificates that had been consigned to a shredder for destruction but which had instead found their way into the hands of a Los Angeles scrap-paper dealer named Gerald Kassap. He had turned them over to two friends with underworld contacts, Alan Charles Levy and Stephen Berg, in exchange for a third of their profits, and they immediately sought out Ricky Jacobs as the man who could turn that paper into cash for everyone.

Jacobs called Mantell and Shinwell, told them he had exactly what they needed, untraceable securities, and if they sent their people to Los Angeles, the certificates would be waiting. But, he added, this time he could not operate on promises and faith. This time, he would need to see some cash up front.

Mantell told him not to worry, everything would be worked out satisfactorily, and the couriers would be on the way in the next few days. Once more, Mantell dispatched Herbert Creekmore; Shinwell sent his closest associate, John Westcott. Once more, they met at the Century Plaza, Jacobs carrying a bulging briefcase from which he poured out securities onto a bed. Both Creekmore and Westcott were impressed. This package, they said, would serve admirably. Not so fast, Jacobs said. As he had told Mantell, the stocks would be turned over only after money had been paid up front. He was getting very tired of people, and especially Ernest Shinwell, making promises and never living up to them. He was certainly willing to turn this new batch over, but not until he saw cash.

How much did he want? Westcott asked.

Well, Jacobs said, he would give them $3 million worth of the securities in exchange for fifty percent of the market value, or $1.5 million. He did not want to argue about it. He did not want to negotiate. Those were his terms. Take it or leave it.

Creekmore and Westcott were stunned. They had expected to have to pay Jacobs something, but nothing on that order. They had not carried that kind of money with them, were not ready to go out and try to raise it without orders from Mantell and Shinwell.

Then check with Mantell, Jacobs said.

They checked. Mantell told Creekmore to get on a plane back to Miami, to tell Jacobs he could keep those stocks and they would look elsewhere for what they needed.

Jacobs shrugged, said that was their choice, but he had no intention of throwing anything more into the scheme until he got something out, and specifically the shares Salamero was holding.

Mantell said he should not worry, he would get them back as soon as they worked out another arrangement.

So, Creekmore and Westcott went back to Florida, and when they arrived, an enraged Shinwell, in town from Panama and waiting for Jacobs's stock, called Creekmore and asked for a meeting at his hotel. Creekmore arrived. Shinwell poured him a drink, then pulled out a forty-five automatic and pointed it at Creekmore's head.

"I shot Rogers because he talked," Shinwell said (though that didn't happen to be true), "and if you open your mouth, you'll wake up with a bullet in your head, too." Creekmore was sure Shinwell meant exactly what he said. He tried to convince him that he had not said a word to anyone and would never say anything about the securities or anything else he knew. Shinwell paid little attention, grew more threatening. The phone rang in the other room of the suite. Shinwell went to answer it, returned without the gun, grinned at Creekmore, shook his hand and said, "Dominic says you're okay."

Jacobs's demands for an immediate solution to the problems, for the prompt return of the Coca-Cola stock, grew more strident with every passing day, and now he was joined by Rizzo, who called Mantell himself, explained his own interest. With the word of Rizzo's involvement, Mantell decided to move quickly to close out the matter.

He summoned Phillip Morell Wilson to Miami. Wilson had two things going for him—the Bank of Sark and the First Liberty Fund. He had bought the charter for the Bank of Sark in 1968 for $15,000, had set up a one-room office on the Island of Guernsey, complete with fancy nameplate and Telex machine, and had proceeded to print millions of dollars of bank drafts, letters of credit and bills of exchange on the bank, which he sold to innocent and gullible investors, and other swindlers who could make their own use of them, for $50,000 to $100,000. The only difference between First Liberty Fund and Bank of Sark was that the fund had its headquarters in the Bahamas.

Mantell and his associates had made good and profitable use of Wilson's worthless paper over the years, and so when Mantell called, Wilson came running. He met Mantell, Shinwell and their associates in a suite at the Americana Hotel on Miami Beach, listened as Shinwell explained his problem: Salamero was "extremely upset because he's sitting on top of stock that's too hot to handle," and he'd advanced Shinwell a lot of money on that stock. Salamero, Shinwell said, was very anxious to get rid of those shares and replace them with something that was not on the hot sheet.

How much did Shinwell need? Wilson asked.

How much could Wilson supply?

Would $2 million in Bank of Sark drafts and $10 million in First Liberty Funds be enough?

It would, indeed.

A week later, Wilson was back at the Americana, presented Shinwell with the drafts and the shares, received as payment five letters of credit on Shinwell's Bahama-based Zurich International Investment Corporation, which was a fair exchange. (Later, Wilson reproduced those letters of credit, turning the five into a hundred and five, which he proceeded to sell around the world at a substantial profit.)

Shinwell's immediate problems were solved. He carried the Bank of Sark and First Liberty Fund paper back to Panama, turned it over to Salamero. The Panamanian stashed it in Banco Exterior's vaults, retrieved the stolen securities and handed them back to Shinwell, along with the advice to take his business elsewhere.

And then Shinwell was gone. He called Ricky Jacobs, told him he was on his way back to Europe and if Jacobs wanted the stock back, he could pick it up in Zurich.

The swindle in Panama had not reaped all that Shinwell, Mantell or the others had hoped. But, for Shinwell, at least, it had not been totally devoid of profit. How much he got away with was uncertain; probably even Shinwell himself did not know. But the cost to those he had taken was high. For Ricky Jacobs, it meant feeling growing enmity and distrust from Rizzo and Raia and the possibility of some form of retribution, as well as the loss of his own potential profit. With the return of the stock, he had the hope, finally, of once more allaying suspicions and anger, and even of realizing profits, but there were all those wasted months.

For Salamero and even Panama itself, the potential losses had been vast and the real ones were not minor, though neither Salamero nor any Panamanian official would ever admit to them or even discuss what had happened and how they were taken.

For Mantell, his dream of rivaling Meyer Lansky as master of a Latin gambling empire had been shattered. Furthermore, as he would later tell Herbert Creekmore, he had lost a lot of money on the Shinwell scheme, more than he cared to think about, and the one thing he regretted was that there was no way he could get to Shinwell and teach him the cost of swindling Dominic Mantell. By then, Shinwell was locked securely in a prison in Luxembourg.

It was a long time before authorities were able to piece together the story of the Panama swindle—from the secondhand leads provided by Tony Grant, from isolated bits related by Herbert Creekmore, William Benjamin and others, from the grudging and often enigmatic confirmations wrung from Ricky and Jerry Marc Jacobs, and from Shinwell himself. When Joe Coffey, during the long hours of a night, related the tale to his wife, Pat, she listened with incredulity. It seemed so unreal to her, as did so much of this case, revolving as it did around pieces of paper worth millions of dollars passed around so cavalierly by so many people.

To her, the real world was a small house in Levittown with a lawn her husband labored over with the same dedication to perfection he brought to everything. It was counting pennies, worrying about bills or what would happen if an appliance broke down, trying to make one dollar do the work of two. To her, the real world was an occasional short vacation close to home, was never having been on an airplane—not because she was afraid to fly but simply because they could never find the extra money for the price of tickets to fly to a vacation spot. The real world was one where people scrimped and saved and made do with what they had, where people were honest and moral and instilled those virtues in their children.

And now Joe was telling her stories of men who dealt in millions as though they were pennies, who traveled first-class everywhere, who boarded planes and crossed oceans on a whim, who stayed only at the best and most expensive places, who spent money without thought. They were people who cared nothing for anyone else, to whom dishonesty was first nature, for whom morality was a thing to be sneered at and despised. She had lived with Joe long enough, and learned enough about his work, to know that those people existed. Still, she found them hard to comprehend; everything about them was thoroughly alien to all she was. The one satisfaction she had was the knowledge that her husband was after them, and if Joe Coffey was casting a net, there was no way they would not one day be caught.

1 5

• • • • • • • • • • • • •

*O*n a freezing afternoon in the middle of February 1971, three
travelers arrived in Zurich. The first two, from Los Angeles, were
Ricky Jacobs and his wife, Evelyn, with a large collection of expensive luggage in tow; he had much business to do and he was planning
to stay on for at least six weeks. An hour later, the third, Ernest
Shinwell, hurried through the gate into the terminal. For him,
Zurich was only a brief stopover on his way from Panama to London.
He spotted Jacobs waiting just beyond the gate, waved a warm
greeting. Jacobs responded with a cold nod. When they came together, Shinwell handed him a heavy attaché case, offered to share a
cab into the city, where he had some business to transact at his bank
before going on to London. Jacobs, holding tightly to the attaché
case, rejected the offer. They went their separate ways.

A little later that afternoon, Jacobs and his wife checked into
the luxurious Hotel Eden au Lac, overlooking Lake Zurich. He was
welcomed with the courtesy and friendliness merited by an old and
frequent guest. The Eden au Lac was a particular favorite of Jacobs,
and he had specifically requested it when an old friend, Richard
Meyer, president of Karminex-Handels, a small but seemingly respectable company in Zurich, had offered to make the hotel reservations a few days before.

Once in his room, Jacobs carefully set the attaché case on the
bed and checked the contents. He gave a deep sigh of relief. Everything was there, everything was in order. Shinwell had kept one
promise at least: he'd returned all the shares of Coca-Cola Bottling
Company of Los Angeles, Occidental Petroleum and Norton Simon.
Jacobs then opened one of his suitcases and looked with satisfaction
on the millions of dollars in stocks it held—the shares that had once
been tendered to Shinwell, as well as IBM, IT&T, Xerox, Unishops

and a lot more, some stolen from the vaults of Merrill, Lynch some months earlier, some stolen from the registered mails.

Jacobs felt a return of the confidence that had been shaken in recent months by the affairs in Germany and Panama. He was looking over a potential fortune and he was sure he was just the man who could realize it. He intended to move those shares until his pockets and everyone else's were overflowing with cash.

But he had little time to lose. And that realization was reinforced within a day, for his phone rang and he was ordered to get on the first available plane to London and appear at the Churchill Hotel.

Waiting in London were Benjamin, Peter Raia and his ever-present enforcer, Mike Affinito. With Rizzo's blessings, they had come to retrieve their stock from Jacobs and do their own trading. Jacobs might have shown them the glitter of the foreign markets, but so far he had come up with only fool's gold, and had screwed up two major deals. They were convinced that anything Jacobs could do, they could do better, including making the right contacts.

Raia had been given the name of someone who knew all the angles, and within hours of their arrival, he was on the phone to John Michael Devereaux de la Pena, American born but for most of his adult life a resident of England and the Continent and an expert in trading hot securities. De la Pena was, indeed, interested in taking on the Jacobs cache. He suggested that while they waited for Jacobs to arrive, they have a night on the town. He said they should meet at the Victorian Sporting Club, an exclusive gambling establishment, where he was well known. "The manager will make all the arrangements," he said. "We'll have a drink, I'll get somebody to take you into the rooms, and then we'll do the town." The man who met them at the club, who provided them entrée and showed them that night on the town, was Hyman "Tony" Grant.

By the time Jacobs arrived two days later, de la Pena had convinced Raia that he was just the man to turn a tidy profit in the stolen securities. Raia's first words to Jacobs when they met at the Churchill were, "I want twenty-five percent of what those stocks are worth. I want it on the table right now, or I want that paper back. I got a guy here just dyin' to get his hands on them."

That ultimatum was precisely what Jacobs had expected, and

feared. He couldn't comply, he told Raia. The stocks were back in his hotel in Zurich, and, of course, he was not carrying that kind of cash around with him. Raia ordered him to go back to Zurich immediately and return with the stock. Jacobs said he couldn't do that. He was on the point of making a dozen deals himself for those shares, deals that were better than any de la Pena could make. All Raia needed was a little more patience and he would discover just how a master operated.

For three days in that hotel suite, hot words and arguments and threats resounded between Raia and Jacobs. At last, Raia relented just a little and told Jacobs he would give him one more chance. But if it didn't pay off, he'd do well to start watching his back because Affinito or even Raia himself would be on the way to pay him a visit.

Jacobs was on the spot and he knew it. If he was to remove the doubts, he had to start pulling in big money. Back in Zurich, he set out his lines, certain the fish would swim toward that beautiful bait the moment they knew it was there. When they bit, he would pull in the lines hard, would not be gentle this time. He would insist on cash up front, cash on delivery, or, at the very least, an ironbound agreement that would have to be fulfilled. And he made a decision to deal piecemeal this time. The big buyers, those who offered to take millions of dollars in stocks, always seemed to have some excuse to avoid payment, were always begging for more time. If he dealt in amounts of no more than a million or a million and a half, nobody would be able to plead difficulty in raising the necessary down-payments.

The selling, trading, bartering began within a day after his return to Zurich from those difficult sessions with Raia. His old Munich friend, Rudolf Schoppman, and Schoppman's American-born partner, Stanley Myron McCabe, heard that Jacobs was back with a trunk full of the best-quality merchandise. They rushed to Zurich, argued about paying cash up front, finally agreed to put up a downpayment when Jacobs adamantly refused to relent, and went off with shares worth several hundred thousand dollars.

Jacobs then turned to an old friend and associate, Jacques Suesans from Amsterdam, with whom he had done much dealing in the past. (Coming across that name, the reels of the Munich tape spun in Coffey's mind once more, stopped at Rizzo saying to Ense, "I told Ricky whatever I do with Jacques, he gets something out of it." Another identification had been made, another mystery cleared away.)

Suesans, as it happened, was in Zurich only because Jacobs was there. He was in a room just down the hall at the Eden au Lac, reserved for him at the same time the reservation for Jacobs had been made by their mutual friend, Richard Meyer, whose Karminex-Handels had a very close relationship with Suesans's own company, Karminex, of Zug, Switzerland. Suesans dropped by Jacobs's room, looked over the stocks, chose a few certificates, took them down to a Zurich bank and offered them as collateral for a personal loan. The offer was accepted with few questions asked. Convinced that Jacobs was, indeed, in possession of very valuable merchandise, Suesans summoned some of his friends to share in this golden opportunity, confident they would accept, that they would have their own ways of making a killing.

Over the next days and weeks, the Jacobs cache was steadily depleted, the stocks pouring out to those who could peddle them across Europe, into Africa, the Middle East and elsewhere. Among the deals that later come to light (and then there were others about which nobody ever spoke) were these:

- More than $1.5 million were funneled by a Swiss businessman, Enrico Friedlander, through a French journalist and onetime counterfeiter, Sylvaire Galardi, to a group of businessmen in Lebanon who intended to use them as collateral for loans to set up a company that would sell arms to the warring factions in the Middle East.
- A couple of hundred thousand dollars' worth were bought by a Swedish businessman, Bertling Nordling, who had customers in Africa who dearly wanted American corporate securities and were willing to pay high prices for them, no questions asked.
- About $30,000 worth of Coca-Cola shares wound up in the hands of the Royal Canadian Mounted Police in Vancouver, British Columbia, when a naturalized Canadian of Dutch origin, Hendrik Jacobus Offers, turned them in and claimed a reward. He had gotten them, he said, from a Swiss business associate named George Konig in exchange for new Nigerian pounds, only to learn that the stocks were stolen and were on the American hot list. He did not get his expected reward. Both American

and Canadian authorities theorized that "Offers may be nearer the source of those documents than what has appeared up to this time . . . it is possible Offers and/or his 'business associates' may have arranged the 'surrender' of the stolen certificates in Vancouver as a test to learn whether a safe manner of financial gain had been developed from those stolen certificates."

- Another $250,000 from the Jacobs cache, this time in shares of IBM, appeared at the Swiss Israel Trading Bank in Zurich, offered as collateral for a loan sought by Franz Visney, a commercial traveler for an East German textile firm. He explained, when questioned, that he had bought them at a large discount from some casual acquaintances he met at the Hotel Jolly in Milan. (These "acquaintances" were never identified.)
- Another four thousand shares of Coca-Cola were offered for sale in Switzerland at the Union Bank of Lugano by a surveyor from Milan named Edoardo Cattaneo. They were, he said, part of the estate of his recently deceased father. When Swiss authorities sought to ask him some embarrassing questions, he hurried across the border back into Italy. The Italian police refused to act on a Swiss request that he be picked up for attempted swindle.

But of all the friends and associates Jacobs and Suesans dealt with during those weeks when they were operating out of the Eden au Lac, none was more important or crucial to the scheme than these three men: Winfried Ense of Munich; Maurice Ajzen, born in Paris, living a tenuous existence in Munich as an illegal immigrant, survivor of Hitler's concentration camps, sometime wine salesman, sometime dealer in metals, old and close friend of Ense, always on the lookout for but rarely finding the big money and the important deal; and Rudolph Guschall, a middle-aged, not very successful lawyer and notary from Frankfurt who, despite an innate timidity and cowardice, steered a treacherous course along the borders of illegality that forever placed him in peril of disbarment or worse.

Never one to miss any opportunity, Jacobs, despite the experience of the previous autumn, saw in Ense another potential customer for all those securities that filled his Zurich hotel room. And Ense, the moment he learned what Jacobs had, was determined to share in the gold. He called and in his most winning manner said that if only his friend Ricky would journey to Munich, they might be able to strike a very profitable arrangement.

Jacobs went to Munich to meet with Ense, and was introduced to Ajzen. Both Ense and Ajzen were sure they knew just the right way to handle at least a million dollars' worth of those stocks, perhaps even more. But they would have to work cautiously and a bit deviously to bring about the best deal. Ajzen's friend, Rudolph Guschall, had clients who invariably needed some means to raise capital or to create the appearance of solidity and worth. Guschall, however, was an easily frightened rabbit. If a deal were presented to him that smelled of illegality, he would run for the nearest hole. But if it were presented with just a slight veneer of propriety, he could be swayed. The important thing was the pretense, so that later, if anything happened, Guschall would be able to plead that he had been taken, had not known he was dealing with thieves.

With Jacobs's blessing, Ajzen went to work on Guschall. Learning that the Frankfurt lawyer was about to go to Paris, Ajzen arranged to be there at the same time, to run into him by chance at a bar, to mention over drinks that he had become close to an American who was staying in Munich. The American, named Mr. Evans, was in Europe representing some other Americans who had just come into a large inheritance. He was in need of the advice and assistance of a lawyer and notary. Having run into his friend, Ajzen said, it occurred to him that Guschall might be just the man to recommend to Mr. Evans. If Guschall was interested, Ajzen would bring Mr. Evans to Guschall's office in Frankfurt when they were both back in Germany.

A few days later, Ajzen appeared in Frankfurt with Mr. Evans (who was in fact, as Guschall would soon learn, Ricky Jacobs). Jacobs spread the net. His American clients, he explained, had inherited large blocks of stock in several American companies and they wished to use them in Europe somehow to avoid the heavy American taxes. But he was uncertain how to go about it, and so he was seeking advice and ideas.

Guschall rushed into the net without hesitation. He was sure, he said, that he knew just the man who could help Mr. Evans with those securities and would be helped in turn. He had a client named Alfred Barg, and Barg was an important officer in a large Swiss firm, Finag Akhiengeselschaft, and several of Finag's subsidiaries. Right at that moment, Guschall said, he knew that Barg was in need of a substantial infusion of funds of one kind or another to assist him in the completion of a land deal in southern France. It was very likely, then, that Mr. Evans had arrived at a most propitious moment. Guschall would arrange to bring them together and would work out the details of how to proceed should they agree on a deal.

Guschall was, of course, right. Barg was desperate for funds. The negotiations had come to an impasse between Finag, Finag's subsidiary, Ferienstadt Bel Air, and the French government and French banks for permission to purchase more than a million and a half acres near Montpellier and build there five thousand expensive vacation homes. What was holding them up were some questions about Finag's, and Bel Air's, financial structure and, thus, its ability to carry forward the project should it be approved. The project was to be financed with the proceeds of a major bond issue Barg and Finag intended to float, but until the French had approved the sale of the land and the construction, the bond issue could not be floated. Thus, Barg was caught in a vicious circle and was searching frantically for some way to break out.

Guschall brought Barg and Mr. Evans together, and the pretenses were quickly dropped—Ricky Jacobs resumed his true identity. With Guschall working out the legal language of a contract to satisfy both Jacobs and Barg, the two negotiated the deal. Jacobs turned over to Barg shares worth between $900,000 and $1 million—stock in Coca-Cola Bottling of Los Angeles, Occidental Petroleum, Norton Simon, First Union, General Portland Cement, Unishops, Capital Holding Corporation, Beneficial Finance Company, National Aviation Corporation, American Hospital Supply Corporation and California Computer Products. In return, Barg agreed to pay a fee of forty percent, or $350,000, for the right to use those shares for three years for whatever purpose he desired, the only limitations being that he could not collect any dividends, could not sell them, could not return them to the United States. At the end of the three-year lease, Jacobs would buy the stock back for $250,000. His profit, then, would be $100,000, and he would once more be in possession of the securities and once more be able to deal them to someone else for more profits.

The terms agreed to, the contract signed, Jacobs turned the shares over to Guschall, and gave Guschall his fee for arranging the deal and handling the paperwork—a one-hundred-share certificate of IBM stock. Guschall took the stocks to Barg and then with Barg and another Finag officer, Werner Kalin, journeyed to Glarus, Switzerland, where Finag had its headquarters. At the Glarner Bank, in front of a bank official, Guschall wrote down a list of the stocks and their serial numbers, placed them in large orange envelopes that he handed to the bank official who then deposited them in the Glarner safekeeping accounts and entered them into the books of Finag as assets of the company.

That was exactly the use, and the only use, that Barg intended for them. Finag's balance sheet took on a rosier hue. The French government, seeing that sudden injection of nearly a million dollars in assets, withdrew its objections and approved the land purchase and gave the go-ahead to the construction of the homes. With that, Finag was able to obtain major financing from French banks and more financing through the successful sale of the bond issue that had until then been held back. At Montpellier, ground was broken, the homes began to rise, and customers began to appear. And all the time, the stolen stocks rested in the bank vault in Glarus, never examined by anyone, never sold, serving only the purpose of improving the look of a corporate balance sheet.

Because he had a contract, and thus a legal agreement, Jacobs had broken his promise to himself: he had not demanded that Barg make at least a downpayment on the rental fee for those stocks. He had assumed that Barg, supposedly a reputable businessman, had every intention of honoring that contract. He had assumed that Barg's trip to Switzerland with the stocks had been for the purpose of using them as collateral for a major loan at his company's bank, and that as soon as the loan went through, he would pay the $350,000 rental fee, or at least a large portion of it with the balance in regular installments. A loan, of course, was the farthest thing from Barg's mind, and nearly as far was any intention of paying Jacobs. There was no way, he reasoned, that a swindler could sue if a contract was violated, and so he was safe.

As weeks passed and there was no payment from Barg, Jacobs began to worry. He called Barg and asked for his money.

Barg hedged, said he would pay soon.

When Barg still did not pay, Jacobs called again, demanded his money.

Barg resisted, said he was working on it.

Jacobs insisted he pay immediately.

Barg said, not yet, soon.

Jacobs asked when.

Barg said later.

Jacobs began to wonder whether all the Germans he dealt with weren't swindlers and if Barg weren't the most accomplished of them all. Jacobs took the next step. He began to threaten Barg.

But Barg was still not concerned. He continued to make excuses. Jacobs's threats took on a strident tone.

Barg decided that perhaps he ought to do something to soothe Jacobs and stop those phone calls. He offered to cut Jacobs in on the profits from the sale of the homes in Montpellier, up to $750,000.

Jacobs said that was very nice and generous and he would, of course, accept the offer. But there was still the outstanding question of the rental money Barg had signed a contract agreeing to pay.

Barg claimed he was having difficulty raising that much cash all at once. The demands on him and his company, because of the building project, were heavy and cash could not be diverted.

Jacobs said that Barg had better try to raise it. And now he raised the specter of sinister, vengeful and powerful Americans behind him who were becoming very impatient for their money (which, of course, Rizzo and Raia were), men who might do something quite drastic if they didn't get it. He was a gentleman, but if Barg didn't pay up immediately, the next people who came to see him might not be gentlemen.

Barg considered that, decided that perhaps the time had come to relent just a little and forestall any such visits. He made a payment to Jacobs of $67,000, and promised that he would henceforth pay regular installments until the balance had been paid in full.

That promise was worthless. Barg had no intention of making any further payments. When Jacobs realized that, he knew he had no choice but to seek help, to dispatch others to call on Barg. He sent his son, Jerry Marc, but Jerry Marc Jacobs was not one to inspire fear. He departed with nothing more than other vague promises.

Realizing he would get nothing from Barg unless drastic measures were taken, Jacobs at last turned to Rizzo. Rizzo listened, sneered at Jacobs, told him he should have come sooner. Rizzo would get the matter settled the right way. Rizzo sent Benjamin to see

Barg. But Benjamin did not impress the German. He gave Benjamin his expenses and a few more worthless promises. But Benjamin had been told what to say should that happen. As he was leaving, he told Barg that a very big mistake had been made. It was inevitable now that the next callers would be those Jacobs had threatened him with, men Barg would not enjoy meeting. And then Benjamin said something that sent an icy wave of terror streaming through Barg. He said it would be well for Barg to remember what had happened to Kurt Huber.

Barg's memory did not have to be prodded. A native of Zurich, Kurt Huber had been an employee of Finag. He had also been involved in spreading stolen and counterfeit currency and securities around Europe. There had been some rumors that he was holding out on the profits. One fall morning, he stepped out of his Zurich home to go to the Finag offices, got into his car, turned on the ignition, and the neighborhood quiet was shattered by a tremendous explosion. What remained of Huber's body was scraped from the wreckage.

So, Barg waited with growing terror for the next arrival from America. He still resisted paying the rental fee, and now he could no longer even return the stocks he had rented. With the French government's approval of the land purchase and construction, and with the success in gaining French bank financing and in selling Finag's bonds, Barg had no further need of the shares he had rented from Jacobs. In late October 1971, he had journeyed to Glarus once more, accompanied by Guschall and Ajzen. At the Glarner Bank, he had retrieved the stocks from the safekeeping account, had turned the envelopes over to Guschall, saying with relief that he was glad to be rid of them and hoped never to see or hear of them again. Guschall had passed the envelopes on to Ajzen, and then all had gone their separate ways.

But now Barg understood that he could not dismiss those stocks, nor his obligation for them, quite so easily. He worried and wondered what to do, talked with his friend Winfried Ense, who advised calm, who said perhaps it would all pass.

And then one day in February 1972, Vincent Rizzo was in Munich and Barg and Ense knew it would not pass. Rizzo so terrified Barg that once the American had departed, Barg never traveled alone anywhere, was constantly on the alert for potential assassins, and he reluctantly came to the conclusion that he had to give Rizzo something. And thus he opened the bank account at Otto Dierks Bank, and thus he signed the agreement cutting Rizzo and de Lorenzo in on the profits of Bel Air. He knew that all he was doing was playing desperately for time, praying to be rescued through some divine intervention. Had he dared, he would have gone to the authorities for protection. But that would have meant public exposure and disgrace, for his part in the affair would have come to light, and he could not face that. He did not know that the intervention he was praying for was on the way.

For, as Barg and Ense were confronted for the first time by Rizzo and his threats and demands that winter day in Munich in 1972, Joe Coffey was two rooms down the hall, listening to it all. He learned of the deal between the American mobster and the Germans that day. He heard about Coca-Cola and was soon following those stocks on their long and tangled trail backward to Panama and before. What he heard not only confirmed his hunches but provided the answer to Barg's prayers.

What happened to the shares that Barg rented, or at least most of them, remains a mystery. Ricky Jacobs maintained that he never saw them again after he put them into Guschall's hands when the deal was made with Barg in Frankfurt. Barg maintained he never saw them again after he gave them to Guschall at the Glarner Bank in Glarus on that October morning in 1971. Guschall maintained that he never saw them again after handing them to Ajzen later the same day. Ajzen said nothing, only smiled.

That was the last that was ever heard or seen of the stocks that had traveled that long and twisted road from Security Pacific Bank in Los Angeles and Union Trust Company in Saint Louis and Merrill, Lynch, Pierce, Fenner and Smith in New York, to Peter Raia and Vincent Rizzo, on to Ricky Jacobs and then to Panama and Ernest Shinwell, and then back to Jacobs in Zurich, and on to Guschall in Frankfurt, to Barg in Munich, to the bank in Glarus, Switzerland, and then to Maurice Ajzen.

But all that was later. In the spring of 1971, when Jacobs was striking that deal with Barg, he had no premonition that he was about to be taken by his European friends. His overdeveloped ego led him to assume that he was dealing with honest swindlers who would live up to their bargain. He carried that assurance back to the United States, to Benjamin, Raia and Rizzo, and for a time they believed him, especially in light of the success he had had dealing all those other securities, in light of the hundreds of thousands of dollars he had put into their pockets with that success.

Besides, there was something else to think about during that spring of 1971. Something more important. Dr. Leopold Ledl of Vienna had just come to Jacobs with an unbelievable proposition.

Part Five

. . . .

TO THE
VATICAN

1 6

. . . .

*I*n the pantheon of swindlers, there is a special place reserved for Leopold Ledl. Though he had been at the game full-time for less than a decade, by the beginning of the 1970s this small, portly, dark-haired, always affable Viennese was already a legend among his peers, those who knew and had dealt with him, and those who only knew of him.

Born in Vienna in 1935, he had come relatively late to the trade. It had taken him nearly a quarter of a century to find the role that suited him best, that would lead to the making of his name and fortune. He was the only son in a poor family, grown poorer during those traumatic years of the Hitler *Anschluss*, World War II and its aftermath, and driven into the squalor of abject poverty like so many others in the wreckage of postwar Austria and the occupation of Vienna by the conquering Allied powers. The only opportunity that seemed open to him then was some kind of semiskilled labor. After completing his primary education, he set off into the world as an apprentice to a neighborhood butcher. It had been a choice made not because of a special talent or interest, but because it was all that was available to him. But after he sliced off the last joints of four fingers on his right hand, he knew he was not cut out to be a butcher, that the cleaver in his hands was a dangerous weapon only to himself, and that he had better look elsewhere for a career if he was to survive in the world. (Learning that, Coffey remembered Ense telling Rizzo in Munich, "You know that he had only three fingers? He lost three fingers. . . . What is it, he kills animals. His profession is a butcher. He makes meat.")

He tried a dozen other trades briefly, and eventually went to sea as cabin boy, cook or whatever job he could pick up on freighters and passenger liners. Aboard those ships and in ports of call around the globe, he studied the ways of the rich at their leisure, watched the manner in which they made their way along the decks and in the salons, as they wandered with such assurance through the markets, shops, bazaars. He determined that he would find a way to be one of them. The rich had manners, exuded an air that marked them as successful, as people of means and stature. He would master those attitudes and attributes until they became part of him. But studying them so carefully, he discovered something else. If there was something for sale, there was always a buyer; and if that something seemed exotic, appeared to have some special value, the price inevitably spiraled far beyond the intrinsic worth and the avid customer would pay with little argument.

By the mid-1960s, not yet thirty, he had put his seafaring days behind him and settled in a small flat in Vienna with his new wife, a tiny, attractive, blonde woman. He was soon the father of two small daughters, was eking out a meager living at inconsequential, dull jobs while trying to find the right path to riches. In his spare time, he tinkered, drawn to the idea that he might invent something that would make that fortune. Invent he did, developing and patenting a new massage brush. It was not much, not anything revolutionary, but it did not have to be, for Ledl had realized by then that the important thing was not the invention itself but how it was parlayed.

Everywhere he went, he touted the magical properties of his new brush in glowing, extravagant phrases. If there was one thing Ledl now understood about himself it was that the magic lay not in the brush but in Leopold Ledl, in his ability to convince the skeptical. He was, someone would later say, the proverbial man who could sell air-conditioners to Eskimos in the middle of winter and furnaces to the Congolese in midsummer.

He came upon one especially fascinated listener, a Budapest-born Swiss resident named Karoly Kacso, a man who knew everybody and who saw the permutations in any good idea. Kacso invited Ledl to his villa in Aarau, Switzerland, to demonstrate his miracle brush and explain its potential to a gathering of investors. Ledl did not hesitate. He was sure he had acquired the necessary polish that would enable him to mix easily in the company of the very rich. And so in that villa in the Alps, he gave his demonstration, made his winning pitch, left with promises of financial backing for his yet unborn enterprise.

Something else happened during that trip to Aarau that was to unlock the doors that had been tightly shut against him. He met King Wammi. Once the absolute ruler of the central African kingdom of Burundi, Wammi was in Swiss exile, driven from his home and his throne by a revolution with the avowed aim of turning Burundi into a republic. But Wammi still claimed the throne, for himself and for his son, Natari V. He insisted that those who ruled in Burundi were usurpers and he was the one true and legitimate leader of his people.

Ledl sat with him through long hours of harangue, listened with sympathy, nodded in agreement, sighed in sorrow, offered to help in any way he could. King Wammi—who supplemented an already vast fortune sequestered in Switzerland by selling titles and peerages from his former kingdom to rich and gullible Europeans with a longing for position, however ephemeral—was so entranced by this compassionate young Austrian that he offered to make him, for a fee far lower than the usual one, an honorary consul of the kingdom of Burundi. A title was one of the things Ledl craved, not so much for itself but because it would increase his stature immeasurably in an easily impressed world. Still, he was shrewd enough not to bite the moment the bait was dangled before him. Wammi sweetened the offer. He would grant Ledl, as well, the power to confer the title on others and issue diplomatic passports from Burundi, car and driver's licenses and the other amenities that come with the rank of diplomat. Ledl still did not leap at the hook. Wammi, intrigued and now anxious to win Ledl to his camp, added something. He was, he said, prepared to name Ledl his personal financial counselor. That was what Ledl had been waiting for.

Back in Vienna, no longer plain Leopold Ledl, inventor and would-be businessman, but now the Honorary Consul Leopold Ledl of the Kingdom of Burundi, financial adviser to his majesty, King Wammi, he set about exploiting what he had gained. With the money from those investors he had met through Kacso, he set up shop as Caravelle Service Company to turn the patent on the massage brush into a viable piece of merchandise and, if he wished, to export and import a wide variety of other things. He also went to work turning his new position with King Wammi and the nonexistent kingdom of Burundi into hard cash. He printed three hundred decrees conferring the title of honorary consul of the central African kingdom and proceeded to sell them in Austria, Greece, Italy, wherever he traveled, for prices ranging up to $100,000. Of course, for an additional fee, the buyer also got from the Ledl printing presses diplomatic passports, drivers' licenses, license plates and more.

But Ledl was still not satisfied. He needed something more attached to his name than honorary consul, something that would bestow the fillip of distinction, that would proclaim him to be truly a man of standing, class and learning. So, it was worth the few thousand dollars he turned over to a friend who knew somebody who could arrange such things to receive in return a piece of parchment proclaiming him an honorary doctor of laws from the National University of Canada in Toronto. Over the next few years, other friends helped him amass a collection of degrees, and by the time he was finished he was an honorary doctor of philosophy, of theology, of canon law, with degrees from the University of Rome, from the University of the Vatican State, from Saint Thomas in Laterano, from Antoniana College and from two universities in London. And his own printing presses were turning out parchment, too, conferring honorary doctorates from universities around the world on whoever was willing to pay the price.

Honorary Consul Dr. Leopold Ledl was in business, and business was booming. Before anyone quite knew what had happened or how, he was head not only of Caravelle Service Company but also of Interterra, a shipping line operating out of Monrovia, Liberia; Westropa Construction Company of Vienna, a home building operation; Intercontinental Rami Etablissement and Etablissement Proco, both with headquarters in Vaduz, Liechtenstein, both with charters granting them the right to do just about anything they wanted, including public relations, market research and analysis, insurance, patent exploitation, banking, commerce, manufacturing. Ledl was into more ventures than anyone could count, all of which resulted in large profits to him, though most seemed to falter somewhere short of completion. There were hotels, warehouses, truck manufacturing plants in Indonesia and Malaysia, a shipbuilding operation in Spain, a home construction scheme in Greece, some mysterious deals in Ghana, Kenya, Nigeria, Zaire and elsewhere in Africa. He did not forget his magic brush and negotiated its license and sale wherever he went, was even at one time striking an agreement with Aristotle Onassis for its distribution in Greece; that deal, like so many others, faded away before the brush reached the market, but not before some of

Onassis's cash found its way into Ledl's pocket. As his fame spread, and his fortune grew, there were some who said much of his new-found wealth was coming from gunrunning to wherever there was trouble (in association with a high-ranking American officer with the NATO forces in Europe), from stolen and counterfeit securities and currency, from financial manipulations of all kinds, and from narcotics. There was hardly an illegal activity that, according to someone, Ledl was not involved in.

If anything was certain it was that within a very few years, the Honorary Consul Dr. Ledl had become very rich, indeed, and very well connected. He had moved his family from Vienna into a luxurious wooded estate, valued at over $1 million, in Maria Anzbach, Austria, and had hired private tutors for his growing daughters. He was serving his guests the best food and wines, and the bar was always stocked with the best liquor, though he drank only milk. He was driving the best cars, traveling first-class all the way. And he even claimed a few more titles—counsel of the patriarchate of Alexandria, and counselor of the archbishopric for Central Africa.

Most important of all, he had cultivated some very important new friends, especially in Rome, to which he journeyed often on business of one kind or another. There was, for instance, the count of San Francisco, Mario Foligni, Honorary Doctor of Theology. His titles and degrees were about as legitimate as any of Ledl's and he had come by them in much the same way. Perhaps that was what had drawn them together and turned them into close friends. Perhaps, too, it was that Foligni had the knack of emerging from unsavory episodes—and there had been a few—completely unscathed. On one occasion, checks that were part of the loot from a bank robbery had been found in his apartment. He simply said that he had no idea how they had come to be there, and the authorities accepted that explanation and never looked any harder in Foligni's direction. On another occasion, he was suspected of having manipulated the fraudulent bankruptcy of a company in which he had an interest. The suspicion was strong enough for the court to have ordered a search of his premises for incriminating evidence. His safe was opened. Inside was a signed blessing from Pope Paul VI. The safe was closed. The investigators apologized for the intrusion and the inconvenience, and departed.

What attracted Ledl most, though, were the people Foligni

knew well, people who might one day prove of considerable value to a man with foresight. Foligni worked every side of the street, maneuvered his way with ease through all strata of Italian society, could count among his friends and associates people well placed in business, government, the church, and the less savory professions. From one world, there were men like Dr. Tomasso Amato, Milanese lawyer and swindler, who specialized in bogus paintings, documents and securities, and Remigio Begni, Rome stockbroker who was not too concerned where the stocks he dealt in came from or where they went. From another world there were the commander-in-chief of the Italian armed forces and the head of the country's tax and revenue enforcement service. A very close friend was Carlo Pesenti, cement and insurance tycoon whose fertile mind overflowed with investment schemes involving tens and even hundred of millions of dollars and who was not averse to cutting in his friend Foligni and Foligni's highly placed friends in the Vatican for a share of the profits if they could help him bring off the deals. There was, too, Alfio Marchini, millionaire owner of Rome's Leonardo da Vinci Hotel, a man whose left-wing sympathies had turned him into one of the major financial backers of the nation's Communist party at the same time that his religious convictions led him into very generous support of the church and its good works and brought him into such a close relationship with those who ruled in the Vatican that he was widely known as "The Red of Saint Peter's." And there were priests like Father Salvatore d'Angelo, head of a charitable organization in Naples called Maddaloni, who spent part of each week in Vatican City and who was on such close terms with the Vatican's assistant secretary of state, Archbishop (soon to be Cardinal) Giovanni Benelli, that he could pass messages and suggestions from Foligni directly to Benelli and know they would quickly reach the right places.

Foligni ran an insurance and finance company called Nuova Sirce, with offices in Rome and Munich, and an investment firm, the Intercommerce Group, operating out of his Rome office. The nominal president of both was an American industrialist and hotel man from Bristol, Connecticut, named Joseph Vetrano, a close friend of the highest-ranking American in the Vatican hierarchy, Bishop Paul Marcinkus. Among the more prominent directors of Nuova Sirce was Monsignor Mario Fornasari, a noted Vatican lawyer with a lucrative practice representing the rich in divorce and matrimonial actions before the sacred rota and, on the side, a manufacturer and distributor of rosaries and other holy articles. He was a good man to know, for he had done many favors for people in the right places. He had, for instance, successfully represented Vetrano in a divorce case on the recommendation not only of Foligni, but of Pesenti, Marchini and Bishop Marcinkus. Of them all, Marcinkus was the one with the potential for doing everyone the most good.

Born in Cicero, Illinois, in 1922, the son of a Lithuanian immigrant window-washer, Marcinkus had early manifested an interest in a church career, had been ordained a priest at twenty-five after graduating from Saint Mary's of the Lake Seminary in Mundelein, Illinois. His career as a parish priest was short, however. He quickly came to the attention of those in charge of the Chicago diocese and became a personal protégé of Samuel Cardinal Stritch and those who followed him in command of America's largest Catholic enclave, Cardinal Meyer and John Cardinal Cody. All took an interest in fostering his career, steered him from the parish priesthood into church government, and particularly into the financial stratum where he seemed most at home, used their influence to situate him in the Vatican itself and advance him up the administrative ladder. Marcinkus hardly looked the part of the ascetic scholar explicating the fine points of theology. A hulking, burly man, towering more than six feet four inches and weighing well over two hundred pounds, he looked more the football player, and, indeed, in high school and college there were some who thought he could make a mark, if he desired, on the football fields or in the rugby scrums, to which he devoted much combative energy. His interests had always been more worldly than scholarly; he had a fondness for good Havana cigars, expensive Scotch, and other things temporal, including the golf links to which he adjourned as often as possible and which he toured with a score that distinguished him as no high-handicap duffer.

That awesome, even frightening aura of physical strength and power won Marcinkus the nickname in the Vatican of "The Gorilla" and won him, as well, the position of personal bodyguard to Pope Paul VI, in charge of security whenever the Pope journeyed forth from the Vatican. He assumed the responsibility of placing himself as an imposing physical barrier between Pope and populace, and he exercised the right to decide who would get to the Pope and who would not. And he was more than just a bodyguard. He was president of the Institute per Opere Religiosi (Institute for Religious Works), more familiarly known as the Vatican Bank. As such, he had virtually a free hand in directing the financial affairs of the Vatican and was, unlike all other church administrators, answerable for his decisions and actions only to the Pope himself.

Perhaps Marcinkus's closest friend outside the church was the Italian banker, financier and industrialist Michele Sindona, whom he would later describe as "well ahead of his time as far as financial matters were concerned." So implicit was Marcinkus's faith in Sindona and his vision that he turned to him often for financial and investment advice and was never discouraged, never had any doubts about Sindona's sagacity, even when later events revealed that following Sindona had resulted in disastrous losses for the Vatican. And he had no hesitation in sending others to Sindona when they were faced with financial problems. He recalled one occasion when an Italian friend was trying to sell to an American group his part ownership in an Italian bank. The deal was foundering because of the intricacies of diverse Italian and American tax laws. Marcinkus suggested a simple solution: his friend should sell his interest to Sindona and Sindona, with his international banking experience and holdings, would easily find a way around the difficulties and consummate the deal. As far as Marcinkus was concerned, Michele Sindona was a master of his craft, a model to emulate.

Just what kind of a model Marcinkus had chosen to listen to and emulate came to light in 1974 and thereafter, when the wreckage of Sindona's adventures lay strewn across the Italian and American financial landscapes, and he was on his way to an American prison.

But, during those years when he was so close to Sindona and relying on him so heavily, could Marcinkus have suspected or known the route Sindona was traveling? Or was there reason why he ignored the whispers that kept arising? There were knowledgeable people in Italy all during those years who were very leery of Sindona, afraid to stand against him, and there was considerable evidence about just what kind of a man he was. Mario Foligni told Leopold Ledl, who had heard the stories from other friends in Italy, Germany and all over Europe, that Sindona was a merciless man, capable of ordering any act, legal or illegal, if it served his purpose, and that he controlled an organization not dissimilar to the Mafia, an organization international in scope and limitless in power. So many were aware of it, Foligni said, that Marcinkus could not have been ignorant of Sindona's character. But there was much gossip, and it seemed to be based on fact, that explained why the bishop appeared oblivious. Sindona and Marcinkus, Foligni said, were partners in many deals that profited both, and though it could not be proved, and Marcinkus would certainly deny it if a question were ever put to him, there were indications that the two men shared a private numbered bank account at Interbanca in the Bahamas and perhaps others elsewhere.

So, Foligni said, if Ledl was interested in doing major business in Rome, the man to know and cultivate was Bishop Paul Marcinkus.

Through Foligni, then, Ledl had come into the orbit of people in power in every sector of Roman society, people whose friendship could lead to new business and great profits. And he had come into even more exalted company through another new friend, Monsignor Alberto Barbieri. (Barbieri's identity and his relationship to Ledl were unearthed only years later, at the end of the 1970s, by two reporters for Germany's *Stern* magazine. That he existed had been known; what had not been known was who he was.) Journalist and lecturer for the Vatican's publishing house, Edizione Paoline, Barbieri was in instant rapport with Ledl, for they had much in common. Like Ledl, Barbieri had a special fondness for the better things of life and reached for them greedily. Like Ledl, Barbieri drove big, fast, expensive limousines. Like Ledl, he wore only the best clothes, his priestly vestments tailor-made in an exclusive shop in Rome. Like Ledl, he enjoyed the company of beautiful women, was seen frequently with them at the best restaurants and night spots, even had a mistress whose existence he hardly kept secret. Like Ledl, he was a doting father, providing only the best for his teen-age daughter. And like Ledl, he was more than a bit of a swindler. According to reports in Italian newspapers, never disputed or denied, Barbieri turned a fancy profit for himself and several associates in 1969 when he helped divert sixty tons of European Economic Community surplus butter from their intended destination—the Vatican's Pontifical

Relief Organization, which was planning to distribute the butter to hospitals, old-age homes and children's shelters—to the black market. Despite an ensuing outcry, he received only the mildest of reprimands. But, then, he had powerful friends in the administration of the church to protect him, friends who had a special fondness for this urbane priest and had no intention of seeing him disgraced.

Barbieri was not slow in introducing his new friend, Ledl, into his circle, especially to those in the Vatican. He arranged for Ledl to stay while in Rome at the Vatican's guest quarters, in room 338 of the Hotel Columbus, very close to Saint Peter's. It was not as lavish as the Excelsior or the Hassler or the Leonardo da Vinci, which Ledl preferred, but it was comfortable and it was the Vatican's own, which was no small thing.

Barbieri made certain, too, that Ledl was entertained well and often and by the right people. It was not long before the Austrian was on intimate terms with some of the most important and influential dignitaries in the Roman Catholic church, so close that he knew he could drop in on them without an appointment, at both their offices and private quarters, and receive a warm welcome. He could count on dinner invitations and, after a sumptuous meal, long hours of convivial and confidential conversation with the likes of Edigio Cardinal Vagnozzi, head of the Vatican's office of economic affairs, and Amleto Giovanni Cardinal Cicognani, secretary of state emeritus, in his late eighties and oldest of all the cardinals. And a special bond seemed to grow between him and Eugene Cardinal Tisserant, dean of the college of cardinals, only a year younger than Cicognani yet still actively running the Society for the Propagation of the Faith and disbursing funds to the church's foreign missions. Instantly recognizable by his long, white beard and patrician bearing, the scholarly, sophisticated French-born Tisserant, perhaps the cardinal closest to Pope Paul VI, appeared to be charmed by Ledl and saw in him, perhaps, a man he might one day put to good use. Whenever they met, Tisserant would grab Ledl's shoulders, and bellow, "Ah, my friend, Johann Strauss from Vienna, is here again," and then lead him away for some pleasant hours of dining and quiet discussion.

This was exalted company, indeed, for a once poor butcher's apprentice turned international swindler, and Ledl luxuriated in it. He did not at first suspect that those venerated church leaders valued him for anything more than his pleasant company and his abil-

ity to tell an amusing story. He did not even think it when Cardinal
Tisserant, during those afterdinner sessions in his quarters and during their meetings in the office (the only other person present an
archbishop assistant to the cardinal—his name has never been revealed), began to tell him sorrowful stories of the declining state of
the Vatican's treasury, of how Bishop Marcinkus had made a series
of ill-considered investments that had cost the church untold millions
of dollars at a time when there was such a drain of the Vatican
treasury, what with the need to support the foreign missions and
the commitment to shore up the stagnating Italian economy, the
shaky banking structure, the collapsing lira and so save the church-
supported Christian Democratic government.

It was only when, according to Ledl, Tisserant dropped the sub-
tleties and pretenses that the Austrian understood why he had been
so welcomed, understood at last the role in which he had been cast.
Early in 1971, in Tisserant's office, only the archbishop with them,
the cardinal concluded one of the tales of the church's woes and
turned directly to Ledl. As Ledl related it later to Joe Coffey and the
FBI's Dick Tamarro, Tisserant asked whether his Austrian friend
had any suggestions or ideas as to how the church might find the
means to solve some of its pressing monetary problems, and those of
Italy, as well.

Ledl had plenty of ideas, but not the kind he cared to put to a
man like Cardinal Tisserant in the heart of the Roman Catholic
church. Despite his own cynicism, grown naturally from his dealings
with men of standing and power, and despite the cynical observation
of his friend Foligni that "they trade in everything; the Vatican
couldn't care less," Ledl was still in awe of the person he was with
and the place they were in. He hesitated.

"No ideas at all, my friend from Vienna?" Tisserant pressed.

Ledl could not bring himself to give voice to those ideas.

Tisserant sighed, looked at the archbishop. Surely, he said, Ledl,
with all his vast experience in such matters, must know how to obtain a great many securities that would assist the Vatican and the
Italian nation.

Ledl asked what kind of securities?

Tisserant laughed. "First-class securities, of course," he said, "in
large American companies."

Ledl sensed the drift of the conversation, but he wanted to be
sure. He said it might be difficult to obtain such paper.

"If they are counterfeit?" Tisserant asked mildly.

Now, Ledl knew. He asked what amounts was the cardinal talking about?

Close to a billion dollars, Tisserant said. To be precise, the figure they had in mind was $950 million. Half, he said, would be channeled through Bishop Marcinkus and the Vatican Bank, to make up for some of the losses the Vatican had suffered as a result of Marcinkus's investments and to provide a base for new and better investments abroad in the future. The other half would go to the Bank of Italy. As a result of its lengthy labor troubles and bad investments, it was in arrears more than $4.5 billion. The infusion of these new assets would be a major step in helping the bank through this crisis. Ledl would be put in touch with the governor general of the bank to work out the arrangements with him as to how delivery to the bank would be made.

Weren't the cardinal and the others, Ledl asked, at all concerned what might happen if it were discovered that the Vatican was dealing in counterfeit American securities? It was one thing for a businessman, or even a large company, to venture into such treacherous waters. But for an institution such as the Vatican to do so. . . .

Tisserant waved that away. He was not at all concerned, he said, nor were any of those he had discussed this with. They all agreed that the American government would never accuse the Vatican of knowingly dealing in counterfeit stocks and bonds. In fact, if it was discovered that such paper existed in the Vatican, the United States would undoubtedly believe the church had been taken by some unscrupulous swindlers and so would secretly step in and make good the losses.

If he could, indeed, find such first-class counterfeit merchandise, Ledl asked, how much was the church willing to pay for it?

If Ledl could make such a delivery, which the cardinal and his friends were sure he could, Tisserant said, then the Vatican and the Bank of Italy would pay him and his sources sixty-five percent of the face value, or about $625 million. Of course, Ledl and his people must understand that they would be expected to kick back a quarter of that amount, or about $150 million, to Tisserant, Marcinkus and the others who had developed this plan. Still, that would leave Ledl and his people about $475 million. That should be enough to pay for their troubles.

Ledl considered it. It was, of course, irresistible. He told Tisserant he thought it might be possible.

Tisserant wanted to hear a stronger and more confident word than *possible* (and in the months to come, whenever they met, and Ledl said there were at least ten more such meetings, the cardinal used all his powers of persuasion to impress on Ledl the urgency of completing the arrangements without delay).

Ledl said, yes, he thought it more than probable that something could be worked out. Since the Vatican, in the persons of Cardinal Tisserant and Bishop Marcinkus, wanted American securities, the best place to go for them was to his friends in the United States.

Ledl was certain he knew exactly the American who could fill the church's order. Manuel Richard Jacobs.

1 7

• • • • • • • • • • • • • •

*L*eopold Ledl and Ricky Jacobs had first met a year and a half before, in late 1969, at the Statler Hilton Hotel in New York. Ledl was in the United States ostensibly to find new markets for his massage brush, though actually to make new contacts and extend his true interests across the Atlantic. A mutual friend brought Jacobs to see him. For a little time, they fenced, danced a pavane around those brushes, Ledl trying to sell Jacobs on their potential, Jacobs expressing an interest in perhaps handling them in California. It did not take long, however, before the brushes were packed back in Ledl's luggage. Jacobs was more interested in Ledl's dealings in the international financial markets, of which he had heard much, and Ledl was more interested in Jacobs's American operations and what Jacobs had to sell. This latter interested Ledl very much, indeed, for Jacobs was then in possession of a large block of American blue-chip securities and a bundle of $100,000 United States Treasury notes.

Thus began a good and profitable relationship. There was just one hitch. Ledl was an entrepreneur, his own man. He dealt with others only as equals or inferiors. While he might temporarily link his fortunes with someone as a partner, he would never hire himself out as an employee. In those early days, however, Jacobs, with his supreme self-assurance, saw himself as the boss, the man who used others for his own ends, who might, if he had no other choice, go into partnership with a Rizzo or a Raia, but not with a European. In his commerce with Ledl, that was the posture he assumed. He continually tried to put the Austrian in a subservient position. When he learned that the honorary consul of the kingdom of Burundi carried a diplomatic passport, the issue came into the open and precipitated their first clash.

They were in Rome then, Ledl cultivating his new friends in the

Vatican and throughout Italian society, Jacobs on business of his own. They had dinner together one evening at the Cavalieri Hilton Hotel with Jacques Suesans and Jacobs's son, Jerry Marc. Ricky Jacobs had something he wanted Ledl to do for him. He had several bundles of securities that he wanted to get to Panama and South America. If Ledl, with the immunity from search his diplomatic status ensured, would carry the securities, Jacobs would pay for first-class flight all the way, would give Ledl $10,000 for every trip he made and would provide him the services of beautiful women at every stop. Ledl was outraged. He told Jacobs he would never consider such a proposal. Jacobs should never think to make another one if he wanted to continue to do business with him.

Jacobs apologized. But he did not abandon the idea that Ledl's real value would be as a servant to him. And so a few months later, he had another proposition: Ledl should move to Southern California. Jacobs would pay all his expenses, set him up in an expensive home, provide him with everything he needed. All Ledl would have to do would be to put himself and his contacts around the world at the disposal of Jacobs and Jacobs's friends. Ledl could hardly believe that Jacobs was serious and snapped, "I am not that hungry." If Jacobs ever made another suggestion of the kind, Ledl would leave and turn elsewhere for his American business. They either dealt as friends and partners or not at all. Since Ledl had proved such a good friend and valuable partner, Jacobs reluctantly abandoned his dream of Ledl as employee and servant.

After that, they continued to deal regularly and profitably together. Early in 1971, Ledl got the news from Suesans and Maurice Ajzen that Jacobs was back in Zurich and was sitting on a very large cache of securities that he was dealing piecemeal. Ledl, who was never one to turn from a profitable opportunity, flew to Zurich, met Jacobs at the Eden au Lac, examined the paper, told Jacobs he was willing to take about $200,000 worth. He had a client, he said, who could use those securities in Italy. As soon as they were disposed of, he would pay Jacobs thirty percent of their value. Knowing that Ledl, unlike the others, stood by his promises, Jacobs gave him the shares on credit. Ledl departed for the south, sold them to Tomasso Amato, the Milanese lawyer, swindler and friend of Foligni.

(The tape ran through Coffey's brain again, and another identification was made. He could hear Ense telling Rizzo about the friend of Ledl's, Dr. Amato from Milan, who had taken possession of merchandise and had not paid for it because he had said it was "bad merchandise.")

About a month later, Maurice Ajzen showed up at Jacobs's room in the Bayerischer Hof in Munich. He was carrying a $30,000 payment from Ledl for the Coca-Cola of Los Angeles stock sold to Amato. But Ajzen had something much more important than that money to pass on. He had a message. Ledl was very anxious to meet Jacobs as soon as possible. He had something so important to discuss it could only be done face-to-face.

If Ledl said that, Jacobs knew it was urgent. But there were a few other things that had to be taken care of first. He had to get back to the United States to resolve some important business with Rizzo and Raia. And there was important business to take care of with the federal government. His appeals on his conviction in the Friar's Club affair had been lost and the authorities were pressing for his surrender to begin serving his prison term. He was sure he could put them off for another few months, at least until summer, but doing that would require his personal presence. He told Ajzen he was sure he could take care of everything expeditiously and Ledl should be informed that he would be back in Zurich no later than the end of April.

Jacobs managed as he had hoped, and so at the end of April, he and Ledl came together at the Dolder Hotel in Zurich, with the multilingual Ajzen as interpreter, for Jacobs spoke little German and Ledl's English was not very good, and it was essential that there be no misunderstandings. Jacobs had never seen Ledl so intense. Almost without preliminaries, Ledl asked Jacobs how much counterfeit paper he could come up with on short notice.

Jacobs replied that Ledl ought to know that he had unlimited paper at his command. How much did Ledl want?

Ledl said slowly that he needed at least $950 million worth. He repeated it slowly and listened intently to make sure that Ajzen translated it exactly.

Jacobs was stunned. He was used to dealing in millions of dollars' worth of paper. But a billion dollars, or close to it, was something else. He demanded to know what Ledl intended to do with so much paper.

Ledl told him.

Jacobs stared with disbelief. "People in the Vatican want it?"

"Yes," Ledl said. "Very important people in the Vatican."

"Who in the Vatican?"

"That I cannot say. But they are very important. They are in a position to make such a deal."

"You're sure?"

"I am sure. I have talked with them many times. They have asked me many times."

"Are you absolutely certain they want counterfeit?"

"I am certain. They ask for counterfeit. That is what they want."

A dozen times Jacobs asked the question, coming at it from every angle he could devise, and a dozen times Ledl gave him the same answer. Finally, Jacobs said, "It's a big order. I'll need help."

"That is to be expected."

"My people will want to meet with you to be sure."

"That, too, is to be expected," Ledl said.

"They'll want some proof."

"I will get them proof."

"Will you meet with them in the United States, in New York?"

"It is better if they would come to Europe."

"Okay," Jacobs said. "I'll go back and talk to them. I'll get back to you as soon as I can."

Over the next months, Jacobs met several times in New York with Vincent Rizzo and Rizzo's superiors, explained that Ledl was willing to split the $475 million take down the middle if they would supply the merchandise. It was an unheard-of proposition, one they were certainly not going to let pass by. But they were not sure they could really believe it, Rizzo told Jacobs. They would have to meet Ledl, talk to him, see his proof before they could totally commit themselves. They would try to adjust their schedules so they could fly to Europe for that meeting.

Jacobs agreed to the necessity of that and said Ledl agreed, too. There was, though, he stressed, an urgent need for speed. It would be wise even before the meeting to make the arrangements to put the plan into motion—to get the engravers, the printers, the forgers for signatures, stocks of the best-quality certificate paper and all the rest. Rizzo said not to worry, he would take care of some of that in New York and Jacobs should make additional arrangements in California.

Jacobs was in regular contact with Ledl, by transatlantic telephone, by courier and, on a few occasions, in person, Jacobs making hurried trips to Vienna, Zurich and Munich to assure Ledl that there was progress, and the meeting would take place very soon.

"You know," Jacobs said at one point, "the people I'm dealing with in this are the Mafia."

Ledl smiled and nodded. "I was sure of that," he said. "Who else would be able to do such a thing but the American Mafia?"

All those messages of optimism from Jacobs were carried by Ledl to Rome, with the assurance that the wait would not be much longer. And in Rome, working with Foligni and Barbieri, Ledl began to put together an organization to handle the logistics of the delivery when the time arrived. From Italy, he recruited Remigio Begni, Foligni's young stockbroker friend, Tomasso Amato and the woman Amato lived with, Marina Giuriati Neubert, a tall, heavyset blonde in her late forties, born in Venice, the widow of a high-ranking German officer in the NATO high command, and herself one of the most trusted assistants to the deputy attorney general of Italy, Dr. Spadaro. From Germany, he enlisted both Ajzen and, without enthusiasm, Winfried Ense. The moment Ajzen mentioned the pending deal with him, Ense insisted that he be made part of it; his familiarity with Italian and Italy, he declared, would make him indispensable. Then both Ense and Marina Neubert suggested one more recruit. They would need, at various points along the way, the services of a pliant attorney and notary. Nobody could fill that role better than Rudolph Guschall of Frankfurt.

By June 29, 1971, all the preliminaries had been taken care of and the time for the meeting was at hand. That afternoon the major figures gathered in a suite at the Churchill Hotel in London. There were Ricky and Jerry Marc Jacobs. His son was there, Ricky explained, because he would soon begin acting as Ricky's surrogate. The federal government had had enough of Ricky's evasions and delays and had ordered him to surrender and begin serving his prison term in just a few days, and there was no way he would be able to hold them off any longer. There was Vincent Rizzo, sitting to one side, silent, deadpan, not revealing the excitement that raced through him. There was another American, a short, fat, older man who sat by himself in a corner and said nothing, who watched everything with narrowed sleepy eyes, who was referred to as Dr. Greenwald from Los Angeles, but who was really Matteo de Lorenzo. There was the husky Maurice Ajzen, the interpreter. And the last to arrive was Leopold Ledl. He apologized for being late, for keeping the Americans waiting. His plane from Rome had been delayed, he explained.

Once more, Jacobs put the questions about the deal to him—its size, whether it really did originate in the Vatican, more. But it took Ledl only moments to understand that the questions did not arise with Jacobs this time, that before asking anything, before saying anything, Jacobs invariably turned and held a whispered conversation with, and received instructions from, the silent man Ledl would later be introduced to as Vincent Rizzo.

Ledl's answers appeared to satisfy Jacobs and Rizzo, and even the man in the corner. But they wanted more than his word. Arranging a deal of this magnitude was going to cost a lot of money—for the plates, the paper, the printing, the couriers, the bodyguards, etc. What they had come to see was some kind of proof so they would know Ledl was not being stupid enough to try to swindle them.

"That," Ledl said, "is why I was just in Rome. I have brought with me what I knew you would want to see." He opened a briefcase and extracted two documents dated that day in Rome and passed them to Jacobs, who read them and passed them to Rizzo, who read them, and passed them to de Lorenzo.

The first was on the letterhead of the Sacra Congregazione dei Religiosi. It read:

To whom it may concern:

Following our meeting which took place today, we wish to confirm the following points:

1) We are willing to buy the complete stock of merchandise up to the sum of $950,-mio.

2) We are agreed upon the terms and dates of consignment, as indicated below:

9.3.71 per 100
10.9.71 " 200
10.10.71 " 200
10.11.71 " 250
10.12.71 " 200

It is understood that the last two consignments, most probably, could be made together on 10.11.71.

3) We guarantee that the merchandise will not be resold up to and not after 1.6.1972.

Yours faithfully,

[Illegible signature]

Rome, Jun. 29. 1971.

The second document was on the letterhead of Rami Etablisse-ment, FL-9490 Vaduz/Fürstentum, Liechtenstein. It read:

Rom deo 29.6.71

According to your letter, we declare that we will perform the delivery of the established items exactly in that terms referring above:

9.3.71	100,-Mio %
10.9.71	200,-Mio %
10.10.71	200,-Mio %
10.11.71	250,-Mio %
10.12.71	200,-Mio %

We point out that with an approximation of 90% the two last deliveries will be performed together.

In case we wouldn't be able to satisfy all conditions and terms of delivery—as established—we declare ourselves ready to pay a penalty in the worth of 1% of the selling price, if the delay in the delivery should be performed.

[Illegible signature]

As Jacobs, Rizzo and de Lorenzo read and studied those two documents, there were expressions of incredulity, which quickly changed to relief, belief and joy.

Rizzo spoke for the first time then. They were in, he declared. What did Ledl want? What was the necessary first step?

He had discussed that with his people in the Vatican, Ledl said. The Americans should go home and begin turning out the counter-feits as rapidly as possible so that the agreed delivery dates could be met. They had committed themselves to paying a one percent penalty if they were late, and that amounted to $9.5 million; natu-rally, they did not want to be faced with paying that. The very first thing, though, was a sample package. The people in the Vatican would like to see and examine what they were getting, and as soon as possible, certainly no later than the end of July. They thought that a $14.5 million sample of the various types of securities ought to suffice.

Rizzo assured Ledl that would pose no problems. The sample could be turned out and work started to meet the delivery dates on the full package. But, Rizzo asked, how did Ledl intend to handle the delivery?

The Americans had nothing to worry about, Ledl said. He had been gathering a group of reliable people for that purpose and, of course, he would direct the operation personally.

Ledl would have no objections, Rizzo said, if the Americans decided to send some of their own people along?

That might make for a cumbersome crowd, Ledl said, and might attract unwanted attention. But, still, he understood the desire of the Americans to safeguard their merchandise and so he would not object as long as the people were reliable. Did they have anyone in particular in mind?

They did, indeed, Rizzo said. Jerry Marc Jacobs would be one of their people, acting for his father. And they intended to include one of their European associates, a man they knew they could depend on. Did Ledl know Tony Grant?

No, Ledl said, he did not know Grant personally. But he had heard of him. He knew that Grant had recently worked on a deal in Milan and elsewhere in Italy with Jacques Suesans and with several others he and Jacobs both knew, including the Swiss Enrico Friedlander and Richard Meyer. Suesans had told him that despite numerous efforts by everyone at banks in Switzerland, England and Italy, and despite Grant's own efforts through his private sources in Italy, they had not been able to find a market for several hundred thousand dollars in worthless drafts and bills of exchange that had been issued on the bankrupt Banca Populaire di Foggia. Even though the certificates had been signed by Mother Superior Remigia Guercia of the Apostolo del Santo Rosario Institute and there was a letter from a cardinal attesting to Mother Remigio's and Santo Rosario's honesty and respectability and responsibility, nobody—not even on the illegal market—wanted to touch the paper once it was learned that it was worth nothing.

Nevertheless, Ledl had been told of Grant's strenuous efforts on behalf of that paper and he had been impressed. If the Americans wanted to include Grant, he would have no objections except those he had already raised.

(And thus another enigma from the tape had been cleared away, and Coffey and the other investigators understood at last what the references by Rizzo and Ense to "the bills of exchange" from "the nuns and the saints of the Bush" and "Rosario" had been all about.)

1 8

• • • • • • • • • • • • •

*L*edl hurried back to Rome from London to tell Cardinal Tisserant that the Vatican should be prepared to accept delivery of the sample package soon after the middle of July.

Jacobs, Rizzo and de Lorenzo headed home, and before they landed, they had come to their own decision. Because of the size of the job and the need for dispatch, the work should not be given to a single supplier but should be split in half. One part of the engraving and printing was assigned to Louis Milo, whose printing plant on Avenue A at Twelfth Street was hard by Jimmy's Lounge and Rizzo's L and S Coffee Shop. The other half was handed to Ely Lubin, a friend of Ricky Jacobs in Los Angeles who worked with a shop of black printers and engravers on Melrose Avenue. Working from authentic certificates, the engravers on both coasts carefully duplicated the originals, leaving blank only the serial numbers, ownership and signatures. From these plates, Milo in New York and Lubin's printers in Los Angeles set their presses rolling and soon that authentic bond paper had been transformed into the sample package of $14.5 million in securities—American Telephone and Telegraph Company, $10,000, 7% bonds; Chrysler Corporation, $5,000, 8⅞% bonds; General Electric Company, $10,000, 7½% bonds; and Pan American World Airways, $10,000, 11 ⅛% bonds. The printing took a little longer than usual, but the demand had been for care, and there had been the promise that this was only a beginning, barely a start on the work that would consume the next weeks and months, until October.

In New York, Milo neatly stacked and packaged his bonds and turned them over to Rizzo. Rizzo handed them to a courier who boarded a plane for Los Angeles, where they were merged with the bonds coming off the presses of Lubin's people. Once Rizzo had seen them off, he called his master forger, William Benjamin, in Philadelphia. The first part of the job was done, he said. Now it was up to Benjamin to finish the work, to make the certificates ready for delivery to Rome.

Benjamin had been waiting for that call, passing the days by showing a visitor, Tony Grant, the sights of Philadelphia. With Rizzo's call, he moved. Taking Grant with him, for the ride and because Grant would soon have his own role to play, Benjamin hurried to New York, stayed only long enough to confer with Rizzo and buy an almost new IBM typewriter and sequential numbering machine from a private source. Then he and Grant were on their way to California.

Louis Gittleman was waiting for them at Los Angeles Airport. Benjamin ordered Grant dropped at a hotel and told him, "Have a good time. You won't be seeing me for a couple of days because I have a lot of work to do." Grant knew exactly what Benjamin meant.

Gittleman detoured to pick up Jerry Marc Jacobs, then drove to an apartment house on Melrose near Normandy Avenue. While Gittleman and Benjamin waited outside, Jacobs, following the instructions he had been given by his just-imprisoned father and by Lubin, went to an apartment on the second floor, rang the bell, identified himself to the black man who opened the door. There were several other men and two women in the apartment. They paid no attention to Jacobs as he was led to the back bedroom. On the bed was a new cardboard carton. Jacobs opened it. Neatly stacked inside were the counterfeit bonds. The black man told him to take it. Jacobs tried to lift it; it was heavier than he thought and the black man helped put it into his arms, steered him back through the apartment, held the door open for him to leave. Jacobs thanked him politely, went down the stairs, joined the waiting Benjamin and Gittleman in the car.

For the next two days and nights, in a room in Gittleman's sister's apartment, Benjamin labored, while Jacobs stood over him and tried to supervise, an intrusive nuisance, Benjamin thought. Wearing surgeons' gloves so he would leave no fingerprints, Benjamin carefully numbered and dated all the certificates on the IBM typewriter and the sequential numbering machine, though after a while he turned that job over to Jerry Jacobs, ordering him to put on a pair of surgeons' gloves before touching the certificates. Then, picking up a pen, Benjamin signed each certificate, precisely duplicating the signatures on the originals so that when he had finished it would have been hard for an experienced investigator to tell those bonds from legitimate ones. He looked at his work of two days and two sleepless nights and was satisfied. There was just one more thing for him to do. He stacked the bonds in neat packages, sealed each package with a bank label. His part of the job was over. Exhausted, Benjamin collapsed onto a bed and went to sleep.

Now it was up to Jerry Jacobs and Tony Grant to see those bonds to their destination. Grant went to a luggage shop in Beverly Hills, bought a large suitcase, which he and Jacobs filled with the bonds, so full it was hard to close and Grant wondered if he shouldn't have bought an even larger one. That done, Jacobs reserved two first-class seats on Pan American Airways from Los Angeles to London, with a change in London to Lufthansa for Rome via Munich. They headed for the airport, checked their suitcase through with the ordinary luggage. It was mid-July and they were on their way.

What they did not know, what nobody knew, was that at almost the same moment, Vincent Rizzo was on his way from New York to Rome. According to immigration stamps on his passport, he arrived in Rome on July 17, stayed only a few days before returning to the United States. What his purpose was he revealed nearly a year later in a room at the Palace Hotel in Munich to a startled Winfried Ense, and to Joe Coffey and a group of German detectives listening a few rooms away. "I was sitting in the other half of the Excelsior," he said. "I was watching all of you. . . . They told me, 'Do you want to meet him?' I says, 'I don't want to meet him. I just want my money. What do I want to meet anybody for?' " Thus, from a distance and in secret, Rizzo saw some of the events that followed and learned about the rest from those he trusted.

More than once over the years that followed, Joe Coffey wondered what would have happened had he been turned loose on Rizzo that February of 1971 when he had first had his hunch. If he had been given the license he wanted, he would have been on Rizzo while all these events were taking place, might have been able to follow on this trip to Rome or the one a few weeks before to London, might have been able to discover enough to blunt the scheme in its infancy. But he was held back, and so the plot went forward unobserved.

1 9

•   •   •   •   •   •   •   •   •   •   •   •   •   •

*I*n Europe, the preparations were complete. At the beginning of July, a courier arrived from the United States and delivered to Ledl a list of the securities then flowing from the presses in New York and Los Angeles. This was the moment to enlist the last recruit, Rudolph Guschall, the lawyer and notary who would put a gloss of legality on the affair.

Marina Neubert called him at his room in a Frankfurt hospital, where for nearly a month he had been recuperating from a serious illness. They had known each other for two years, from the time Guschall had been handling the legal end of the sale of an Italian aircraft plant to some German clients and had found himself trapped in the maze of conflicting international regulations. He had turned for help to the Italian attorney general's office, and Neubert, as assistant to Deputy Attorney General Spadaro, had been instrumental in guiding him through the labyrinth. Now, during that call to his hospital room, she told him that she needed his legal help. She launched into a disingenuous story, knowing that Guschall would never participate in a scheme that was patently illegal. A friend named Leopold Ledl, she said, was the European representative of an American firm, the Evans Import Trading Company of New York. It was his desire to turn over to her a large number of bonds in several American corporations, to sell or use as collateral for loans. In order to expedite the transaction, they needed the services of a lawyer to draw up a power of attorney for Ledl and the Evans company, which named her as the recipient of those securities. She had immediately thought of Guschall because they had worked together so successfully in the past.

On July 9, Neubert, carrying with her a portable typewriter, and Ledl appeared in Guschall's hospital room. As Ledl dictated, Neubert typed out a document. Guschall read it and though Ledl had brought no securities with him—they were still being worked on by Benjamin in Los Angeles—he notorized the agreement. It declared that the Evans Import Trading Company was turning over to Marina Neubert 498 bonds of American Telephone and Telegraph Company, valued at $4,980,000; 259 bonds of General Electric Company, valued at $2,590,000; 412 bonds of Chrysler Corporation, valued at $2,060,000; and 479 bonds of Pan American World Airways, valued at $4,780,000—a total of $14,410,000 worth of bonds. Neubert was empowered to act as Evans's agent in the sale of those bonds or to obtain loans against them and for her services would be paid one-quarter of one percent of what she raised.

The need for such an agreement had been evident to Ledl for some time, though it could not have been implemented until he received word of just what securities his American partners were going to supply. It would be tempting fate, he knew, for anyone to walk around with so many securities worth so much without proof of ownership or the right to possess them. A notarized agreement relating to their possession was, then, an essential precaution. And the use of Neubert's name was another, for with her trusted position in the Italian attorney general's office, any searching inquiries would probably be blunted.

All that was needed then were the bonds, and they were on the way. Jerry Marc Jacobs and Ense were in daily telephone contact during the time they were being prepared, their final conversation taking place only hours before Jacobs and Grant departed, Jacobs giving Ense their flight number and time of arrival in Munich. The moment he knew they were moving, Ense alerted Ledl in Vienna and then, leaving Ajzen behind in Munich to meet Grant and Jacobs and accompany them the rest of the way, summoned his car and chauffeur and headed south for Rome.

Ledl called Tomasso Amato, told him to inform Cardinal Tisserant's assistant, the archbishop, and Bishop Marcinkus that the securities would be arriving within twenty-four to forty-eight hours and that they should be prepared to take delivery. Then he boarded a plane for Munich, with connecting reservations for Rome.

Early on Sunday, July 18, 1971, Grant and Jacobs, with the suitcase crammed with $14.5 million in counterfeit bonds, landed in Munich. Ajzen and Ledl were there to meet them. For the next three hours, they sat around the airport, had lunch, talked idly, barely referring to the contents of that suitcase. Then Ledl continued alone on a plane south. Jacobs, Grant and Ajzen made a flight a little later.

Early that evening, all the conspirators reached Rome. Ledl was with Amato and Neubert in their apartment. Jacobs, Grant, Ajzen and Ense were at the Cavalieri Hilton Hotel, the suitcase on a bed in Jacobs's room. All seven met later that evening for dinner in the rooftop restaurant of the Hilton, dined leisurely, talked calmly about the impending events, trying to control their mounting excitement. Ledl casually asked if he might see some of the merchandise. Ajzen and Jacobs obliged, went downstairs, returned with a few packets. Ledl looked at them, smiled with satisfaction, handed them back. Had they been arranged in serial order?

Jacobs didn't know. It might be well, Ledl said, if that were done. As Ledl, Amato and Neubert were preparing to leave, Ledl said that the initial contact would be made in the morning, the first step toward consummating the deal.

Jacobs, Grant and Ajzen worked until two in the morning to group the certificates by corporation and then by serial number. When they had finished, the bonds were put back into the suitcase and Grant took it with him to his room for the night.

Now it was all in Ledl's hands. In the morning, he, Amato and Neubert appeared early at the Cavalieri Hilton. Ledl asked for the suitcase. Grant brought it to him. Ledl said there was no need for Jacobs, Grant or Ense to go along on this errand. Ajzen might accompany them; he was a powerful man and might prove useful as a bodyguard if that were necessary, but the others should stay behind.

Jacobs objected. He and his father had not done so much and he had not traveled so far only to be cut out at the last moment. He did not want to let that suitcase out of his sight until the exchange had been made.

No exchange was to be made that morning, Ledl said. This was only a preliminary meeting for the purpose of an examination of the certificates by one of the interested parties. There was no need for Jacobs to be there.

That didn't matter, Jacobs said. He was determined to be present.

It would serve no useful purpose, Ledl said. Jacobs did not know the man they were to meet, did not understand Italian, would merely be in the way.

He was in charge of the securities, Jacobs said.

Very well, Ledl said. If Jacobs thought he could handle the deal himself, Ledl would bow out and Jacobs could try.

Ledl knew that was impossible, Jacobs said. It was just that he had his instructions from his father and Rizzo and the others in America.

But they were in Rome now, Ledl said, and the people in Rome were the people that Ledl knew and who knew Ledl. They would do it Ledl's way or they would not do it. He had had arguments about things like that with Ricky Jacobs and Ricky had learned that Leopold Ledl did not joke about important things. It was time for Jerry Jacobs to understand what his father already knew.

Jerry Jacobs understood when to retreat. He did not relish doing so. He was not happy watching Ledl, Amato, Neubert, Ajzen and the suitcase disappear down the avenue. But, he told himself, what else could he do?

Within a half-hour, Ledl and his companions were at the office of Fondinvest-Begni on the Via Nazionale, near the Bank of Italy. Remigio Begni greeted Ledl, Amato and Neubert warmly, ignored Ajzen, whom he did not know. He asked to see the merchandise. Ajzen hefted the suitcase onto a desk. Begni opened it, took a sample certificate from each package, studied the samples. They looked very good to him, he said, expert work. But, still, he would like to take the samples over to their man at the Bank of Italy for his expert opinion.

Did Begni have any doubts? Amato asked.

No, Begni said. But they looked so legitimate he wanted to make sure they were counterfeits and not stolen ones that might be on the hot list.

They were exactly what Cardinal Tisserant had asked for, Ledl said.

Then there should be no objection to the man from the Bank of Italy examining them, Begni said, just to be completely certain. They were very good, he repeated, so good, in fact, that he thought it essential they be checked against the American hot list. One never knew when the Americans were trying to put something over on the Europeans.

If Begni insisted, Ledl said, then, of course, he would have no objections.

Begni left. For two hours, they waited in that small office for his return. When he reappeared, he smiled with satisfaction and nodded. The man at the bank, he said, had examined the bonds very carefully. They were absolutely first-rate and would serve admirably. The news would be passed on and the deal could now proceed.

Where, Amato asked, were the samples?

He had left them at the bank, Begni said.

Why had he done that?

Since some of them were destined for the bank anyway, Begni said, their friend had asked if he might keep them.

Had their friend at the Bank of Italy paid for them?

No, of course not.

If he had not paid, Amato said, then Begni must go back and reclaim them.

Begni objected.

Amato slapped him across the face, hard, then slapped him a second time. They were not giving the paper away, he said. If Begni did not want something worse than a few slaps, he had better return to the bank and get those certificates immediately.

Begni began to frame another objection, but when he looked at Amato, at Ledl, at Neubert, he kept silent, turned and left the office. Within ten minutes he was back, the certificates in his pocket, full of apologies for what had obviously been only a minor misunderstanding, one that would certainly not affect the deal. The Vatican had been informed and in the morning they were to call at the cardinal's office to seal the transaction.

With the contents of the suitcase once more intact, Ledl, Amato, Neubert and Ajzen returned to the Cavalieri Hilton, to the anxious Jacobs, Grant and Ense. Ledl assured them there was nothing to be concerned about. Everything had gone well. The next day, the bonds would be turned over to the Vatican, where they would be approved so that the rest of the deal could then move forward. Meanwhile, he said, he wanted to take them all for a drive, at the end of which they would have lunch and "meet a very important person."

The group piled into Amato's car, headed out of Rome into an isolated area in the hills above the city, stopping at a small café, only a terrace with four tables. Spread out in the distance was a view of the city, its towers and domes reflecting the brilliant glow of the summer afternoon sun. A couple of tables were pulled together to accommodate them. Aperitifs were brought. Amato told them their guest would be arriving momentarily.

It was a half-hour before a new BMW sedan turned off the mountain road and parked beside the café. A priest emerged, saw them, smiled broadly, waved. Amato, Neubert and Ledl rose and hurried to greet him. Amato called him "Your Excellency." Ledl addressed him as "Monsignor Alberto." He was introduced to the others only as "the man who has helped us make the deal for the merchandise." He was Monsignor Alberto Barbieri, friend to those in high places. He had joined them not merely to share a good lunch but also to bring the instructions for the delivery of the suitcase the next day.

Early Tuesday, July 20, the conspirators set out for Vatican City. In one car were Jacobs, Grant and Ense. They were merely to wait outside, watch and hope. Jacobs did not like that arrangement, wanted to accompany Ledl directly into the Vatican and be present at whatever transpired. Ledl would not hear of it. Jacobs was forced to capitulate. But he had one final word for Ledl. "Don't take lire," he said. "We don't have a truck big enough to hold that many lire." Even after kicking back the Vatican's share, Jacobs was expecting to take away nearly $6 million, and at the current rate of exchange that would add up to more than 3.5 billion lire. "We'll only accept dollars or German marks," he said.

Ledl appeared a trifle surprised, said, "Do not worry. I know what must be done. Leave it to me." He got into the second car with Ajzen and Amato (Neubert remained home this day). They paused once along the way, to pick up Begni, then drove across Trevere and on to Vatican City, parking just outside the wall, near the Bancus Spiritus Sanctus. The four left the car, walked into the city, made their way to the office of the archbishop. He was not there. The priest in the outer office explained that unfortunately the archbishop had been called away from the Vatican and would not return for three or four hours. If they liked, they could wait or go away and return in the afternoon.

They stood outside the office in the corridor, uncertain as to their next move. Suddenly, the priest appeard, hurrying toward them. He had been mistaken, he said. The archbishop was not out of the Vatican as he had believed. He was actually with Cardinal Tisserant and was waiting for them in the cardinal's office. Ledl led them in that direction.

Cardinal Tisserant greeted them jovially, slapping Ledl on the shoulders, bellowing his inevitable, "Ah, my friend, Johann Strauss from Vienna, is here again." He spied the suitcase in Ajzen's grasp. "Ah," he said, "I see you have brought what we ordered."

"Yes, Your Eminence," Ledl said. "In that suitcase is the sample of the merchandise for your inspection."

The suitcase was opened. Tisserant and the archbishop peered into it, lifted a few of the packets, inspected them closely. "They are very good," the archbishop told Ledl.

"They are acceptable?" Ledl asked.

"Yes," the archbishop said. "And you will be able to deliver the rest on schedule?"

"Certainly," Ledl said. "There will be no difficulty."

"Good," the archbishop said. "I assume," he added, "that you would like to be paid for the sample."

"Yes, of course," Ledl said. "But I must tell you something. My associates say they will not accept payment in lire. They desire dollars or deutsche marks."

The two prelates exchanged surprised looks. This was an unexpected development. What Ledl's associates were asking for, even after the twenty-five percent kickback, was about $6 million. The archbishop shook his head sadly. If Ledl would agree to accept lire, the payment could be arranged within a few hours by Bishop Marcinkus. While he could appreciate the physical difficulty entailed in transporting that many lire, still . . . dollars or deutsche marks? There were just not that many in Rome, and certainly not in the Vatican, that could be easily diverted at a moment's notice without prior warning.

The archbishop went into a whispered conversation with Cardinal Tisserant. He turned back to Ledl. They had come up with a possible solution, he said. If Ledl would travel to Turin, the archbishop would meet him there and they would get together with the official in charge of the Italian banks. That man should be able to supply the requested dollars and deutsche marks. Of course, the Vatican would not think of keeping the securities at this point. Ledl should take them away until the meeting in Turin. Was that acceptable?

Was there any alternative? Ledl said they would meet again in Turin.

Yes, the archbishop said. And Ledl could inform his associates that the Vatican was pleased and they could proceed with the rest of the arrangement.

Meanwhile, outside the Vatican walls, Jacobs, Grant and Ense were growing very nervous as time passed and there was no sign of Ledl or the others. They had seen them walk away, had not seen exactly where they had gone. Because of the spot where they were parked, there was an assumption that they had gone into the Bancus Spiritus Sanctus, and they had not emerged. Grant was told to go into the bank and cash a traveler's check, see what he could see. He recognized nobody in the bank, returned to the car and took up the watch once more. "We started feeling funny about being outside of the bank for such a long time," Grant would later say, "figuring that the police would stop us as possible bank robbers." Grant told Ense and Jacobs they could stay and keep vigil if they wanted, but he was going back to the hotel; maybe the others had somehow returned already, even though Amato's car was still parked just down the street. Just as Grant was entering the Cavalieri Hilton, he heard Jerry Jacobs being paged for a telephone call. He took it. It was Ajzen. Grant told him where Jacobs and Ense were. Ajzen said he would gather them and then they were all to meet at the bar in the Excelsior Hotel.

At the Excelsior, Ledl waited until everyone had had a drink, refused to answer their questions until they had relaxed. Then he said, "There were a few problems. It is nothing important. But we must go to Turin. There, you will get your money."

2 0

• • • • • • • • • • • • • •

And so it was on to Turin. Jacobs, Grant, Ajzen and Ense (who had ordered his chauffeur to drive his car back to Munich) traveled by plane with the suitcase; Ledl, Neubert and Amato went by car. They checked into separate rooms at the Piemonte Hotel. A few hours later, they were joined by Monsignor Barbieri. The party occupied almost an entire floor of the hotel.

From the outside and with the perspective of time and distance, it is possible to see the events of the next days as a silent-film slapstick comedy. But a sense of humor was not a strong point of any of these conspirators, and the issues themselves were so serious it is doubtful whether then or later any of them ever saw any of the humor.

It began that morning in Turin as Ledl once more told Jacobs that he, Grant and Ense were not needed. Jacobs objected strenuously, but Ledl ignored him, drove away with Amato, Neubert, Ajzen and Barbieri—and the suitcase. They stopped at a monastery on the outskirts of the city. Barbieri left the car and rang the bell beside the massive entrance doors. The doors opened. Cardinal Tisserant's assistant appeared. Barbieri bowed, his manner one of respect and deference. The archbishop greeted him warmly, beckoned to those in the car, led them down passages to a large room. A few moments later, they were joined by a slim, short, expensively dressed man of about sixty. He was introduced as a deputy in the National Assembly, a very important man in the government and in banking, very close to those in power in the Vatican. He and Amato were obviously old and good friends.

They remained in that room only long enough for Ajzen and Neubert to be told to make themselves comfortable and wait. Ledl and Amato, now carrying the suitcase, followed the archbishop, the deputy and Barbieri to another part of the monastery. They were together for three hours. When they reappeared, Amato still had the suitcase, seemed a trifle distressed. Ledl displayed no emotion, nor did the others. They bowed, shook hands. The deputy, the archbishop and Barbieri escorted Ledl and his companions back to the car, watched as they drove off. On their way back to the hotel, Ledl and Amato said only that they were all going to Milan the next day.

Some by car, some by train, they continued north through the Italian peninsula, checked into the Excelsior Hotel in Milan and for a day did nothing, seemed to be without direction or purpose. Ajzen later said that the deputy they had met in Turin appeared suddenly the next afternoon, beckoned to Amato, Neubert and him, took them into the bar and told them that somehow a high official in Milan had learned about the scheme and wanted to be cut in. Ajzen was very worried. He hurried to find Jacobs, Grant and Ense, told them he had just learned something so upsetting he had to talk to them in private without delay. He was going to get into a cab and they should follow in another until they reached someplace where they were sure they could not be overheard. In a zigzag pattern, he led them around Milan, finally ordering the cab to pull into a narrow side street and stop in the middle of the block. He got out, gestured to those in the trailing cab, which had halted just at the turning, to meet him half-way between the vehicles. There, he told them what the deputy had said.

"How did that man find out?" Ense asked.

"I don't know," Ajzen said. "Maybe the priest told him. Maybe the deputy. Maybe a banker. I don't know."

"Are you sure he knows?" Jacobs asked.

"The deputy says he knows."

It was a very unhappy group that headed back to the Excelsior. The four gathered in Jacobs's room to try to chart a course for themselves, a road to safety. It took them only minutes to decide that they must put the whole deal on the shelf until things cooled off. Too many outsiders were getting involved, too many people were learning about it, and the more people who learned, the greater the danger. The thing to do, Jerry Jacobs said, was to split up, seek some guidance and new orders from those at the top, like his father and Rizzo.

That decision was quickly relayed to Ledl. He offered no objections, did not seem particularly concerned. If that was what they wanted to do, he said, then they should do it. Jerry Jacobs suggested that Ledl ought to try to arrange a meeting with Ricky as soon as possible, as soon as Ricky could arrange a furlough from prison. Ledl said he would try to do just that, though he made no effort later to follow through.

In the morning, the group went their separate ways. Ense got on a plane for Munich. Grant boarded a flight for London. Jacobs made the first available plane that would take him to Los Angeles, though before leaving he turned the suitcase with the counterfeit bonds over to Ajzen, explaining that he had no desire to carry it and risk a customs inspection when he arrived home. Just before Jacobs left, Ledl told him to be sure to inform his father and the others in America that there was nothing to worry about, that everything would turn out well.

A few hours later, Ledl, Amato, Neubert and Ajzen, carrying the suitcase, were on their way back to Rome. Once there, Ajzen handed the suitcase to Amato and asked what he ought to do now. Amato and Ledl both suggested that he find an apartment some-where in Rome and remain for the next few months, at least through the middle of October.

Ajzen would later say that once he put the suitcase into Amato's hands at the airport in Rome that July afternoon, he never saw it or the securities again. Though he was in daily contact with Amato until he finally left Rome to return to Munich in the fall, all Amato ever said to him was, "Trust me. Everything will be all right and you'll be taken care of."

The crucial moments during those days would seem to have been the three hours at the monastery in Turin when Ledl and Amato disap-peared with the archbishop, the deputy and Barbieri. What hap-pened during those hours? Though he would later talk about many things and reveal much, Ajzen said he was never told. Amato and Neubert, who shared so much so intimately with him, were never asked by the Italian authorities and outside investigators never got near them. Ledl, who would later have much to reveal about many facets of the operation, had nothing to offer about those hours in Turin.

On the basis of events that ensued and a few enigmatic hints that were dropped, it is, nevertheless, possible to pierce that veil. Dollars and deutsche marks were, as the archbishop and Cardinal Tisserant had said, not easy to come by in Italy in those days, and with the tenuous position of the economy, the government and the banks, it would have been no simple thing to divert $6 million in hard currency without arousing considerable suspicion. There had been no time to prepare for the demand for such currency, and that only compounded the difficulties.

But there is something more crucial. Though the bonds in that suitcase had a face value of $14.5 million, they were just a sample of what was to come, had been brought to Italy, shown to the official of the Bank of Italy and to those in the Vatican only as a sample of the $950 million in securities that were to be delivered in September and October. A sample is only a sample, not the whole, and a business transaction turns not on the delivery of the swatches or the blueprints, but on the delivery of the finished product. Thus, while $6 million is a considerable sum, and the conspirators would not have been averse to walking away with it in return for the sample, it was as nothing against the $475 million that would be due them with the final delivery on October 11 and 12, less than three months in the future. It is, then, possible to surmise that during that long conference in the monastery in Turin an agreement was reached between Ledl on the one side and the archbishop on the other. The sample had been shown and was acceptable. The suppliers—Ledl, Rizzo and the others—would now proceed, would amass the full compliment of merchandise and when it was delivered, the full payment would be made, and meanwhile, the suppliers would retain possession of the sample.

That Ledl did not reveal this to Ense, Ajzen or Grant, or to Jerry Jacobs is not surprising. They were, after all, only underlings, along to play minor roles, not involved in the setting of major policy, and so there was no need to inform them. If Ledl told anyone, it was Ricky Jacobs and Vincent Rizzo, and they were no more likely to take these peripheral characters into their confidence than he was. After all, Ledl had not wanted Ense or Grant involved in the first place; he had accepted Ense only because he demanded a part once he had learned of the deal and had accepted Grant only because Rizzo had insisted. And, as Joe Coffey overheard in Munich the following winter, Rizzo's opinion of Ajzen and Jerry Jacobs was something less than complimentary. He agreed with Ense's comment that while Maurice Ajzen was somebody who could be trusted, nevertheless "he is a fool, this Maurice. He is very, very stupid. He makes mistakes a lot in a lot of places. . . ." As for Jerry Marc Jacobs, Rizzo had few kind words. "Jerry is a son of a bitch," he told Ense. ". . . And when I saw his father, I told his father that. . . . I says, 'All right, your son's out of it. Push him out.' "

Part Six

. . . .

BEYOND THE VATICAN

21

• • • • • • • • • • • • • •

Suddenly the central pivot was gone. Late in July, after ordering Amato and Neubert to do nothing with the securities in their care until they received further instructions, Ledl returned to Vienna to see to other business. He had hardly arrived home before he was warned that he should put everything else to the side. Something urgent had come up that he would have to deal with immediately. The police were closing in on him at last.

On August 11, the honorary consul Dr. Ledl was arrested by the Austrian police. They had not come after him for any of those vast enterprises that had carried him into the inner sanctums of high finance around the world. Ledl was arrested for fraud and extortion. Two of the Austrians to whom he had peddled that fictitious title of honorary consul of the kingdom of Burundi—a salesman who had paid $35,000 for his and a manufacturer whose $100,000 bought him an honorary doctorate from the National University of Canada in Toronto in addition to the diplomatic rank—had discovered to their dismay and horror when they applied to the Austrian government for accreditation as Burundian consuls that everything Ledl had sold them was worthless. The foreign ministry was incredulous and not a little amused when the applications were received for processing and told the two they were either trying to put something over on the government or they themselves had been taken. Enraged, the two would-be diplomats filed charges against Ledl for swindling them.

But that was just the start of Ledl's troubles. After his arrest, his home and office were searched, a safe-deposit box opened and, while nothing was found about the Vatican operation or most of his other dealings, several intriguing and potentially incriminating things did turn up. There were stocks in several American corporations that had been stolen about two years before from the home of a Petaluma, California, doctor named Victor di Carli. These stocks had traveled a twisted path: one of the burglars and the original fence, both small-time operators, had been murdered, and a low-level punk in the New England syndicate controlled by Raymond Patriarca was in prison, convicted of one of those murders; some of the shares had turned up in Glasgow, Montana, others in Las Vegas, at Bache and Company in New York, at Franklin National Bank on Long Island. Just how Ledl happened to be in possession of more of those shares remains a mystery; it was one of the many things he refused to talk about, then or later, and nobody seemed very interested in digging to discover answers.

Other papers in Ledl's safe-deposit box indicated that he had swindled First National City Bank of New York out of $17,900 by reporting the theft of traveler's checks and receiving a reimbursement at the same time an accomplice was cashing those checks all over Paris.

Perhaps most fascinating, though nobody picked up on it then and if anyone later did, the implications were never explored, were papers that pointed to Ledl's possession of several counterfeit one-hundred-share certificates of IBM. They had been turned over in a circuitous manner to Ledl's Viennese lawyer, who eventually passed them on to authorities, who failed to explore the details of Ledl's link to them. But what was particularly intriguing was that nine more of those counterfeit IBM certificates, in the same series, had turned up two months earlier, in mid-June, in Luxembourg. The man who had them was Ernest Shinwell. The man who gave them to Shinwell was Maurice Ajzen.

Soon after his departure from Panama, Shinwell, never idle, had devised a scheme to swindle a swindler, Robert Vesco, whose own operations were soon to collapse in disarray and scandal. It was a typical Shinwell maneuver. He had become friends with a Swiss lawyer, Italo Tresch, and a Luxembourg banker, Jacques Wollner, both associated with Vesco's Investors Bank of Luxembourg—Tresch as the attorney, Wollner as a director. The scheme was simple. They would deposit counterfeit securities in Investors Bank and, using them as collateral for loans, would take the bank for millions and split the proceeds. With the arrogance that few but Shinwell possessed, the Englishman contacted Ricky Jacobs and asked him to

supply part of the counterfeits; the balance Shinwell obtained from
Alan Charles Levy and Stephen Berg, who were touring Europe trying to unload the stocks they had gotten from Kassap Rag Company
in Los Angeles and which they had reclaimed from Jacobs when his
attempt to turn them over to Shinwell in Panama had failed. Jacobs
listened to Shinwell's request, agreed to do what he could, did not
even ask for payment up front despite his earlier experience.

In June, Shinwell and his aide, John Holmes, journeyed to Luxembourg to put the swindle into operation. They met Tresch and
Wollner, went to the bank. Ajzen was waiting for them there with a
package that contained the counterfeit IBM stock. He handed it
to Shinwell and went his own way. Shinwell took those IBM shares
and part of the Kassap haul and with the help of Tresch and Wollner deposited them in the bank as collateral and walked out with a
$150,000 loan.

It was so simple that a few days later they decided to up the
ante. Another $7 million of the Kassap paper was taken to the bank,
deposited and a request made for a bank credit of $3 million to be
put into an account for Shinwell's Agricultural and Industrial Management Company of Panama and a new firm he was then establish-
ing, the Zurich International Holding Company, of Luxembourg.
Unfortunately, the size of the deposit in a bank whose own structure
was extremely shaky created a little suspicion in the mind of one of
the officers. He did a little quiet checking and what he discovered
sent him to the police and sent the police to the bank in time to meet
Shinwell on his next appearance.

And so Ernest Shinwell's career as an international swindler
was brought to a sudden, if temporary, halt. And perhaps Ricky
Jacobs and Dominic Mantell had a few smiles and a sense of vindic-
tive satisfaction. Shinwell was tried in Luxembourg for swindling
the Investors Bank with the counterfeit IBM and Kassap stocks and
was convicted, as were Holmes, Tresch and Wollner, and sent to languish for the next four years in the grand duchy's ancient, decrepit
and forbidding dungeons that some have said make Devil's Island
seem like a vacation spa.

If the Austrian authorities seemed unconcerned with Ledl's ties to
those counterfeit IBM shares, his swindle of First National City
Bank, and his tenuous link to the di Carli robbery, they were very

concerned, indeed, about the way he had taken his fellow Austrians and had used fake titles and degrees. These were particularly heinous crimes in their eyes. They announced that he would be prosecuted to the full for these actions, and for the next year, most of Ledl's time—some of it spent in jail and the rest free on bond under surveillance and restricted to his home in Maria Anzbach and his office in Vienna—was devoted to seeking a way out. But he could find no way and in September 1972, after a month-long trial, he was convicted of fraud and extortion, and of posing as something he wasn't, and sentenced to three years in prison.

So, Ledl was preoccupied during those crucial months of late summer and fall of 1971, unable to play a role in the Vatican operation. A sense of uncertainty seemed to overcome his friends in Rome. Amato was holding a suitcase with $14.5 million in counterfeit bonds in his apartment. Within six weeks, if all went according to schedule, enough additional bonds would arrive to make up the initial $100 million delivery, and a month later still another $850 million. Ledl had been the pivot, the link between the American suppliers and the Vatican customers. Who would replace him?

The man who attempted to fill the vacuum was Mario Foligni. He summoned Amato and Begni to a meeting, informed them that Bishop Marcinkus had passed word to him indirectly (Marcinkus, Foligni declared, never stepped into the open himself, always used others as emissaries and covers) that he and the others in the Vatican wanted to float a trial balloon to test how far they might go with the securities. They had decided, Foligni said, that he should take about $1.5 million of that counterfeit sample held by Amato to Switzerland, open an account and see if the bonds would pass inspection.

On July 27, Foligni, Amato and Neubert flew to Zurich. Outside Handels Bank, to which Foligni had an introduction from his attorney in Rome, Amato turned over to Foligni the sample—10 bonds each of American Telephone and Telegraph, Pan American and Chrysler, and 128 bonds of General Electric. Foligni went into the bank, met with an officer, Lino Buzzolino, deposited the bonds with him and opened a joint account in his name and that of Monsignor Mario Fornasari. With those bonds as collateral, Foligni requested a loan of five percent of their face value to his Nuova Sirce company, a relatively minimal amount chosen to given an aura of legitimacy to the transaction yet not so large as to make the bank want to take a close look at the securities. Buzzolino said the bank would be glad to accommodate Foligni and Fornasari, would lend the sum without interest for eighteen months. But, he said, the normal banking procedures would have to be followed, of course, and the authenticity of the bonds would have to be verified before the loan could be made.

Naturally, Foligni agreed. He expected no less, was prepared for that. He told Buzzolino to immediately Telex the serial numbers of the bonds to Handels Bank's correspondent institution in New York for verification. Those serial numbers would not be on any hot list and so Foligni had no reason to be concerned. Indeed, the next morning the Swiss banker reported that the Hanseatic Bank in New York had confirmed that the bonds were authentic and were not stolen. If Foligni would drop by, he could pick up a checkbook in his name and Fornasari's, for the account was now officially open.

As Foligni was leaving the bank a few hours later, prepared to report back to Rome that all had gone without a hitch, he was brought up short. Buzzolino told him something that he had hoped his careful planning, the use of Fornasari's name, and thus the Vatican imprimatur on the account, would have forestalled. The bonds, Buzzolino said, were about to be sent to New York for a physical examination; it was normal banking procedure and certainly Foligni would have no objections.

Foligni had plenty of objections, but he was afraid to voice them. He knew exactly what would happen in New York when the experts took a close look at those bonds, no matter how beautifully they had been fabricated. But if he were to object now, to close the account in order to prevent those bonds from crossing the ocean, he knew it would only arouse great suspicion, might even cause considerable unpleasantness in Switzerland, where bank swindles are not taken lightly. He agreed, but promptly rushed back to the hotel, collected Amato and Neubert and, without a pause, headed south across the border back into the safety of Italy.

It did not take long for the Bankers Association in New York to recognize that the bonds were forgeries. Foligni, back in Rome, tried to devise ways to meet that problem. He sent Fornasari to Marcinkus to find out what to do. The monsignor returned, Foligni said, described Marcinkus as not overly alarmed, as saying, "We made a mistake in Switzerland. We'll have to be more careful in the future."

That was not precisely what Foligni had hoped to hear. He was going to receive no protection and not even any advice from the bishop, would have to rely on his own wits and resources. But, then, that was what he had been doing for years. When Handels Bank called early in August to tell him the bonds were counterfeit and it would like him to appear in Zurich to discuss the matter, he blandly agreed to make the trip, even set a day and hour for the appointment. He simply did not bother to show up, certainly not when he knew his appearance was very likely to lead to no little inconvenience, and considerable trouble from the Swiss authorities. Instead, he composed a careful letter, explaining how he had become innocently involved, had been duped by a pack of apparent swindlers, and handed that letter to Interpol in Rome.

An old friend, he wrote, had introduced him to a stockbroker in Rome named Remigio Begni, a man with a sterling reputation. Begni told him that a client, a wealthy German heiress named Marina Neubert, owned a number of American corporate bonds. For reasons neither Begni nor the heiress specified at the time, she wished to remain in the background and keep her identity a secret. She was seeking a discreet person who might deposit those bonds in a Swiss bank where she could use them as collateral to obtain larger advances than were possible in Germany. If Foligni agreed to handle the arrangements, he could expect a sizable commission. Begni showed him a document notarized by a Frankfurt attorney named Rudolph Guschall confirming the heiress's right to dispose of the bonds as she wanted. Based on the document and an expert's opinion that the bonds were authentic, Foligni agreed to the proposition.

He met Neubert for the first time, he wrote, in front of Handels Bank in Zurich on the day of the transaction, was handed an envelope containing the bonds by a young man who was her companion. The heiress, who identified herself as Marina Neubert, "declared that she did not intend to appear in the deal and that is why she had contacted other people. She stated that her motives were of a purely personal nature and had to do with her relations with other heirs."

When he received the alarming phone call from Buzzolino, Foligni continued, "I was surprised and concerned. I informed Mr. Begni about it and phoned my lawyer who was on vacation. The lawyer told me to forward immediately a written statement to Interpol." Finally, Foligni wrote, he was going to file a criminal complaint with the Italian authorities against Neubert, Tomasso Amato and Begni for having involved him in such a deal. He was informing Begni of his intentions, though he was sure Begni had been only "an innocent go-between."

Interpol forwarded Foligni's letter without comment to Switzerland, then turned over a copy of the letter and a Swiss report about the Handels Bank affair to an Italian assistant attorney general in Rome to see if he thought any action was warranted. He read the reports, asked Interpol for information about several people, including Leopold Ledl, Maurice Ajzen, Rudolph Guschall and Jerry Marc Jacobs, as well as the Evans Import Trading Company of New York. What little information Interpol had was promptly supplied. A few days later, the assistant attorney general quietly revealed his findings. Since no crime had been committed on Italian soil, there was nothing the Italian authorities could or were prepared to do about the affair or about anyone who might have been involved in it.

The only people on either side of the Atlantic who seemed at all concerned when an item appeared in the Paris edition of the *Herald-Tribune* were Jerry Jacobs in Los Angeles and Winfried Ense in Munich. Ricky Jacobs seemed thoroughly blasé when he was told, and Vincent Rizzo acted as though the news were of no importance to him. But Jerry Jacobs, perhaps because no one confided in him or in anyone on the lower echelon of the Vatican operation, was sure that something terrible must have gone wrong. He called Ense in Munich. Ense echoed his concern, said he would try to find out something and get back to Jacobs. A little later, Ense met Amato in Munich. Amato told him to calm himself. "Our people know everything," Amato said, "and they'll find a way to make everything okay. We're still working with those people in the Vatican and the deal's still on."

A month after the fiasco in Zurich, Foligni and those above him decided to make one more try with the samples. This time it would be much closer to home, at the Banco di Roma, in which the Vatican Bank had a major interest, and whose chief executive, Mario Barone, was very close to both Marcinkus and Michele Sindona. (Barone's Banco di Roma poured hundreds of millions of dollars into Sindona's grab for an international financial empire, some as late as the eve of the collapse of the Sindona fortunes. A few years later, Barone was arrested by Italian authorities for trying to conceal just how deep his and the bank's involvement, and losses, had been.)

Early in September, just as Rudolph Guschall was finally being released from the hospital in Frankfurt where he had been recuperating all summer, he received another call from Neubert. His legal expertise and notary's seal were needed once more, this time in Rome. Guschall boarded a plane, was met at the Rome airport by Neubert and Ajzen and driven to Amato's apartment. Amato and Foligni were waiting for him. Over the next two days, there were a series of meetings at the apartment and at the Ritz Hotel. According to Guschall, he had no idea what was being discussed, though he was present at all those meetings. They were conducted entirely in Italian and French, and he spoke only German. About all he managed to understand were repeated references to the Vatican.

Then Guschall was informed that the moment had arrived to put his skill to use. He was driven by Neubert and Amato to the Leonardo da Vinci Hotel. Foligni arrived about the same time, greeted them, told Guschall they were going to "meet with a very rich and powerful man who owns this hotel." Foligni led them to the private suite of Alfio Marchini, the millionaire of the left, the special friend and emissary of Bishop Marcinkus.

Within moments, Marchini and his son, Sandro, entered the room. Neubert passed the ubiquitous suitcase, which she had been carrying, to Sandro Marchini. He opened it, removed the stacks of bonds and spread them on a table. Guschall was then put to work. He prepared a letter in German, which Neubert translated into Italian, listing the bonds by name and serial number, stating that they were the same ones he had vouched for in July, were owned by Neubert and were authentic. He then affixed his notary's seal to the letter in German and to the Italian translation. His next task was to draw up an agreement between Neubert and Marchini, turning over control of the bonds to Marchini and giving him the power as trustee to do with them as he wished.

From those stacks on Marchini's table, another selection was culled, a representative sample worth $2.5 million The rest of the bonds were put back into the suitcase. Sandro Marchini closed it and carried it away, to some other part of the suite. When he returned, he no longer had the suitcase.

The loose bonds chosen at random were turned over to Foligni.

He carried them to the Banco di Roma, deposited them into a new account he opened in his name and that of Alfio Marchini. No one had any doubt that Marchini's name, position and reputation would successfully constrain the kind of check that had been made at Handels Bank in Zurich; after all, who would want to take a step that might embarrass a man of Marchini's standing? They were depending on that, and on Barone's ability to circumvent anything more than a Telex to New York verifying that these bonds were not on the American hot list.

What they were not counting on was an overzealous bank official who, seeing a deposit of such magnitude, took measures of his own without talking to Barone. He followed the normal banking routine and sent the bonds to New York for examination.

The distressing results were passed on to Marchini. He declared himself appalled, declared that he must have been duped by unscrupulous swindlers.

As for Mario Foligni, the scrupulously honest Count of San Francisco, he was later to claim that it was actually he who had alerted authorities the moment he learned from Begni that a second attempt was going to be made to deal those counterfeit securities. He had done so, he said, in order to protect not just the Banco di Roma but, more importantly, to protect the Vatican. He was convinced from all that he had heard that if the deposit had gone undiscovered, millions of dollars in counterfeit bonds and stocks would then have flowed unchecked into the Vatican Bank, with disastrous consequences for the Holy See. In good conscience, he could not let that happen. Indeed, the only reason he had participated in the operation in the first place, and had urged that ever-larger numbers of bonds be allocated to that deposit, had been to make certain that as many of the forged certificates as possible would be seized and thus not be available to taint the Vatican's reputation.

The authorities in Rome, however, had no record of any report by Mario Foligni prior to the discovery that counterfeit bonds had been deposited at the Banco di Roma. Even so, no charges were ever brought against Foligni, Marchini or anyone else.

In Zurich and Rome, then, some $4 million of that sample package of $14.5 million in counterfeit bonds turned up. Of most of the rest of those bonds, the last anyone would say he saw of them was the moment that Sandro Marchini closed the suitcase and walked out of that room at the Leonardo da Vinci Hotel. And the bonds in that suitcase vanished from public view.

But what the Marchinis, father and son, and those in Europe and the United States who conceived, carried forward and directed the operation did not know was that the suitcase the Marchinis took control of that September morning in Rome was missing additional bonds. At some points during the summer, while the suitcase was in the possession of one or another of them, the foot soldiers—Tony Grant, Maurice Ajzen, Tomasso Amato—fearing that the deal was collapsing and, along with it, their expectations of any financial gain, all dipped into it. When they heard no more of the Vatican arrangements after that day at the Leonardo da Vinci, they all, individually and on their own, decided to use what they had and so make at least a little profit.

On February 15, 1972, Edoardo Cattaneo, the surveyor from Milan who five months later would try to palm off four thousand shares of Coca-Cola Bottling Company of Los Angeles stock on the Union Bank of Lugano, claiming they were an inheritance from the estate of his father, appeared at the Commercial Credit Bank of Muralto, Switzerland, bearing bonds of American Telephone and Telegraph Company, Pan American World Airways and Chrysler Corporation, with a face value of $25,000. He desired, he told the bank's Elio Colombi, to sell them. But a check by Colombi showed that the bonds were counterfeit. "In my opinion," the bank official said, "Mr. Cattaneo and the persons whom he represented were cheated." Cattaneo was permitted to return to Milan.

Two days later, an Italian named Stefano Colombo presented three more of those bonds to Bonea Commerciale Italiano in Milan and asked that they be sold. The bonds were turned over to Merrill, Lynch, Pierce, Fenner and Smith for trading, but when they were examined in New York, there was no doubt that another $25,000 of the bogus issues had surfaced. Back in Milan, Colombo was questioned, said he had received the bonds from an attorney in Milan named Oswald Pedroni. Pedroni said he had received them as payment for services from a client named Adriana Radaelli. She said she had gotten them as a guarantee for a financial deal from someone named Ulysses Bifani. He said he had obtained them from someone he preferred not to name in Switzerland. It had become such a tangled and confusing affair that the authorities in Milan decided to drop the matter and not press charges against anyone since the securities had been confiscated.

About a month later, John Michael Devereaux de la Pena, Tony Grant's friend and the man Peter Raia had chosen to replace Ricky Jacobs in dealing securities in Europe, arrived in New York from Paris in time to keep a prearranged business date. He sat down at a table in the French Quarter of the Americana Hotel with his contact, someone he thought was named Joe Morgan, but who was really an undercover FBI agent named John E. Houlihan. When Houlihan asked if de la Pena had the merchandise with him, de la Pena gestured to a briefcase he had set on the floor close to his chair, said the securities in it were so beautifully done they could not be told from originals. Houlihan said his man was in the bar at that moment and offered to bring him over to the table. De la Pena agreed.

A few minutes later, Houlihan returned with somebody he introduced as Jim, but who was actually FBI agent John J. Hauss. Hauss sat down, said he understood de la Pena was asking fifteen percent of the face value for the merchandise.

De la Pena said he knew that had been the agreed price, and it would stand in any future deals, but for this initial purchase he had to get eighteen percent. The additional three percent, he said, was a tax in England. Whatever the price, he added, Jim would agree it was well worth it once he saw the merchandise. He picked up his briefcase, put it on his lap, opened it a crack and withdrew two pieces of parchment—an orange Chrysler Corporation bond and a blue American Telephone and Telegraph bond. They were just a sample, he said, of what was in the briefcase and what was available to him from his sources. If things worked out, "this may be the beginning of a beautiful friendship."

Whatever it was, it was not the beginning of friendship. As de la Pena was retrieving the bonds and putting them back in his briefcase, Hauss gave a signal. Other FBI agents stationed around the room moved toward the table, surrounded it, arrested de la Pena and seized the briefcase. Inside, they found twenty bonds each of Chrysler, American Telephone and Telegraph and Pan American, worth $500,000 at face value.

De la Pena decided that the better part of valor was to become a federal informant and tell the American authorities what he knew about the illegal securities market. Unfortunately, he said, he really knew very little about those particular counterfeits. About all he could say was that he had gotten them just before leaving Paris from a friend and business associate, Sylvaire Galardi. Where Galardi had gotten them, he did not know.

But when Galardi's name was fed into the FBI computers, the information that spewed out sent the agents back to de la Pena, for on the print-out were the Coca-Cola stocks that had surfaced in Lebanon the previous year to fuel the Middle Eastern arms race. De la Pena, though, said he could add nothing to what they already knew about that. He knew a lot of the people involved, but knew nothing about that particular project.

It was not until five months later that more of those counterfeits surfaced. Early in August, a lawyer from Biasca, Italy, Francesco Bignasca, telephoned a young Swiss stockbroker, Giovanni Mahler, in the Lugano offices of Loeb Rhoades and Company. He had some clients, Bignasca said, who owned about $100,000 worth of American bonds they wanted to sell. Mahler had been recommended to him as a broker who could handle the transaction.

Mahler asked Bignasca to forward to him either the securities themselves or photocopies for shipment to the main office of Loeb Rhoades in New York for authentication. Once that was done, the sale could proceed. Bignasca dispatched the photocopies—one American Telephone and Telegraph debenture, four Chrysler and seven Pan American.

According to Mahler, a few days later, the New York office of the brokerage firm sent him a message that the photocopies were not sufficient, that the originals would be needed for examination. He telephoned Bignasca with the news and within a few days, the lawyer arrived in Lugano with two men he said were his clients and the owners of the securities, Virgilio Lucchetti and a lawyer from Rome, Dario Pietrantoni. The bonds were turned over to Mahler and he was told that once they were authenticated and sold, the funds should be deposited in Bignasca's name at the Swiss People's Bank of Lugano and Bignasca notified so that he or Lucchetti could draw on the account. Nothing was ever deposited, of course, for Loeb Rhoades in New York quickly realized the securities were bogus. "I am not in a position to say whether or not Lawyer Bignasca was aware of the fact that the securities were forged," Mahler said, "but he displayed an intense and continuous interest, not only at the time of the transaction, but also after he had been informed by me as to the fact that they were forged securities."

Bignasca had a slightly different story. The whole affair, he said, was a terrible shock because he had known Pietrantoni for years and had implicit trust in him and so had no reason for suspicion when Pietrantoni brought Lucchetti to him. Further, he said, Mahler's actions surprised him and were contrary to his instructions and expectations. The Swiss stockbroker had told him that the photocopies were sufficient and that New York had raised no objections to them, and so when the securities were delivered to him in Lugano it was with the anticipation of an immediate sale.

The affair never went much beyond the filing of charges in Lugano against Bignasca, Pietrantoni and Lucchetti for attempted fraud. They were Italians and had no intention of appearing in Lugano to respond to and fight those charges, and without the cooperation of Italian authorities, who did nothing but take a statement from Bignasca, there was nothing the Swiss could do.

On four separate occasions in 1972, then, a total of $650,000 of those counterfeit bonds that had been secretly lifted from the suitcase appeared in relatively small amounts in Switzerland, Italy and the United States. Whether there were attempts to deal more, attempts that were successful, no one can say, for after the aborted try in Lugano, there was only silence—a silence that has remained unbroken.

2 2

• • • • • • • • • • • • • •

Did it end there? Did the nearly $10 million of that sample package of counterfeits that remained in the suitcase carried off by Sandro Marchini simply vanish forever into some impenetrable darkness? Did the men in the Vatican, and Vincent Rizzo and Ricky Jacobs and the others who had set up the deal, merely cancel it without discussion or argument? Did they just forget about the remainder of those $950 million in securities that had been scheduled for delivery in September and October of 1971? Did they forget, as well, the profits they were to reap?

No one in a position to know has ever said and there is no way to know for certain. But, if one listens hard enough, there are clues—some clear, some subtle, some implied in acts of commission, others in acts of omission.

In mid-September 1971, little more than a week after the first delivery—$100 million of the $950 million package of counterfeits—was to have taken place under the terms of the contract between the Vatican and Leopold Ledl and his American partners, rumors began to circulate, and hints to appear in the Italian press, that Michele Sindona and his good friend Bishop Paul Marcinkus and the Vatican Bank were off and running in tandem once again. That Sindona and Marcinkus might be allied, even partners, in a huge venture surprised no one. It was accepted dicta that wherever Sindona went, Marcinkus and the bank were usually only a short step behind. Not only had Marcinkus relied repeatedly on Sindona for advice, he had poured millions, perhaps hundreds of millions, of dollars of Vatican funds into many of Sindona's 140 companies in ten countries, in everything from banking to real estate to photography. Though

Marcinkus might later claim that he had had "only limited financial dealings" with his friend, few experts thought that more than a self-serving attempt to deflect the criticism directed at him as a result of the heavy Vatican losses (the Italian press estimated these to be in excess of $100 million) when the Sindona empire finally collapsed. And, indeed, Sindona himself did not credit it, saying on several occasions that Marcinkus and the bank had been particularly strong backers, were substantial if minor partners in a number of his ventures.

Among those enterprises in which Sindona and others said that Marcinkus and the bank had a heavy stake was Società Generale Immobiliare, Sindona's major Italian holding company, from which radiated a vast complex that included, among other things, the Watergate complex in Washington, the Meurice Hotel in Paris and a string of other European luxury hotels as well as a number of industrial concerns in the United States and Europe. Sindona, in fact, had bought his initial one-third interest in Società Generale Immobiliare in 1969 from Marcinkus's Vatican Bank. He had also bought control of Condotte Dacqua, the company that supplied Rome with its water, from the Vatican Bank. In addition, Sindona and Marcinkus shared interests in Finabank of Geneva, a general banking and securities management firm; Edilcentro International, a Bahamian banking institution (where Marcinkus was also a director of the lay Cisalpine Overseas Bank of Nassau and where, according to rumors, he was co-holder with Sindona of a private account at Interbanca); Fasco International Holdings, of Luxembourg, through which Sindona was making his international grab; Banque de Financements de Geneve in Switzerland; Banca Unione of Milan; and Banca Privata Finanziaria Italiana, the centerpiece of Sindona's banking empire that had entered into international banking partnerships with Continental Illinois National Bank and Trust Company of Chicago and Hambros Bank of London.

There were many knowledgeable Italians who were sure that Marcinkus and the Vatican Bank were doing a lot more for Sindona than merely following his advice and putting a considerable fortune into his ventures. They believed Marcinkus was so close to and so involved with the Sicilian-born financier that he could not possibly have been unaware of the road his friend was traveling. Indeed, early in 1981, Marcinkus's major lay assistant, Luigi Mennini, the

Vatican Bank's chief lay administrator and highest-ranking non-cleric, was arrested in Rome on charges of complicity in the Sindona swindles and fraudulent bankruptcies. To many, that was merely the last of the revealing road signs. As Sindona rose to prominence, wealth and power, there were repeated allegations in both the press and the National Assembly—especially from members of the opposition to the Christian Democratic regime, which was strongly backed by the Vatican and which was a prime beneficiary of Sindona's financial benevolence—that the financier had been using the Vatican Bank to transfer funds secretly and illegally in and out of Italy in his quest for international suzerainty. They further alleged that Sindona had been using the bank to wash money—by depositing securities and other paper of all kinds into the bank and receiving letters of credit that could be used for whatever purpose he wanted anywhere in the world—and that the money that was being laundered was not just his but funds channeled through him and the bank by the Sicilian and American Mafias. And there were stories, louder than just whispers, that Sindona and Marcinkus were linked in more than a few deals that emitted a decidedly rank aroma.

It was just such an aroma that pervaded the events of the fall of 1971. They began with reports that somebody was trying to buy the giant Italian holding company Società Italiana per le Strade Ferrante Meridionali, more commonly known as Bastogi, and its wide interests in real estate, mining, chemicals, cement and more. Soon, the identity of that somebody was widely known—Michele Sindona, and along with him, Bishop Paul Marcinkus. If they succeeded, Bastogi was destined to become a jointly owned venture of Sindona and the Vatican.

These rumors raced through the European banking community, and they were soon accompanied by a much more disturbing story. The bankers heard, and veiled references to what they heard began to appear in the European press, that Sindona and Marcinkus were in the process of depositing $100 million in counterfeit American corporate bonds in West German banks, particularly in Westdeutsche Landesbank Gerozentral, and on the basis of those deposits, the banks were prepared to advance the funds for the purchase of fifty percent of Bastogi's stock. Torchiana Tullio, president of Bastogi, tried to determine whether there was any truth to those stories, but all his efforts failed, for the bonds were out of Italy and in German banks that would not cooperate with him. Though neither Tullio nor other bankers in Europe had any doubts that the rumors were based on fact, they were powerless to thwart the takeover.

But then events worked in their favor. The news that Bastogi was going to be swallowed up sent its stock spiraling, to two or three times the real value, and that made it too rich a purchase even for Sindona and Marcinkus, even using the kind of paper that was to have financed it. The deal was aborted, the bonds were withdrawn from the German banks and were, according to reports, then deposited in the Vatican Bank in the custody of Marcinkus. (About two years later, Marcinkus on his own made another move for Bastogi, this time succeeding and adding it to the Vatican's own industrial empire.)

But a central question remains unanswered. If, as the European banking community so firmly believed, the purchase of Bastogi was to be financed by $100 million in counterfeit Amerian corporate bonds in the fall of 1971, where did those bonds come from? In fact, was the Bastogi plan already under discussion when the deal for the bonds was being made with Ledl?

As each marking along this twisted trail appears, it becomes evident that Bastogi was but a single stopping point. It was not long after the Bastogi maneuvers collapsed that Sindona turned his gaze across the Atlantic, to Long Island and the Franklin National Bank, the nineteenth largest bank in the United States with assets of $3.3 billion. The first overtures were made just after the start of 1972. As the months passed, Sindona's intentions became clearer and his determination to take Franklin National stronger. By mid-1972, through Fasco International Holdings, he had acquired a controlling interest in the bank for $40 million—$40 a share for 21.6 percent of the bank's stock, or $8.25 a share above the then-quoted price on the Over-the-Counter market.

It took Sindona a mere two years to drive Franklin National to the edge and then into the abyss. Out of the debris of the bank's failure—the first for a major American bank since the Depression days of 1933—came the revelations that he had fraudulently removed at least $15 million from the bank, had manipulated its foreign-currency speculations to such an extent that the bank lost $30 million on them, and had bought the bank in the first place with $40 million illegally transferred out of Italy. It could never be proved, but experts were convinced that the transfer had been accomplished through the Vatican Bank.

The collapse of Franklin National was only the American facet of the shattering of the Sindona empire. Almost simultaneously, his entire empire was falling, and all the kings horses and all the kings men could not put it together again. All banking experts could do was try to figure out what happened and why. Sindona had, it was discovered, illegally removed at least $225 million from his banks in Milan. His Banca Privata went under when its losses topped $200 million. The Banco di Roma was near collapse after funneling $200 million to Sindona in a futile rescue effort on the eve of the disaster. The list of financial destruction was nearly endless wherever Sindona had his hands. But most sinister of all, five Italian investigators looking into the empire were murdered, and Italian authorities were later to indict Sindona for those murders. One of those charged with having murdered on contract from Sindona was an American hoodlum who escaped from Riker's Island, where he had been locked up on another charge while Sindona was in a nearby cell; while on the street, that hoodlum, William J. Arico, had long been in the employ of Vincent Rizzo.

Despite the charges and revelations, Sindona's friends in the Vatican did not abandon him. On the eve of his trial in New York—which ended in 1980 with his conviction on sixty-seven counts, a twenty-five-year prison sentence and a $207,000 fine—Bishop Paul Marcinkus and two cardinals offered to appear, not in person but on videotape, as character witnesses. Their appearance was vetoed just prior to the taping by the Vatican secretary of state, Jean Cardinal Villot, who felt it would be neither fitting nor proper.

During his two years at Franklin National, before he fell, Sindona did manage to accomplish something that, at the time, won him some praise. He lured massive foreign deposits into the bank. In a laudatory article less than a year after he took control, *The New York Times* said that through his efforts, those foreign deposits had totaled several hundred million dollars.

There were some in Italy and elsewhere, however, who read that and saw in it confirmation of their belief that Sindona had been merging Franklin National into his vast money laundry operation by depositing into it letters of credit issued by his own Italian, Swiss and German banks, by the Vatican Bank and other institutions where he had considerable sway, and backed by securities of, perhaps, a dubious nature. If they expressed that conviction privately and not for attribution—Sindona was, after all, a dangerous man known to take sudden revenge on those who crossed him—it was finally spoken loudly and publicly at his trial in 1980. Chief United States prosecutor John Kenney declared then that Sindona "was, indeed, a launderer for the funds of prominent Italians and other people," and among those involved with him was the Vatican Bank, which had engaged in transactions "which would not comply with the religious tenets of the Vatican or the Roman Catholic Church."

And so the questions arise: Was there a relationship between those hundreds of millions of dollars in foreign deposits that found their way from Europe to Franklin National and the counterfeit bonds that had been marked for delivery to the Vatican and the Bank of Italy? Were some, or many, of those deposits, based on the letters of credit, indeed backed by those worthless securities? If these questions cannot be answered, still Joe Coffey and a lot of banking experts are sure that the collapse of the Franklin National Bank can be traced, at least in part, directly to those bonds, and so they are convinced that those bonds were delivered.

If what Sindona and Marcinkus and others were doing in Rome in the fall of 1971 and later suggests that the bonds were delivered, perhaps as significant were more subtle emanations from New York—the little signs of change, the things that were not done.

Vincent Rizzo was neither a forgiving nor a charitable man. No one who knew him or had ever dealt with him doubted that the only thing he valued more than his pocketbook was his own life. The surest way to stir Rizzo to wrath and violence was to put him in physical peril or to attack his wealth by welching on a debt, being slow in the payment of money owed, cheating him or doing harm to those he used for profit. These had been the facts of life about Rizzo for years and the world he traveled was filled with people, and corpses, who had learned the hard way. Where money was concerned, it was unwise to play games with him; he had neither patience nor a sense of humor; he responded quickly without mercy.

The fall and winter of 1971-72 were busy times for Rizzo. He was into a dozen different rackets and all seemed to be doing well, lining his pockets and the coffers of those he worked for and who worked for him. If there were some who noted a little more assurance and arrogance, that seemed only natural, given his success and his steadily increasing position in the syndicate. If, as Coffey, for one, observed when he first took out after Rizzo, the bosses were showing him a little more respect and deference than in the past and than his own reputed ranking in the underworld hierarchy might command, then that, too, could be explained by his great success as an earner, by his few failures to come up with large profits no matter what he turned his hand to.

That Rizzo was as merciless as ever, perhaps even more so, was patent. John Calamarus, owner of the Blue Seas restaurant, found that out when he couldn't make his regular payments on his loan-sharking debt. Winfried Ense and Alfred Barg discovered that distance and their Continental sophistication and slickness were no shield when they tried to swindle Rizzo out of $350,000. Jerry Marc Jacobs learned how merciless Rizzo could be when the amount owed was a mere $25,000; he learned it through threats, beatings and the discovery that a contract had been given on his life.

And there was Michael "The Animal" Affinito, Peter Raia's gorilla. In the fall of 1971, Raia and William Benjamin had a few words at Raia's Manhattan shoe store when Benjamin explained that Raia would have to wait for full payment on a stock deal until Benjamin's customers paid him. What Benjamin owed was $18,000, and Raia wanted it then and there. Benjamin insisted that Raia would have to wait. Raia motioned to Affinito, then stood back and watched with satisfaction as the young, muscular Affinito went after the elderly Benjamin with his fists and shoes, punching him until he was on the floor, then kicking him until he was bleeding and unconscious.

It was several days before Benjamin was well enough to move around again. He immediately went to Rizzo. "Those two bastards," he said, "ought to be killed."

"I'll see what I can do," Rizzo said. "I'll talk to my people."

A little later, in the early fall of 1971, Affinito left his girlfriend's apartment in the Bronx early one morning, got into his car parked on the street, turned on the ignition. The block erupted in sound, was scorched by the blazing fire that engulfed the car, incinerating Affinito's body. Two sticks of dynamite had been wired to the ignition.

Tony Grant heard the story a few months later from both Benjamin and Rizzo, was told by Rizzo that he had ordered the murder on approval of his superiors. "I wanted to get that bastard, Raia, too," Rizzo said, "but they wouldn't allow that." Still, Raia got the message. His dealings with Rizzo and others in the syndicate came to a sudden end, and one day when Rizzo heard Benjamin tell Grant to avoid even walking by Raia's store "because he associates you with us and might do something to you just for spite," Rizzo laughed and said, "Don't worry about it. If Raia sees us, he'll die of fright."

This, then, was the Vincent Rizzo everybody knew, the man who was merciless with people who owed him money, with people who crossed him. Yet in all those months of late 1971 and into 1972, Rizzo seemed to be unconcerned about the deal in the Vatican. It was the biggest deal he had ever been associated with, or was likely to be associated with; it stood to earn him and his American associates nearly $250 million if completed; it had already cost him considerable time, effort and manpower, if not outright cash (since Rizzo had means to compel men to do his bidding for little or nothing but his smile and approval). Still, he talked to no one about it, at least no one on a level below him. There were no threatening phone calls to those who had been involved in it—to Amato, Neubert, Foligni, Begni or anyone in Rome; to Ense and Ajzen in Germany; to Grant; to Jerry Jacobs; to anyone. There were no hurried trips abroad to demand payment. There was no violence or threats of violence. There was nothing but silence.

Even after Rizzo's phones were tapped, in all the torrent of words and intimations about deals, past, present and future, words spoken both directly and subtly, there was not once a mention or an implication of that staggering arrangement in Rome. And in February 1972, when Rizzo went to Munich to confront Ense and Barg, it was to demand payment of the $350,000 on the loan of stolen securities and to arrange other deals. The Vatican did not concern him, did not even seem to interest him. When Ense kept trying to bring up the subject and explore it to the full, Rizzo's reactions and responses were those of a bored listener who could not have cared less. They were not the reactions of an angry man who had been cheated.

In fact, the only calls about the Vatican that were ever made from the United States or anywhere were to Rudolph Guschall and Leopold Ledl. Guschall received several, all with the same message: Do not talk about the Vatican deal with anyone; if you do, you may find yourself in the same place as Kurt Huber. To Ledl, the message was only: Do not talk to anyone about the Vatican, ever.

The implications seem clear. Still, there are questions that cannot be answered with any certainty. Had the bonds not been delivered to the Vatican and no payment ever received, would Vincent Rizzo have so cavalierly dismissed the loss and ignored those who had caused it—even continued to deal with them? Would there have been no demands or threats, no insistence at least on some explanation?

And if a deal of such mammoth proportions that had been arranged by Rizzo and that was to bring such enormous wealth to him and to his superiors had fallen apart with no profits, with only losses, would Vincent Rizzo have been shown respect and deference from the men at the top of the syndicate? Indeed, would Vincent Rizzo have walked the streets of New York and everywhere he went with such total assurance of safety? The men for whom Rizzo worked, to whom he had held out such promises of vast profits, were not men to accept the loss of those profits with equanimity. They were as sudden as Rizzo, as dangerous when crossed, when promises were not kept. If Rizzo had not delivered what he promised, there is little doubt that his remains would have turned up in the trunk of a car somewhere, or encased in a block of cement at the bottom of a river.

. . . .

Part Seven

*T*HE LAST PIECES

2 3

• • • • • • • • • • • • • • •

*T*hrough the years, isolated pieces had been put into place—an event here, a name there. But no one, not even the FBI computers, had been able to discern the links, to see that all were part of the same puzzle. Leads were followed without a clear sense of where they were pointing, clues and hints picked up without an understanding of their true import. Then, one spring morning in 1972 in the Manhattan district attorney's office, Detective Joe Coffey lit a cigarette for a nicotine-starved Tony Grant.

In the days before Grant began his recital, Freddy Mayo and Jimmy Heimerle, to save themselves, had talked about stolen and counterfeit airline tickets and credit cards, about the travel agency they operated for Rizzo and others in the syndicate, about trips to San Francisco and Miami and other places. But Grant's statements sparked the realization that these were just the edges of a much larger canvas. Grant stepped up to that canvas and began to sketch in the contours around the edges and toward the center, adding details, filling in empty places, drawing the lines that connected disparate elements. Though he left the center blank because he did not know what was there, still he knew enough to provide the clues and the means by which that center would one day be filled and the painting completed. If what he did was, in some measure, self-serving and self-exculpating, was only as much as he felt he had to do to win gratitude and eventual freedom, still it was enough. He revealed what Coffey and the New York detectives, and Tamarro and the FBI, were looking for and who they were after. He pointed them toward the potential weak links who might turn. The investigators now began to move more steadily and with surer purpose along the avenues Grant had marked.

But the turning of Grant, Mayo and Heimerle also had an immediate consequence. The detectives would have much preferred to move slowly and carefully along the paths laid out for them by Grant until they reached that center, until they knew it all and there were no more questions. That was no longer possible. The leap had to be made from the investigative to the prosecutive stage. Once the three were in custody, it did not take long before suspicion began to grow and spread along Avenue A that they were undoubtedly talking. That suspicion created a new sense of caution, perhaps even a belief that Izzy Marion might have been right all along when he said the phones were probably tapped. The flood that had poured from the phones at Jimmy's Lounge, Rizzo's home, the L and S Coffee Shop and all the other locations for months suddenly began to dry up.

So, the time had arrived to begin to use all that had been gathered since the chase began for its real purpose—to put society's enemies in society's prisons. Certainly, the investigations would continue to move steadily ahead, especially in those areas where uncertainty remained and where the evidence was inconclusive. But the prosecutor, Assistant District Attorney Ronald Goldstock for Hogan's office and Strike Force attorney William Aronwald for the Justice Department, now took the central roles, empaneled grand juries, began to present the evidence and seek indictments, and prepared to go to trial. That they were duplicating each other's efforts often was a calculated decision. They were determined to avoid any chance of a slipup, and so indictments for the same crimes were sought in both jurisdictions and once obtained, the burden of prosecution would fall in the jurisdiction in which conviction carried the stiffest sentence. If that meant that Aronwald and the Justice Department would go to court more often and so win most of the laurels, it had to be; Goldstock and Hogan accepted that, even though they were convinced that the success of the whole investigation was primarily the result of the work of their own detectives.

The first indictments were handed down within weeks after those critical arrests on Staten Island, against Grant, Mayo, Heimerle and several others for dealing in stolen and counterfeit airline tickets and credit cards. They were, of course, merely weapons to ensure the continued cooperation of the three and, indeed, none was ever tried. The indictments were, as well, a means for Hogan to ensure that his office and his men got at least some of the credit before the federal government began to claim the major share when the bigger cases started to break. No longer concerned that he might be tipping his hand to those who were the main targets—the hand had already been tipped, he knew, with the arrests of Grant and the others—Hogan called a press conference and announced that the indictments had grown out of a lengthy investigation that was still in progress and that centered around organized crime's involvement in stolen securities and narcotics. Some of those stolen airline tickets, for instance, he said, had been used by Grant and Mayo for a trip to Argentina to buy cocaine.

If there were still a few on Avenue A who were blind to the significance of the arrests of Mayo, Heimerle and Grant, that revelation by Hogan stripped away the blinders. Some began to run. Rizzo's strong-arm collector, Patty Marino, disappeared within days and it was years before he finally resurfaced. And the phones went completely silent. Along Avenue A, everywhere syndicate leaders congregated, there were muted conversations and wary glances at strangers, and a growing sense of impending trouble.

It came quickly. Hogan's detectives passed through the doors of Jimmy's Lounge and the other hangouts with regularity, bearing subpoenas for appearances before the grand juries. For some of the cops, it was one of the small pleasures at the end of months of frustration; after hearing about so many crimes over those phone taps they were finally able to take some action.

If there was one man who greeted that opportunity with particular relish it was Joe Coffey, whose hunch on a winter night had begun it all. He had been in Jimmy's Lounge before, of course, but that was at the start and he had been dressed as a steamfitter, was unknown and unrecognized. By the time he walked into the bar again on a July afternoon, his name was well known; it had appeared on enough of those subpoenas, had been mentioned frequently enough in the grand-jury rooms to leave a bitter and unforgettable echo in the ears of those who had heard it and repeated it. Some of them had been waiting for him to appear, just to see what he looked like, to hear what he sounded like. But during that initial period of subpoena serving, he had remained in the background, not out of choice but because that was how things fell. Then his turn came: he was to serve a subpoena on one Vincent Rizzo.

When Coffey strode through the door, looming large in the dim light, groomed and dressed in a lightweight summer suit, nobody doubted that he was a cop, and nobody doubted that Detective Coffey had finally come to call. Rizzo was at the bar. He stared. This was the first time they had ever come face-to-face, but he knew it was Coffey. "So," he said, "you're Coffey."

"Yeah," Coffey said. "I'm Coffey. What about it?"

"I want to buy you a drink," Rizzo said.

"I don't want one of your drinks," Coffey said.

"No," Rizzo said, "I want to buy you a drink." He gestured to the girl behind the bar. "Loraine," he ordered, "give Detective Coffey a beer."

"I told you," Coffey repeated, "I don't want one of your drinks."

"Give him a beer anyway," Rizzo insisted.

Loraine poured the beer, put the glass down in front of Coffey. He picked it up and slowly and deliberately turned it upside down, dumping the beer in a large, spreading puddle all over the bar. "I told you," he said slowly, "I don't want your beer. I don't drink with scum like you."

Rizzo's fists clenched, his face turned apoplectic. "Just who the fuck do you think you are?" he raged.

"I know who I am," Coffey said. "And I told you what you could do with your beer."

"Don't give me that shit," Rizzo shouted. "You come in here like you're God almighty himself, like you think you own the fuckin' place. Well, let me tell you somethin', you son of a bitch. You're gonna have to learn. I'll get you, you bastard."

"I wouldn't count on that," Coffey said. "But I've got something for you." He pulled the subpoena out of his pocket, put it in Rizzo's hand, turned and walked without haste out of the bar.

When Rizzo made threats, though, it was always with the intention of backing them up. It was not long after Coffey's appearance in the bar, then, that Rizzo sought out a neighborhood punk everyone knew was an FBI pigeon, told him that the people in the right places ought to know that a detective from the Manhattan D.A.'s office named Joe Coffey had just shaken him down for $50,000. The informant rushed to the FBI with the story. For the next six months, the FBI investigated Coffey, kept him under surveillance, dug deep into his life. The man who did much of the work was Coffey's friend and partner, Dick Tamarro. He turned up nothing to substantiate the story Rizzo had started, nothing that even showed Coffey to have bent the law or even minor rules or regulations, and eventually a report was filed saying the tip had been baseless and Coffey was clean. (It was not until years later that Coffey learned about that FBI investigation of him, learned about Tamarro's part in it. He was furious. "It doesn't make any difference that they found out I was clean," he says. "They didn't even have the decency to come to me and ask me about it. All the time they were working on me, they were working right alongside me—Tamarro and the others. They were supposed to be my partners and my friends, which meant they were supposed to trust me like I trusted them. And all that time they were on me, looking for something. Thank God, I wasn't wearing white socks instead of the department regulation black, or taking two hours for lunch or going home early, anything like that. Who knows what they would have done if they ever found out I was breaking some nit-picking rule?")

All through the rest of the year and beyond, into 1973, the grand juries sat, viewed the evidence, listened to hundreds of witnesses— the innocent victims, the conspirators who became informants to save themselves, the grim and uncooperative men soon to be defendants. Mayo, Heimerle and Grant spread before them twisted tales of stolen and counterfeit airline tickets and credit cards used to make possible an international trade in narcotics and hot securities. The Argentinian Adolf Soboski, now an informant himself, explained the way cocaine and other narcotics travel from South America to the United States and named those who helped them travel. John Calamarus detailed how a man could be trapped when he borrowed from a loanshark named Vincent Rizzo. After a lot of intense persuasion from detectives, Jose Brocero, the Puerto Rican who had been nearly killed with a pool cue for his temerity in walking into Jimmy's Lounge and ordering a drink, decided that it might not be such a bad thing after all to tell what had really happened to him that night. One after another, the witnesses paraded before those grand juries, told their stories and went their ways, and the evidence piled up to staggering heights.

By the start of the 1972 Christmas season, only the securities cases remained unfinished. They were, of course, the most important, with the most far-reaching implications, and the most difficult. But all the others had been dealt with. More than a hundred persons had been arrested during all those months on those other charges, and the grand jurors, having heard the evidence of dozens of crimes, had returned or were about to return indictments of thirty-two defendants on seven federal and seventeen New York State counts, including conspiracy, extortion, counterfeiting, mail fraud, perjury, narcotics, attempted murder, attempted robbery, possession of stolen property, forgery, criminal usury and possession of weapons. (No indictments against the others who were arrested were sought because some had turned informant, or the evidence had not been considered strong enough, or there were some other mitigating circumstances.)

Perhaps most satisfying were the multiple indictments against Vincent Rizzo. Particularly satisfying to Joe Coffey was the assignment to take Rizzo personally. But that December, as the blizzard of charges came swirling out from the grand-jury rooms, Rizzo vanished. He was not at his home at 201 Avenue A, or at his country estate in Wurtzboro in the Catskills; he was nowhere to be seen at any of his accustomed places. There were rumors that he had fled to South America, seeking shelter with his friends in the cocaine business. If he had done that, he would have found a cold welcome, for by then Soboski had become a major government witness. Stops were put on the bank accounts he was known to have, but there was no conviction that that would dry up his funds, for everyone realized that most of Rizzo's money was not kept in banks, at least not under his name. His Mercedes, too, seemed to have disappeared, but Coffey knew where it was; he found it buried under mounds of dirt in a dark corner of the garage where it was usually kept. Then Coffey passed the word along the street: somebody was likely to get hurt if the police had to continue the large-scale manhunt for Rizzo; it would be wise if he turned himself in, would save everybody a lot of grief. A few days before Christmas, Rizzo walked into the Leonard Street offices of the Manhattan district attorney, asked for Detective Coffey and, glowering malevolently, said, "I hear you've been lookin' for me." Barely able to restrain a wide grin, Coffey took him personally through the routine of arrest—the booking, the fingerprinting, the mugging, the search and all the rest.

Hogan's detectives and the FBI agents had done their work well. In every case but the narcotics ones, most of the defendants, faced with evidence so overwhelming there was no hope of combating it, bowed to the inevitable. Advised by attorneys that a jury trial would surely bring upon them not just wide publicity but the wrath of the jurors and long sentences from judges, they pleaded guilty and threw themselves on the mercy of the courts. The advice had been good.

Uncle Marty de Lorenzo went to prison for a year for his part in arranging the supply of counterfeit money that traveled to San Francisco and then to the Far Eastern black markets, and to Miami to buy cocaine; the evidence against him in all the other cases was considered not strong enough to warrant indictments. Sam Salli went away for two years for supplying those counterfeit bills.

Izzy Marion got a five-year suspended sentence, five years' probation and a $3,000 fine for his part in trying to force Jerry Marc Jacobs to pay the $25,000 he owed Rizzo. The charges against Robertazzi, the man Marion had sent to Los Angeles to put pressure on Jacobs, were dismissed when the judge refused to accept the wiretap evidence.

Vincent "Popo" Tortora earned three years after pleading guilty to multiple counts of possession of stolen and counterfeit airline tickets and credit cards. Most of the other defendants in most of the other cases received similarly short sentences.

Rizzo, however, did not get off so easily. He was sentenced after guilty pleas to twenty years for extortion of John Calamarus, five years for his role in the counterfeit money scheme, and five years for the attempted murder of Jose Brocero. He elected to fight the narcotics charges, went through a two-week trial and lost. That cost him another fifteen years in federal prison. But he knew that, as heavy as those sentences appeared, they would run concurrently and if he was a model prisoner, he would be back on the streets in about seven years.

The results, then, amounted to little more than slaps on wrists. It hardly seemed to have been worth the effort of a year and more in the time and work of so many men. In a year or two, everyone but Rizzo would be back at the old stands, refreshed after a short vacation at public expense, and even Rizzo would not be away long.

But still ahead, still obscure and tortuous even after the revelations of Grant and the informants who followed him, lay the trail that led to the center of the securities swindles, the most important cases of all.

2 4

● ● ● ● ● ● ● ● ● ● ● ● ● ●

*T*he trade in stolen and counterfeit securities was international in scope and the crimes had been committed in the United States, Latin America and Europe. Though the other cases were being closed, so much about those monetary schemes remained unknown that there was no thought of going to a grand jury, let alone before the courts. The government had what Coffey had learned on his two trips to Munich, in February and May. It had the transcript of that bugged conversation in the hotel room, but much of the conversation was still enigmatic. It had what the German authorities had supplied, but much of that dealt with the activities of foreign nationals and their crimes in the Federal Republic. And it had the revelations of Tony Grant. What was desperately needed was corroboration, and the answers to those still-puzzling questions—about the way Coca-Cola stock and the other stolen securities had been used, who had used them and who had supplied them. And most important of all were those questions that remained about the Vatican.

To get the answers, Coffey was ordered back to Europe one more time, in mid-November 1972. This time he would not go to bug and tap. This time he would go to confront Ense, Barg and others and get some details. Everyone agreed that Tamarro should go along. He was, after all, the FBI agent most knowledgeable about the case; his presence alongside Coffey could prove essential for the Justice Department, which would eventually be the one to go to court. Everyone agreed that Tamarro should go—except the FBI. It had no intention of deviating from its strict policy of refusing to send agents outside the United States, of relying instead on its legal attachés stationed abroad. Aronwald went to Washington, directly to FBI acting director L. Patrick Gray, and argued strenuously to bend the rules. Gray listened, thought, finally agreed, though only on condition that Tamarro report to the legal attachés every evening as soon as work was done. (Indeed, Tamarro followed that dictum to the letter all through the trip until eventually Coffey, who had been told only to report back to New York when he had something important to relay, threw up his hands in disgust and began to have his drink and dinner alone.)

Their first stop that November, just before Thanksgiving, was Munich. The first call was to Winfried Ense. They met in the office of Rudolph Pecher at the police presidium. Ense disclaimed knowledge of anything, was uncommunicative. Coffey suggested that Ense have a drink alone with the Americans at the bar in the Munich Hilton. Perhaps he would be more relaxed in less official and forbidding surroundings. Ense agreed, sat down, toyed with his drink, watched and waited warily. He continued to pretend ignorance, invented plausible explanations whenever a question seemed based on knowledge, seemed to strike close. They had been talking for nearly an hour when he rose and excused himself to go to the bathroom. As they watched him leave, Coffey turned to Tamarro. "Let's get him up to the room," he said.

"What good's that going to do?" Tamarro asked.

"If we get him there in private, maybe we can think of something to break him down," Coffey said.

The invitation was extended when Ense returned to the table in the bar. Ense saw little purpose in accepting; he knew so little, he said, of the matters they wanted to discuss. Still, they were guests in his country, and as he did not wish to be impolite, he would go with them.

In the room, they gathered around a low table out on the patio-terrace. Ense continued to claim innocent ignorance. Coffey took a gamble. He picked up the phone, dialed room service, gave the room number, said, "Would you please bring up a bottle of Chivas Regal Scotch—and, oh, some ice and water."

Ense started, stared at him.

Carefully, with deliberation, calling on his memory, Coffey set out to re-create the scene that had been played out at the Palace Hotel nine months before. He began to quote from the bugged conversation, directing the words with calculation at Ense.

Ense nodded slowly. "Ah," he said. "So, you know."

"We know," Coffey said.

"You were listening?"

"We were listening."

"Then, what can I tell you?"

"The details. Everything."

The pretenses were dropped. Ense started to talk. It was past midnight before he finished. He had much to tell, much to make them fully understand and he tried to choose his words with care, to minimize his own role and make himself out an innocent dupe caught in a web of evil spun by dangerous Americans like Ricky and Jerry Jacobs, William Benjamin and, especially, Vincent Rizzo. By the time he departed into the cold of the Alpine darkness, Ense had given them the story in detail as he wanted them to have it—the story of his trade in stolen United States Treasury bills in Brussels, of Barg's arrangement with Jacobs to borrow the stolen Coca-Cola stock, of the visits of Ricky Jacobs and others, of the terrifying appearance of Rizzo. And he had given them the peripheries of the deal in the Vatican, or at least as much as he knew. He had begun to fill in the details of the picture Tony Grant had sketched.

He was back early the next morning, with Alfred Barg. There was little reason to hide much anymore, at least not anything the Americans wanted to hear about. Ense had convinced Barg of that during a long after-midnight call. Now Barg gave his version, a version in which he, too, was only a victim of the dangerous Americans, or at the very most an unwitting accessory.

One thing both Coffey and Tamarro sensed in Barg and Ense during those days in Munich was a wave of relief. It was not the kind of relief that comes with the baring of the soul to wash away sin and guilt. It was the relief that comes with the knowledge that at last that hoped-for miracle, the means to remove the threat posed by Rizzo and his vengeance, was at hand. And it had come without the fear of official retribution, for Coffey and Tamarro had arrived with a promise, guaranteed by their superiors, of immunity from American prosecution if they would tell all, agree to travel to New York at American expense, testify before grand juries and, if necessary, at ensuing trials. They grasped at the offer eagerly.

(A few months later, both made the trip, were put up at the Westbury Hotel in Manhattan, did their testifying before the grand juries and then went back to Germany, relieved, convinced that the

episode was behind them and they had heard the last of it. The day
Ense left for home, he was driven to Kennedy Airport by Coffey and
Tamarro. Just before he boarded his plane, he had presents for them,
expensively wrapped rectangular packages. "Good luck, gentlemen,"
he said as he handed over the gifts. "I have enjoyed meeting you. I
want you to have this with my appreciation and good wishes." In
each package was a bottle of Chivas Regal Scotch and Wyborowa
Polish vodka. Tamarro rejected the gift immediately, declaring that
it was a violation of the FBI code of ethics. Coffey took his with
thanks and a laugh. "After all," he says, "Ense was no longer a
criminal in our eyes. He was a cooperative witness, so if he wanted
to give us a couple of bottles of booze, there was no reason not to
take it. We weren't investigating him anymore, so it wasn't like he
was trying to pay us off or anything or get any favors out of us. We
couldn't do anything more for him and there wasn't anything more
we wanted out of him. But Tamarro couldn't see it that way. So,
I wound up with two bottles of Chivas Regal and two of Wyborowa vodka.")

Now they had Ense and Barg, and a few days later they had
Maurice Ajzen as well, brought to them by his friend and employer,
Ense. Ajzen was willing to tell what he knew, and to repeat it in the
United States, in exchange for the same guarantees.

Now it was on to Frankfurt and Rudolph Guschall. He had been
warned they were coming, that they knew everything, or most of it,
and that all the subterfuge and the thin polish of legality he had
used for so long to protect himself would no longer work. The ve-
neers had been stripped and all Guschall could do was try to throw
himself on their mercy; try, as his friends had done, to tell his story
so as to put himself in the best light. "He was so scared the day we
questioned him," Coffey remembers, "he threatened to commit sui-
cide right in front of us. He ran over to the window and tried to
force it open so he could jump out. Tamarro and I had to physically
restrain him. Then he opened up. He was crying like a baby the
whole time he talked to us. His whole life was falling down around
his ears. He was going to be disbarred and God knows what else. But
he corroborated what other people had been telling us and he gave us
some new names and some new details. It was all filling out, just like
we'd hoped."

There was a side trip to the Grand Duchy of Luxembourg.

There, in Arnheim Prison, was Ernest Shinwell, locked in a dark, dank, tiny cell with only a bare wooden slab for a cot, a single faint light bulb in the ceiling that was never extinguished, a battered tin cup from which to drink cold tea, circumstances that appalled even an experienced New York cop. And Shinwell was ready to talk. "We wanted him to come over to the States to testify," Coffey says, "but they wouldn't permit it. They said they didn't care what he could give us, they weren't letting him out, not when he was serving time for swindling the Luxembourg banks. He didn't like that, but it didn't stop him from talking for hours about Panama and all the rest."

And then in Vienna, in an interview room in another prison where he was serving time for swindling his fellow Austrians and bedecking himself with fake titles, the honorary consul Dr. Leopold Ledl appeared before Coffey and Tamarro. He greeted them warmly, displaying all his renowned charm. He would tell them whatever they wanted to know, he said, would answer all their questions—if only the Austrian authorities would absent themselves. He did not want them present because what he had to say might be damaging and self-incriminating and he wanted to give them no further weapons to use against him. The Austrians agreed to depart. When they were gone, Ledl, alone with Coffey, Tamarro and an Interpol interpreter, began his tale of wheeling and dealing with American swindlers and mobsters, with cardinals and archbishops and bishops and monsignors, with businessmen and others, in the United States, in Italy, all over the world. When at last he was silent, the picture was nearly complete. There were only a few missing pieces. Some, Ledl would not discuss, would not reveal. For others, he showed them where to find them and how to fit them in.

After Ledl, the direction they had to travel was obvious to both Coffey and Tamarro. They had to journey south. They had to go to Rome. They had to find and talk to Mario Foligni and all those others—Tomasso Amato, Marina Neubert, Remigio Begni, Monsignor Mario Fornasari, the mysterious and still-unnamed monsignor who played such an important role, and all the men in the Vatican.

It had to be done. But it was not done. The Italian authorities, then and later, refused to cooperate. They would, they said, handle things their own way. They did not need the interference or the assistance of the American police.

So, on their own, without the necessary official Italian help, Coffey and Tamarro did what they could from a distance. Most of those Ledl and the others had named were impossible to locate without assistance on the scene. But they did manage to reach Foligni. He listened to them, agreed to make a trip to New York and there provide his own version and his own explanation of what had transpired. It was all that could be done then in Italy. It was not enough, but it was something.

Coffey and Tamarro were home by early December. Their trip had been more successful in some ways than they could have hoped. But it had been a traumatic journey. They had known about the Vatican, of course, ever since Coffey had received the first intimations in Munich in February. They had learned more from Tony Grant, who had told them of the almost comical journey with $14.5 million in counterfeit bonds. What they had not known was who in the Vatican was involved, nor had they known how the deal had come to be nor where it was going. Now they had that. For two devout Catholics, raised to believe in the sanctity and unimpeachable honesty of the leaders of their church, this was an unsettling discovery. They had not come upon ordinary criminals, men who lived in a dark world, men who were their usual targets. They had come upon men of great power and influence, who were respected and admired and much honored. Above all, these were men of the cloth whose reason for being was supposed to be the betterment of man and the church. Now Coffey was confronted with evidence that some of these men had committed grave crimes. It was nearly unthinkable.

It was a disturbed Joe Coffey, then, who went to see District Attorney Frank Hogan that December. They had become close, had shared much, and one of the things they shared was a deep and abiding religious conviction. Hogan listened as Coffey talked grimly. "He was shocked, totally shocked," Coffey remembers. "We were both absolutely beside ourselves. We couldn't believe it until we went over everything very carefully and in detail and followed all the lines. Then we were sure it had to be."

Together, then and later, they explored the implications of the discoveries and evidence. If they should follow the trail now, directly into the heart of the Vatican, uncover and reveal to the world the crimes of those revered leaders of their church, the damage they would do to the church itself was likely to be great, to be immeasurably wounding. There were, obviously, many people who would view this as a condemnation of the church itself, would see it as a clear sign that there was rot at the core of the church and that all the leaders were infected, would not see that it was evidence that men are fallible and that the crimes were those of a few, not a reflection of the whole.

They knew they had a choice. They could ignore the role the Vatican had played, the role of those leaders of the church who had been part of the scheme. No matter how much evidence they managed to gather, they knew there was little chance that they would be able to bring a cardinal or a bishop or a monsignor from Rome, from the Vatican, to stand trial in New York. What would it profit them, then, to stir up a scandal that exposed as criminals some of the men who helped direct the Vatican? What profit except to do harm to their church? Would it not be better to concentrate on what they had, to gather the evidence that could be used to convict Rizzo and the others in the organized American underworld and forget about the rest?

Coffey and Hogan talked about that and they talked about much more. But there was never a question in Coffey's mind, or in Hogan's, what course they must travel. "He told me," Coffey says, "and it was the way I felt, too, that we had a duty to the people we were supposed to be protecting to follow every investigation no matter where it went. He said, 'I want to pursue it.' That was fine with me, because that's what I wanted to do, and so did Vitrano and Goldstock and everybody in our office who knew anything about it, and that was what Tamarro and Aronwald and the guys who were in on it at the Strike Force wanted to do."

Part Eight

• • • • • • • • • • • • •

C OVER-UP

2 5

• • • • • • • • • • • • • • • •

*T*hen it all started to come apart.

Coffey and Tamarro had returned from Europe not only anguished by what they had discovered, but outraged, determined that they would do whatever necessary to strip away covers, to follow the lines wherever they might lead, to see that justice was done. They were only too aware that high position often serves as a shield, that power and reputation manage to deflect retribution. And they were now faced with the task of pursuing men who held very high positions, who exuded power and who could cloak themselves in good repute. But they were certain that they would have the backing of Hogan and Aronwald and others and so would be able to break through those formidable barriers, discover and reveal what lay on the other side.

Just before they left the prison in Vienna, Leopold Ledl had casually dropped a bit of information that was potentially as shocking as anything they had heard to that point. He thought they might be interested in knowing, he said, that Ricky Jacobs's circle spread far beyond the underworld. During the spring of 1971, when the preparations were being made for the meeting in London between Ledl and Jacobs's American allies to cement the Vatican arrangements, Jacobs had made a trip to Europe to meet with Ledl and personally assure him that everything was moving smoothly. That meeting took place in Munich, at the Bayerischer Hof. When Ledl arrived at the hotel with Maurice Ajzen, the lobby was overflowing with dignitaries. A major international economic conference was in progress and finance ministers from around the world had gathered in Munich to deal with major monetary issues. Ledl and Ajzen threaded their way through the throng toward the elevators, spotted Jacobs just before they reached the bank of the elevators. He was across the lobby, deep in conversation with a tall, immaculately tailored, silver-haired American. Jacobs glanced up, noticed them, beckoned. When they approached, he introduced his companion, not by name but as his financial adviser, a man he could rely on implicitly to steer him in the right direction in financial matters. For about ten minutes, they chatted idly, until the silver-haired man looked at his watch, said he was going to be late for a meeting and hurried off toward a conference room.

Did Ledl know who that American was? Coffey asked.

Ledl did not. He had never been told the man's name and as the meeting had been accidental and casual, he had never bothered to inquire. But it was obvious to him that the man was a very important government official.

Coffey and Tamarro filed the information in the back of their minds, and in their notes. Several weeks later, Maurice Ajzen was brought to New York to tell his version of the Vatican affair and the other swindles. During those interviews, Coffey and Tamarro, remembering Ledl's story, asked him about it. He recalled it clearly, confirmed all that Ledl had said. They gathered a stack of photographs of American officials as well as ordinary people, and asked Ajzen to go through it to see if he could identify the silver-haired man. Ajzen studied the photographs, shaking his head, then came upon one and pointed to it, said with absolute conviction, "That is the man. I would know him anywhere. It is a face you cannot forget."

The photograph was of John B. Connally, Jr., onetime governor of Texas and, at the time of that encounter in the lobby of the Bayerischer Hof, United States secretary of the treasury. Though he had left the cabinet six months before the November elections, he was still one of the nation's most powerful politicians, called on constantly for advice by President Richard Nixon, considered by some to be the president's most trusted and relied-upon confidant. And it was no secret that Connally was a man of enormous ambition, that his eyes were fixed on the Oval Office itself and that if he decided to seek it in 1976, he would probably have the blessing of Nixon.

It seemed incredible that Connally might have any relationship with Ricky Jacobs, that such a relationship might be as close as Jacobs had indicated in Connally's presence, without a denial from Connally to Ledl and Ajzen. But then the whole case had been filled with incredible revelations. Whether the Connally-Jacobs tie, if it indeed existed, had any bearing on the events they were investigating was impossible to know at that moment. They would have to dig to find out. But an investigation of John Connally was not a thing to be undertaken lightly nor something Coffey and Tamarro could initiate on their own. They went to Hogan and Aronwald, spelled out the little they had, the enigma it presented. Both officials agreed that the story and the identification warranted a closer look. Hogan was prepared to turn Coffey loose, but obviously the search fell within the federal jurisdiction. And Aronwald, though holding a high position in the Strike Force, was an agent of the Department of Justice and he knew full well that authorizing an investigation of John Connally was outside his province and would require the approval of his superiors in Washington.

He went to the nation's capital to seek that authorization from Attorney General Richard Kleindienst. He was, he told Coffey and Tamarro, prepared to argue for that approval, to do battle to win it if that was necessary.

Aronwald was not warmly received by Kleindienst or anyone else in the administration. Richard Nixon might have won reelection in a massive landslide. He might be starting his second term on a high note with an outward display of supreme confidence. But there were signs that his strength was not as solid and his hold on power as unassailable as he pretended.

Watergate was in the air. The administration was trying to dismiss the spreading rumors as mere speculation with little significance. But the evidence was mounting that it was something much more serious. The burglars might have pleaded guilty to the break-in, but the *Washington Post, The New York Times, Time* magazine and other publications were charging a direct link between them and the White House, were saying that the burglars had been promised financial support and other rewards if they kept their mouths shut and pleaded guilty. And it was not just the press that had begun to discern unplumbed depths in the Watergate affair. The Senate had authorized hearings into it and other charges of political espionage and sabotage during the 1972 campaign, and Senator Sam Ervin of North Carolina had been named to chair those hearings.

But Watergate was only the most public of the scandals beginning to batter the administration in what should have been its most triumphant moments. There were growing revelations about massive illegal contributions to the 1972 Nixon campaign, contributions that had been given reluctantly and only under the pressure of reprisals if they were not made. There were loud whispers about the reason why the administration had decided to drop an antitrust action against International Telephone and Telegraph Company, and that when the truth finally came out, among those who would be tarnished by that affair would be Kleindienst, Connally and other powerful men in government. And the stories that had arisen the previous fall about Vice-President Spiro Agnew being the recipient of bribes from Maryland contractors and others continued to spread despite administration claims that they were unfounded and a smear on the vice-president's reputation.

The last thing the administration needed at that moment, then, was to turn loose a couple of good and determined investigators to uncover yet another tale of corruption and scandal. And it especially did not need to turn them loose on John Connally at a time when the president was coming more and more to rely on him so implicitly.

So, it was a chastened Aronwald who returned to New York. There would be no investigation of John Connally. Coffey and Tamarro were told: "You are to forget you ever heard the name John Connally in connection with this case. You are not to pursue this line of investigation. You have nothing. You will get nothing. You are not to look for anything. And that's an order."

There was little they could do but obey. But they did take one small step on their own just to satisfy their curiosity. They did some checking, learned that Connally had indeed been in Munich on the day Ledl and Ajzen said they met him with Jacobs. They could go no further and so, reluctantly, they dropped the matter there.

Still, the doubts remained, and there was much speculation as to what they might have uncovered had they been given the free rein they had sought and needed. As the months passed, and the power of John Connally became more and more evident, Coffey's curiosity became mixed with cynicism and bitterness. He became convinced that for Connally, as related to this investigation, power and position had indeed served as a shield. For, in the embattled White House, the Watergate affair growing ever more serious, Connally had emerged as the man who was devising Nixon's strategy for meeting the charges. He was the strongest voice urging the president to stonewall, even to turn the Watergate tapes into a massive bonfire. So close had Connally come to the top that later in the year, when the stories about Spiro Agnew turned out to be true, and the vice-president was forced to resign in disgrace, Connally was Nixon's initial choice to succeed to the vice-presidency; only strong Congressional opposition compelled Nixon to drop that proposed nomination and turn instead to Gerald Ford.

Coffey's suspicion that he might have unearthed something had he been permitted grew, and his skepticism deepened, as the Watergate and related investigations bared the involvement of the former secretary of the treasury in the dropping of the antitrust case against IT&T. And it grew even more when Connally was indicted on charges that he had accepted $10,000 in bribes from the nation's largest dairy cooperative, the Associated Milk Producers, Inc., to use his influence to help raise the federal milk price-supports. The charges were buttressed in one way or another by officials of all twelve of the nation's Federal Reserve regional banks. But Connally was later acquitted because, some jurors said, the government had failed to produce any independent eyewitnesses to the payoff.

So, Connally's involvement with Ricky Jacobs remains an enigma. It is possible that if Coffey and Tamarro had been permitted to follow the leads supplied by Ledl and Ajzen, they might have discovered that the meeting in the Bayerischer Hof had been a casual one with no significance. But they were not permitted to go along that trail, and so were prevented from once and for all allaying all doubts about the nature of John Connally's involvement.

2 6

• • • • • • • • • • • • • • •

One line, thus, was sealed off. They could force themselves to accept that, however bitter the aftertaste, and rationalize that Connally's connection was probably peripheral at most. Besides, there was something much more significant to concentrate on. There was the Vatican.

Three eminent members of the Vatican hierarchy had been cited by Ledl, Foligni and others as prime movers in the plot involving the counterfeit bonds. One, Eugene Cardinal Tisserant, had died in February 1972. A second, the archbishop who had worked so closely with Tisserant in developing the scheme and in making the arrangements with Ledl, had not been identified by name. Ledl had been careful not to divulge this information, just as he had never given Monsignor Barbieri's name—in fact, in most cases, as he told his tale and answered questions, he was careful not to give names until he was certain somebody else had already done so. Still, he had provided Coffey and the others with the means to discover the names for themselves if they wanted to look; he had given a description of the archbishop as a slim, smallish, Sicilian with white wavy hair, in his mid-fifties who was very close to Tisserant, practically his alter ego.

The third principal cited was Bishop Paul Marcinkus and he was still very much a presence, still in charge of protecting Pope Paul VI, still the man who held the reins of the Vatican's finances, answerable only to the Pope. Most important, as far as the American investigators were concerned, Marcinkus was an American citizen and so theoretically subject to United States law. That meant not only that he could be indicted, and the indictment made public, but that his extradition to stand trial in the United States could be demanded. Even though such a demand would undoubtedly be ignored, the resulting publicity created by the indictment and the demand would serve some purpose.

But to move against an official of the Vatican was to wade into very treacherous waters, roiled by religious, diplomatic and political undercurrents. It was not something to be undertaken without considerable thought. After such careful consideration both in the district attorney's office and by the Strike Force, there was hardly a man who was not willing to take that step, regardless of all the potential risks. Hogan was convinced it must be done, and so were Vitrano, Goldstock, Coffey and the others in the D.A's office, as were Aronwald and Tamarro and their associates on the FBI team.

Even with that, they realized that it would be no simple matter to move against Marcinkus or anyone else in the Vatican, or against Foligni, Amato or anyone in Italy. It would not be like going after Rizzo and his minions in lower Manhattan, or against Ricky Jacobs and his people in Los Angeles. The Vatican was a sovereign state and Marcinkus was both a resident and an official of that state. American law, American court orders, American police had no legal standing there, as American authorities had no standing to operate and conduct investigations on their own anywhere beyond the United States borders. To look into the activities of Marcinkus and others, with the aim of gathering incriminating evidence to use against them, would require the permission of the sovereign power, and that could be obtained, at least as regards the Vatican, only through the most delicate of approaches. (As far as Italy itself was concerned, the Americans had written that off. The Italian authorities had already rejected requests for cooperation. Only after some intense pressure had they even agreed to question Amato, Neubert and a few others, though they had not looked very hard for them and when they turned them up, had interviewed them briefly and cursorily, asking few searching questions. They had refused, furthermore, to permit American investigators to operate within their jurisdiction.)

What was required, then, was an appeal at the highest level. Terence Cardinal Cooke, archbishop of the New York diocese, was approached. The outlines of the case were explained to him and he was asked to use his influence to win Vatican cooperation. He thought about it for a few days and then politely declined.

It would, then, have to be a top-level government-to-government approach, an appeal perhaps to Pope Paul VI himself, certainly to the papal secretary of state, Cardinal Villot. Such an appeal, if it were to be heeded, would have to be made by the president and the secretary of state, Henry Kissinger.

Once more Aronwald boarded the shuttle for Washington to seek help and approval from his superiors. If he had fears, he did not voice them. He was, as he had said the last time, going to push as hard as he could to get what he needed.

But Aronwald could not have gone to Washington with such a request at a more unpropitious moment. If there had been only faint tremors earlier in the year when he had been denied permission to investigate John Connally, by mid-April the Nixon White House was in a shambles, tottering toward a collapse. Hardly a day passed that the *Washington Post* did not come forth with new and increasingly disturbing revelations about Watergate, that brought the scandal ever closer to the Oval Office. And the President's counsel, John Dean, determined not to be made a scapegoat, was telling federal prosecutors the details of the Watergate cover-up, and in so doing was tightening a noose around the president's closest advisers in government—John Ehrlichman, H. R. Haldeman, Kleindienst, former attorney general John Mitchell, former commerce secretary and financial director of the Nixon reelection campaign Maurice Stans, Connally and others. Even the president himself was becoming tainted.

And there was more. The fallout from the Watergate affair was spreading wide. A new look was being taken at the dropping of the antitrust case against IT&T, and new light was being shed on the roles played in that dubious decision by Kleindienst and Connally and others. The nomination of Pat Gray as permanent director of the FBI, which he had headed on a temporary basis since the death of J. Edgar Hoover, had to be withdrawn when Congress rose in righteous indignation at the news of his clandestine political activities and the revelation that he had destroyed sensitive Watergate files. Gray was forced to resign even his temporary post in disgrace. The public was learning of the huge, secret Nixon campaign war chest and how contributions to it had been wrung from corporations and individuals through threats of reprisals and promises of favors. The whispers about political payoffs to Spiro Agnew were growing louder.

The government, then, was in near chaos, the president's own position becoming increasingly tenuous. Nixon was looking for support to shore him up wherever he could find it. And among those who backed him most strongly were the nation's Catholics. He was not about to do anything that might alienate them when he most desperately needed their unquestioning allegiance. There was little doubt that an airing of charges against high Vatican prelates, including the highest-ranking American in Rome, by officials associated with the administration would cause a serious reaction in the Catholic community.

And there was another factor, as well. Marcinkus's friend Michele Sindona had carefully cultivated friends in high places in the administration. He had become friendly with Nixon during the 1960s, and Nixon, then in private law practice in New York, began to recommend to a number of clients that they avail themselves of Sindona's expert investment and banking advice and services. In 1972, when Nixon was running for reelection, Sindona offered a secret $1 million contribution to the president's campaign. Though Maurice Stans, in charge of campaign finances, eventually rejected the proffered gift because Sindona insisted on anonymity, knowledge that Sindona had made the offer and was prepared to do more to help the president caused many to look on him as a man to cultivate, a man who could prove very useful in a variety of ways.

And Sindona had hired Nixon's first secretary of the treasury, David M. Kennedy—the former chairman of the Continental Illinois National Bank and Trust Company, with which Sindona had worked in international banking partnership—as an investment adviser and ambassador of goodwill to the American financial community. He had even put Kennedy on the board of his Fasco International Holding Company. As it happened, Sindona and Kennedy had been brought together originally by a mutual friend, a onetime native of the Chicago area and himself a prominent international banker—Bishop Paul Marcinkus. Indeed, so close did the three become that when one of Sindona's Italian aides became a father, Marcinkus baptized the boy, Sindona was the godfather, and the child was named David after Kennedy.

So, Aronwald returned from Washington emptyhanded again, reporting: "We are to forget about the Vatican. We are to stay away from that line."

"Why?" Coffey demanded when he was told. "The Vatican's crucial. Marcinkus is crucial."

"It's an order," he was told. "It's a policy decision. There's nothing we can do about it."

But Coffey did not believe it. He went to Hogan with the word of Washington's refusal to do anything to help. Hogan was furious. Maybe they would never be able to extradite Marcinkus and try him in the United States, but with just a little more evidence, and they were sure that could get it just by asking the right questions on the spot in the Vatican, they would certainly be able to indict him and ask for his extradition, and the ensuing publicity and public outcry might at least go some distance toward preventing him from doing any more, might even force the Vatican to take some steps on its own. Hogan made some phone calls personally and in his iciest manner threatened to make a lot of noise if the decision was not reversed. He even threatened to leak the story to the press. If there was one thing an administration already in deep trouble did not need it was public accusation by a man of Hogan's reputation that it was engaged in yet another cover-up.

Hogan's fury and his threats paid off. A diplomatic request was dispatched to Cardinal Villot for Vatican cooperation. In early April 1973, the cardinal responded. A small party of American officials would be permitted to call on the Vatican.

Hogan was elated when he heard the news. He asked when the investigative team was planning to leave for Rome because he wanted to make sure that Coffey was fully briefed and prepared for those impending sessions in the Vatican.

Coffey's not going, he was told.

Why? Hogan demanded.

This was to be strictly a federal affair, for it was a federal case. Aronwald was going. Tamarro was going. And the man who would lead the team would be William Lynch, boss of the Organized Crime and Racketeering Section of the Department of Justice. Just those three. Nobody else.

Why was Coffey being cut out?

He was not needed.

Hogan seethed. Not needed? Did anybody know more about this investigation than Joe Coffey? Had anybody been working on it longer or harder or in more detail or on more aspects or with better results than Coffey? He had the whole thing at his fingertips. He knew better than anybody else what questions to ask. Without Coffey, the mission could turn into a farce.

They didn't need Coffey.

If Coffey didn't go, then nobody ought to go, Hogan said. Maybe they ought to forget the whole thing, which was probably what they wanted anyway.

Three people were going, he was told, but they were only the federal people, Aronwald, Tamarro and Lynch. Coffey was not part of it. Hogan had insisted on diplomatic approaches to the Vatican and he had gotten them. The Vatican had agreed to see the American investigators. Hogan ought to be satisfied with that.

Hogan wasn't, but there was little he could do. He was a Democrat and the administration in power in Washington was Republican. And, despite his concern that the Vatican affair not be bungled or covered up, he could not devote all his energies to preventing it. There were other things that were making demands on him and they could not be ignored. For the first time in his quarter-century as Manhattan district attorney, he was facing a serious challenge to his continued tenure in the forthcoming Democratic primary. And there was something even more serious: his health was failing. He had cancer and he did not have much longer to live.

So, Coffey remained behind, frustrated and furious, convinced that Henry Kissinger or whoever in the State Department had made the contacts with the Vatican had given assurances that the Vatican would be treated gently by the visiting Americans, that the church had nothing to worry about.

On April 25, 1973, Aronwald, Tamarro and Lynch paid their call on Vatican City. They were ushered into the offices of Archbishop Giovanni Benelli, the assistant secretary of state and friend of Mario Foligni. Benelli remained with them for only a few moments, just long enough to introduce them to three monsignors on his staff— Edward Martinez, Carl Rauber and Justin Rigali.

Tamarro was sent outside, to wait in an anteroom, while Lynch and Aronwald met with the monsignors; Lynch did all the talking for the Americans. He outlined the information in the hands of the authorities and the grand juries, telling them that $14.5 million in counterfeit American bonds had been delivered to Rome in July 1971, destined for the Vatican, that those bonds were only a sample and that the people in the Vatican who were part of the scheme had actually ordered an eventual delivery of $950 million worth of such bonds. Lynch talked about the trial deposits by Foligni at Handels Bank in Zurich and at the Banco di Roma. He said that during the investigation, charges had been made that Bishop Marcinkus had been directly involved in the plot as well as in several other illegal projects in association with Michele Sindona. As an internal FBI report put it, Lynch informed the three monsignors "that indictments in this matter would be handed down in the near future and that some of the allegations concerning the Vatican or of the use of the good name and reputation of the Vatican would then become a part of the public record and possibly would be the subject of some press inquiries."

Monsignor Martinez, the assessor in the secretary of state's office, heard Lynch out, then responded that he had no knowledge whether anyone in the Vatican had previously known anything about this situation. But, in any case, "it was not the intention of the Vatican to collaborate with United States officials in their investigation at this point, since this was considered to be an informal meeting and their purpose at the present time was only to listen."

Lynch had a document he wanted the monsignors to examine, at least for an opinion as to its authenticity. Among the papers that had been seized from Ledl at the time of his arrest in Vienna, and which later had been turned over to Coffey and Tamarro by the Austrian police, was the contract-letter from the Vatican's Sacre Congregazione Dei Religiosi setting forth the details of the order for the $950 million in counterfeit bonds. The three monsignors took the letter and studied it. Martinez said the letterhead appeared to be legitimate and "identical with the letterhead of a legitimate sacred congregation of religious which is located at the Vatican."

But, whether that indicated that a deal had been made, Martinez did not know and would not speculate, nor, he said, did he know if there were any counterfeit American bonds on deposit in the Vatican Bank. When Lynch offered to give him a list of the types of bonds that had comprised the package so that the monsignor might check the records of the bank, Martinez refused to accept the offer. That, he said, was the function of Bishop Marcinkus. There was nothing further to discuss. The interview was closed.

The next morning, Bishop Paul Marcinkus himself saw Lynch

and Aronwald in his private office, while once more Tamarro was told to wait outside. Marcinkus listened intently as Lynch went through the evidence and the allegations once again. When Lynch was finished, Marcinkus said he would try to answer those charges to the best of his ability. To deal with the question of Michele Sindona first, he said, while he and Sindona had been good friends for several years and while he considered Sindona "well ahead of his time as far as financial matters are concerned," they had only very limited financial dealings together. He might mention one or two of those dealings in general terms, he said, but he would not go into any detail about them. Though the charges that had been made against him were "extremely serious, [they] are so wild I do not believe it is necessary that banking secrecy laws be broken in order to defend myself."

Marcinkus was sure he knew exactly what lay behind those charges. His position as head of the Vatican Bank, answerable only to the Pope, "has led to certain hard feelings by other men in responsible positions in the Vatican. That is unavoidable and just part of my job. I am, as you know, the first American to have risen to such a position of power within the Vatican and this also may have caused a certain amount of hard feelings."

Now, Marcinkus said, to deal with specifics. Take Monsignor Mario Fornasari. While he had met the monsignor on several occasions, "some of the people who work for me at the Vatican Bank pointed out Fornasari as an individual to avoid. You know, Fornasari was denounced some time ago for writing slanderous letters, though the charges against him were dropped."

As for Mario Foligni, he had been involved in two transactions with the man, but neither of them had ever come to fruition. One had taken place on or about July 29, 1971, and had revolved around a $100 million investment that was supposed to have benefited the Diocese of Rome. It was to have been a joint venture of the Vatican Bank and Foligni's Nuova Sirce and Intercommerce Group. For various complex and confidential reasons he did not want to discuss, though none was illegal, Marcinkus said, he decided not to pursue the proposal and so it never went beyond the paper stage.

The second deal with Foligni, he said, had taken place about a year before, in March 1972. Again, the bishop said, he could not go into detail because that would be a violation of banking secrecy laws.

What he could say, though, was that the proposition had come to him in a very unusual fashion. He had received personally from Pope Paul VI a letter from Foligni and Foligni's friend, the industrialist Carlo Pesenti, outlining a $300 million investment scheme. The Pope instructed Marcinkus to see if it was worthwhile. Marcinkus said his initial step had been to go to the Pope and ask how he had become involved. He was told that the letter had been handed to the Pope by Archbishop Benelli. Marcinkus immediately called Benelli and "told him that in the future all financial dealings should be worked through me and not the Pope, according to proper Vatican practices."

Still, because of the Pope's interest and instructions, he met with Pesenti and Foligni. The main thrust of the meeting, however, was not a discussion of the deal but how Foligni had managed to involve the Pope. "Pesenti apologized," Marcinkus said, "and said that Foligni was the one who got the letter directly to the Holy Father." Marcinkus said he demanded to know the name of the person Foligni had used as a direct line to the Pope. Was it Benelli? "Foligni gave me a name some time later, but I dismissed that because that person was too far removed from Rome to have any high-ranking Vatican contacts." Then Foligni handed Marcinkus a letter saying "my staff was completely corrupt and dishonest. I was appalled by the letter. It was nothing but a piece of worthless trash which had absolutely no basis in fact." That was enough for him, Marcinkus said, and he informed Foligni that he wanted nothing to do with the Foligni-Pesenti proposition. Soon after, "I found out that Mario Foligni was bad-mouthing me all over town and making wild accusations against my character."

It was obvious to him, then, Marcinkus concluded, that the charges that he was involved with counterfeit American bonds were just more of Foligni's slander. He was certainly not aware of any attempt to deposit such bonds in his Vatican Bank, had never discussed such a thing with anyone and he would certainly accept a list of the types of bonds so that he could be on the alert should they ever appear.

Lynch thanked him for his cooperation. The interview ended.

What Lynch neglected to note and what Marcinkus ignored in his discussion of the two deals with Mario Foligni was a curious and perhaps significant conjunction of dates. That first deal with Foligni, for $100 million, had taken place just two days after Foligni made that initial trial deposit of $1.5 million in counterfeit bonds at Handels Bank in Zurich. Perhaps Marcinkus could have claimed that, at that point, he would have had no way of knowing of Foligni's involvement in such an illegal venture. But the second deal with Foligni, for $300 million, had taken place eight months after the Handels Bank operation and six and a half months after the one at the Banco di Roma. News of those deposits and Foligni's role in them was no longer a secret. Yet, despite that, Marcinkus was still dealing with the man in huge investment schemes.

A little later, back in New York City, Coffey read the reports of those two sessions in the Vatican with growing rage and a certainty his feeling had been confirmed. "My son could read those reports," he says, "and see right through them, see that they never asked the right questions, never pressed, just sat there and let Marcinkus and the others say whatever they pleased, and all they did was nod and say thank you. About the only thing you can say for them was that they at least got the thing out in the open so none of those people in the Vatican could ever claim again that they didn't know about it."

Coffey cornered Tamarro and Aronwald and demanded an explanation. Why had they been so gentle? Why had they willingly accepted everything that had been said to them? Why had they not asked one single tough question and demanded an answer? Why had they done no digging at all?

Tamarro agreed that the mission had been a botch, had accomplished almost nothing except to put the facts and the innuendos directly before the people in power in the Vatican. But, he said, "I wasn't in the room, Joe. They wouldn't let me in the room."

Coffey glared at him. "You're full of shit, Dick," he said, "just like those reports, and you know it. You're supposed to be a good agent. You're supposed to know this case. You believe in it. You fought for it. And you let them get away with that!"

Then he turned to Aronwald. "You're full of shit, too," he raged, "and don't tell me any different. If you had allowed us to go over there and conduct this investigation the way an investigation is supposed to be conducted, we would have had it all. But you wouldn't agree to that and now you've blown it."

His anger had grown from frustration, and eventually he realized he should not have expected any more. He liked Tamarro, respected him, but he knew Tamarro well enough to understand that he had been nurtured in the traditions of Hoover's FBI and that his future in the agency depended on adherence to the rules and to orders. Tamarro would follow directions no matter what his inner feelings; he was not one to make waves. And Aronwald might be a good prosecutor, might be committed to this investigation, as he had shown often enough in the past, but he was still a bureaucrat whose future depended on following the lines laid down for him. There was no way, Coffey understood when he cooled off, that Aronwald would dispute Lynch, his superior, or go against a policy set by his department.

Two years later, Aronwald appeared before a Senate subcommittee in Washington to go through the story of the tangled affair that some called Operation Fraulein. During his testimony, he told the Senators, "Because of the serious allegations that had been made with respect to someone in the Vatican, although the name of the individual was never given, the Department of Justice made contacts with the Vatican and obtained their cooperation. . . . As a result of our visit and a result of the cooperation of the Vatican, we were able to conclude that there was no substance to the allegation that anyone within the Vatican was culpably involved in this scheme."

2 7

. . . .

*F*or more than two years, ever since that night he had followed
Philip Crespino in the freezing rain to the Columbia Civic League
Club and watched that clandestine conversation with Vincent Rizzo,
the investigation had been Coffey's obsession. They had been years
when he had played his hunches and they had almost always panned
out, years filled with high drama and low comedy, with intense grati-
fication and crushing frustration. There had been months of plod-
ding along twisted and tangled pathways that seemed to be leading
nowhere, and moments of sudden and startling breakthrough and
discovery. There had been much elation and no little trauma. Often
during those years, as the scope of the hunt and its consequences
became clear, he had been convinced that this was what he had been
born to do, that this would be the capstone of his career. And now it
was over, ended not with the glittering victories he had foreseen but
on a sour and cynical note. He could no longer deny what he had not
wanted to believe: there are people so powerful and so highly placed
that they are impervious to the law, and that society's rules and
codes do not apply to them.

The long struggle and its small rewards had exacted a heavy
price. There had been none of the glory and honor that so many had
anticipated in those early days when the first hunches were turning
to reality, when the revelations were spewing forth from the phones
in Jimmy's Lounge. There had been no smashing of important parts
of the organized syndicate and its rackets. There had been only some
ephemeral advances and a few words of praise from Hogan and
Vitrano and then assignment to another case.

And there had been personal agonies and tragedies. Those endless hours on the chase, those days when home and family seemed
only a distant dream, had cost one detective his marriage, had sent

the wife of another into the hospital, emotionally distraught. Even Coffey, despite the strength of his own will and his own marriage, and the support of his wife and his family, had not been immune. He had gone to Europe that last time in November flushed with hope and expectations for the future. His wife was pregnant again. He had returned to discover that in his absence she had suffered a miscarriage and had kept the news from him, so as not to turn his mind from the work he had to do. He had returned, too, to discover that while he was gone there had been a fire in his house and that tragedy had been averted only by the quick reactions of his older son.

Had he been a different kind of man, the disillusionment and the personal ordeals might have been enough to send him walking away, not just from this case but from the police force and the wars that inner compulsion had for so long led him to fight. The system itself was designed to deflect and thwart those who reached for that goal and so he knew that the most he could ever hope for were small and temporary gains.

But the police force was Coffey's life. Somebody who cared had to do that job despite all the frustrations and setbacks, somebody had to remain and carry on, hope that someday, somehow, things might change. Coffey knew that change would come only if those who cared remained. The job was too vital to be entrusted solely to the timeservers and the cynics and those who were in it to get only what they could out of it. If he and others like him turned away, who would stand for society against the barbarians at the gates and within the city?

So, he would stay and do what he had to do and try as best he could to put aside the bitter memory of the end of those years. Perhaps it was a good thing, though he did not think so at the time, that he was about to be leaving Hogan's office, the scene of those struggles. In May, after seven years on the district attorney's squad, a long-awaited promotion to sergeant finally came through, and under police department regulations, that meant the end of his tenure on Leonard Street. Promotion required a return to uniform for at least six months and a transfer to some other assignment. It mattered not at all that Hogan wanted to keep him and that he wanted to remain or that there were people like Vitrano and several others who argued to keep him. It was a rule and an unbreakable one.

Coffey looked at the packed boxes beside his empty desk, boxes full of the memorabilia of half-forgotten, more innocent days when he had been so sure of the rightness of his course and the dedication of those who traveled with him. Just before he left the office for the last time, Hogan summoned him. The door was closed and they were alone. There was a hug, some private words of gratitude for all that had been accomplished, expressions of regret for what could not be done and had to be left unfinished. The Vatican affair was passed over with only a shrug of resignation.

"Joe," Hogan said, "the one thing I wish is that I could keep you here with me. But you know I can't do that. I can't go against that department rule."

"I understand that, Mr. Hogan," Coffey said.

"I won't even be able to bring you back here at the end of the six months," Hogan said. "The department only lets me have three sergeants and there aren't going to be any openings."

"I know that, too," Coffey said.

"But I don't want you to worry," Hogan said. "I'm going to make sure you end up in the right place. As soon as your six months in uniform are up, you're going to go to work for Mike Armstrong."

Michael Armstrong had been special counsel to the Knapp Commission, which had conducted a searching inquiry into corruption in the New York City Police Department. He had just then been appointed by the governor as district attorney for Queens County, to replace Thomas Mackell, who had been indicted on charges of corruption. Armstrong had appealed to Hogan for help in setting up a solid, experienced and incorruptible staff. Hogan obliged. He sent one of his most trusted aides, John Keenan, to Queens to become Armstrong's chief assistant. Now, he said, he was going to tell Armstrong and Keenan that the sergeant who could help them establish a crack investigative team was Joe Coffey, and they could have him the moment his six-month tour in uniform was over.

Coffey thought that the best going-away present Hogan could have given him. He put on the uniform with the sergeant's stripes and went up to his assignment in the Twenty-fifth Precinct in East Harlem, sure that he would be there only until November, and then would be back in the detective division, back in the war against organized crime, this time as a sergeant and a boss in the office of the Queens district attorney.

He was in East Harlem only six weeks when he got a call from

Vitrano. The grand juries had finally completed their work on the securities cases. A press conference had been called to announce the indictments. Since Coffey had done so much work, had been instrumental in breaking the cases, Vitrano wanted him to be on the platform when the announcements were made, along with Tamarro, Edward Shaw, head of the Strike Force, Aronwald, Goldstock and Alfred Scotti, Hogan's chief assistant.

Coffey arrived about an hour before the press on that July morning in 1973. Aronwald was waiting for him and beckoned him into a private office. "There's something very important I want to say to you before the press conference starts," Aronwald began.

"Yeah?" Coffey said. If he had once had considerable respect for Aronwald, that feeling had died when he had read the reports of those sessions in the Vatican.

"Under no condition," Aronwald ordered, "are you to talk to reporters, before, during or after the press conference. Do you get that? There is going to be no mention of any involvement by the Vatican. We do not want the Vatican brought into this in any way except the way we mention it. Do you understand that?"

Coffey made a sour face. "You're not my boss," he said tersely. "I'll talk to anyone I want." He turned and walked out.

Still, he made the decision that he would be discreet, would follow instructions and make no waves. But he had no intention of telling Aronwald that and giving the attorney any sense of pleasure and power. It was just that he thought it would do no good to rake through those ashes, would only make trouble that could not be resolved.

Through that press conference, he stood with Tamarro at the rear of the dais and listened. There was at least a little satisfaction in hearing that sixteen persons had been indicted for dealing in stolen and counterfeit securities, including nine Americans—Vincent Rizzo, Ricky Jacobs, Jerry Marc Jacobs, Evelyn Jacobs, William Benjamin, Patty Marino, Louis Gittleman, Peter Raia and Dominic Mantell—and seven Europeans—Tomasso Amato, Remigio Begni, Mario Foligni, Tony Grant, Leopold Ledl, Marina Neubert and Ernest Shinwell. Among the things they had done, Aronwald announced, were to cash stolen securities at various banks and brokerage houses in the United States and Europe, lend for a considerable price stolen securities to a co-conspirator in Germany named

Alfred Barg, use stolen stocks as collateral in banks in Panama and try unsuccessfully to sell counterfeit bonds to the Vatican.

When the press conference was opened for questions from reporters, there were only a few regarding the Vatican, and they were passed over lightly and obliquely and nobody bothered to press very hard.

As Coffey was starting to leave, one of the detectives from Hogan's office who had worked with him on the case approached. "Joe," he said, "would you do me a favor? A guy I know from the *Wall Street Journal* is here and he wants to ask you a few questions. Would you mind if I brought him over?"

"Sure," Coffey said. He would talk to the reporter, but if what he was after dealt with the Vatican, Coffey was determined to remain silent.

That, however, was not the reporter's interest. "Are you the cop who went to Germany and tailed all those people over there and did all the wiretapping and bugging?" he asked.

"Yes."

"Then I have just one question. How the hell could you possibly keep those people under surveillance when you didn't know the language or the geography?"

"It was simple," Coffey said. "I didn't do the visual surveillance. The Germans assigned sixteen of their own detectives to do that."

"Thanks," the reporter said and walked away.

The next morning, a story appeared in the *Wall Street Journal*. It quoted Coffey about the surveillance. But it also went on to say, "Mr. Aronwald emphasized at a press conference that the indictments did not say that a fence actually existed within the Vatican. But a source close to the investigation in Europe said a man of the cloth within the Vatican was suspected." That source was not Joe Coffey.

Aronwald read the story. Coffey had hardly reached his desk in East Harlem before the attorney was on the phone to him. "I told you not to talk to reporters," Aronwald shouted.

"You can tell me whatever you like," Coffey answered. "But you don't run my life and I don't answer to you. The man asked me a legitimate question and I gave him an honest answer. Besides, what's so bad about what I told him?"

"Do you have any idea what you're going to cost me because of what you said?" Aronwald raged. "Now I'm going to have to sub-poena all sixteen of those German detectives and bring them over here to testify at the trials."

"Just a second, Mr. Aronwald," Coffey said. "If you ever go to trial, you're going to have to subpoena them anyway, because of the surveillance they did. But I seriously doubt whether you'll go to trial, because I think that with the evidence we got for you, those guys are all going to take a fall. So, don't bullshit me that because I talked to a reporter I made a lot of trouble for you."

Aronwald had only one more thing to say that morning. "Let me assure you, Joe Coffey, that you will never get out of uniform again. That's a promise. You're going to stay right where you are for the rest of your time on the police force. I mean it. I can make sure of it. And I'm going to."

Coffey was right. The German cops were not subpoenaed because there were no trials. A close look at the evidence convinced most of the American defendants and their attorneys that it would be use-less to fight. Except for Patty Marino, who was on the run and had not been caught, and Evelyn Jacobs, whom the government decided not to prosecute, all pleaded guilty and stood silent while the judges handed down sentences.

Benjamin got a year, to run concurrently with a seven-and-a-half-year term he received after pleading guilty to narcotics charges. But Benjamin decided that the prospect of prison was not pleasing, especially for a man of his advanced years. In exchange for freedom and a new life as a protected witness, he turned informant.

Jerry Marc Jacobs was given three years' probation, and his father, Ricky, had two more years tacked onto the terms he was then serving in California.

Louis Gittleman was put on probation for five years.

Dominic Mantell went to prison for three years.

Peter Raia went away for four years.

Vincent Rizzo had another five years marked against him, though those years would run concurrently with the sentences he had already received for the other crimes.

As for the Europeans:

Shinwell remained in prison in Luxembourg and, when released, returned to his home in England. Requests for his extradition were not pressed.

Tony Grant, when he finished talking, hurried to Kennedy Airport, boarded a plane for home and vanished somewhere in England.

Leopold Ledl finished his time in prison in Vienna and returned to his home in Maria Anzbach and picked up his trade. Because of his cooperation, no attempt was made to extradite him.

Requests to Italian authorities to pick up Amato, Neubert and Begni were ignored. Begni went on with his career as a stockbroker. Amato and Neubert faded from sight. A few years later, Coffey heard they were in South America, doing as they had done before.

No attempt was made to bring Mario Foligni to the United States to stand trial. He had, after all, cooperated with American authorities. And, in Italy, he continued to wield influence, to run his companies, to maintain friends in the best circles. And he got into politics, setting up the ultraconservative Catholic-oriented New People's Party, becoming its spokesman under the banner "The man with clean hands."

About the only one in Italy who paid any price was Monsignor Alberto Barbieri, unindicted in the United States because his identity was not known. The penalty he suffered, however, grew not from his part in the securities swindle but from the fact that the Vatican eventually tired of the many shady deals which had his imprint. He was fired from his job with Edizione Paoline and defrocked. "If something went wrong," Barbieri, now a layman, later complained to a reporter for *Stern* magazine, "they always blamed me for it. But the storm will subside and then the church will take me back."

Coffey's prediction, then, was right. But that did not deter Aronwald from carrying out his threat. Aronwald was close friends with Michael Armstrong, and called to tell the new Queens district attorney that he would be making a big mistake if he took Joe Coffey because Coffey had a big mouth and liked to talk to the press.

So, Coffey was stuck in uniform in East Harlem's Twenty-fifth Precinct. For the next two years, he wondered if perhaps he had made a mistake in staying a cop, wondered if there was any chance ever to get back into plain clothes so he could do the kind of work at which he had proven himself so expert. The road to Queens had been sealed off by Aronwald. (Later, however, he and Aronwald would patch up their differences and their disagreements would vanish, and he would become friends with Mike Armstrong, and John Keenan would tell him sadly whenever they met, "Joe, I owe you one because of what happened.") For a time, he thought he might be summoned back to the Manhattan district attorney's office. Vitrano put in regular requests for his transfer back to the squad and so did others in the office. But at first there were no openings for a sergeant and then Hogan was dead and Vitrano retired and a new district attorney with new men was in charge, determined to build his own staff with loyalty to him. And then a new mayor was in office and a new team in command of the police force, a team that did not look kindly on the detective division and set up rigid rules governing who would get in. Coffey was on the outside and there were only two ways to get back in and regain his gold shield: to spend two years in narcotics, where corruption was almost endemic, or in internal affairs, where the main job was investigating fellow cops. Coffey wanted no part of either. So he resigned himself to a life as a uniformed sergeant, to doing what he could in that job and trying to bury the disappointments.

He had been in uniform for two years when the Puerto Rican terrorists blew up Fraunces Tavern, a historic landmark in Manhattan's Wall Street area. Somebody in the police department remembered that Sergeant Joe Coffey had worked on terrorist cases in Hogan's office, and that Coffey was something of an expert on terrorists and the way they worked. The summons went out and suddenly Coffey was back in the detective division, a supervising sergeant coordinating the investigations.

The years that followed were years of success, honors, promotions and a certain fame. He handled the Fraunces Tavern investigation and then the terrorist bombing at LaGuardia Airport, moved on to become night operations supervisor, a key man in the citywide hunt for the "Son of Sam" mass murderer, a job he performed with such facility that he was promoted to supervisor of detectives. By the spring of 1978, he had become commanding officer of the Organized Crime Homicide Task Force for the city, a special assistant to the chief of detectives. His fame and his reputation spread both within and without the department. More and more often, his name appeared in the newspapers as the cop behind the breaking of important cases, the cop who always gave straight answers to embarrassing questions. More and more, the television cameras sought him out when the views of an important cop were needed on a major issue. The reporters had come to know that from Coffey they would not get the official line, what the department wanted said; from him, they would get bluntness and honesty. When asked about the effectiveness of security for visiting dignitaries, for example, he said there was no way it was possible to completely protect anyone from an assassin who was determined to kill and was willing to sacrifice his own life in the process. It was not the answer that pleased his superiors, for they boasted constantly of the effective security measures they took for important visitors. But they had come to know that the only way to gag Joe Coffey was to order him not to speak, and if they did that, it might create more trouble than letting him talk.

Coffey, then, had reached a kind of pinnacle. He was where he wanted to be once more, where he could use all he knew and all he had learned to the best purpose. It was not even such a bad thing to have come to the realization that there would be no decisive victories, that all he could do was deal with matters as they came up, to try to anticipate, to man the walls and keep the invaders at bay.

But over all he did, there continued to hang the shadow of the Vatican affair. His mind kept returning to it; he never ceased wondering if somehow he might have done something that would have made it come out another way. Even had he wanted to forget it, though, it would have been impossible. Wherever he turned, there was something that brought it back.

For instance: Soon after he was assigned as a sergeant to the Twenty-fifth Precinct in East Harlem, reports of the investigation into the still-unsolved murder of Michael "The Animal" Affinito crossed his desk. Since it touched on the cases he had worked on in Hogan's office, he was temporarily detached from East Harlem and sent to the Bronx on special assignment to look into it. He, after all, knew that Rizzo had ordered that murder; Tony Grant had told him that. But there was no corroboration. Then William Benjamin turned and the reports of Benjamin's revelations were handed to Coffey by one of his friends in the FBI. Reading them, he came upon the corroboration he was seeking: Benjamin's tale of how he had complained to Rizzo after his beating in Raia's shoe store and Rizzo's prompt ordering of Affinito's murder. With Benjamin as a witness, Coffey could now go to a grand jury, seek Rizzo's indictment for murder and so put the man in jeopardy of a twenty-five-year-to-life sentence that would not run concurrently with his other terms. Coffey went to his friends in the Strike Force and asked them to bring Benjamin in as that witness. But Benjamin had vanished into the protected witness program. The government refused to produce him. And so the indictment was never brought and Rizzo never went to trial for Affinito's murder.

For instance: In December 1979, a case was dropped on Coffey's desk in the Organized Crime Homicide Task Force. A man named Louis Milo had been found murdered in the trunk of his car. The name was not unfamiliar. Milo was the New York printer who had turned out the counterfeit bonds for the Vatican. For a day, Coffey looked in vain for a possible connection. But Milo had been murdered because of money he owed and because of his links to a pornography ring.

For instance: In 1978, an article appeared in *Stern* magazine that dealt with the Vatican affair and the stolen securities racket, and pointed to the involvement of Ense, Barg and Guschall. Questions were asked of German authorities as to why these men were still running around loose. The government responded to the pressure by indicting them. Coffey and Tamarro were subpoenaed as government witnesses. Both were outraged. The three Germans, after all, had been promised immunity in exchange for their help in the American investigation. Promises made in the United States, they were told, carried no weight in the Federal Republic. The three Germans had to be brought to justice. Coffey and Tamarro were ordered to make the trip to Germany and testify. Ense, Barg and Guschall were convicted and sentenced to short prison terms.

For instance: Just before Easter 1981, Coffey received a call from his friends at the Justice Department. They wanted his help. A banker in Milan had been receiving calls from America that were so threatening he had gone to authorities for help and had given them permission to tap his phone. The taps had picked up two calls made to the banker in Milan a few days before from a Holiday Inn in Rockville Center, New York, and the content seemed to point back to the old Operation Fraulein case. Coffey was asked to listen to the tapes, determine whether he could identify the voices of the callers or come up with any links.

There were no preliminary greetings in those telephone calls. When the banker picked up his phone, an American voice said, "Why don't you do what I ask? You see what you're causing me? You're going to make me lose everything."

"What can I do?" the banker asked.

"You should get ahold of these people and start working on these documents for me."

"You never told me what you want from me," the banker insisted.

"I want you to straighten out things with the banks over there," the American said. "I tell you, you get in touch with who you have to get in touch with. You know who you have to get in touch with. And you ask what you can do. If I hurt you, don't you want to hurt me?"

"I am not hurting you."

"You are hurting me. Very bad. Indirectly, you know where my money is at."

"I don't know anything," the banker said.

"The only way I can get my money," the American said, "is if this man, and you know who I'm talking about—"

"I told you already," the banker shouted into the phone, "I have nothing to do with Mr. Sindona. I never had anything to do with him. I don't know anything about him."

"I think you're a nice man," the American said. "I'm a nice man. But let me tell you something, if I get hurt—"

"I don't know anything about that. If you gave money to Mr. Sindona and Mr. Sindona hasn't given the money back to you, I don't know what to do. Because you are a fool to lend him money."

"Then I am a fool. Don't you be a bigger fool. I'm desperate, and if I'm desperate and if I have to suffer, I'm going to make other people suffer, too."

"Look here, please," the banker pleaded, "I don't know what to do."

"All right," the American said. "You take care. You have a nice Easter."

Five minutes later, the banker's phone rang again. This time, the voice from America was different. It said, "You got a call from a friend of mine today. Forget about the documents. You're going to have to learn the hard way. Someone's going to have to get hurt. Maybe even die. My friend, he says, forget about the documents. You're going to have to learn the hard way. Remember your son and your daughter. Remember your family. They're going to be hurt, because you're hurting us."

"Listen to me," the banker begged. "Can't you listen to reason? I don't know anything about what you're talking."

"If you don't know, don't worry about it," the second caller said mildly, with practically no emotion. "You'll have to learn the hard way. That's the way you want it, that's the way it's going to be. Have a nice Easter. Have a nice Easter." And he hung up.

Perhaps the banker had a nice Easter. But a few days later, his house was burned down.

When he heard those tapes, Coffey could not be certain. But he had a hunch, and he trusted those hunches, that what they were about probably could be traced back a decade. It would, though, be up to the Justice Department and the Italian authorities to find out for sure.

For instance: When Pope Paul VI died, there were many Vatican watchers who predicted a quick end to the career of Bishop Paul Marcinkus. His position and power had grown from his intimate and abiding relationship with Pope Paul. A new pontiff would surely go through the records carefully and, if only because of the vast sums Marcinkus had lost the Vatican through his dealings with Michele Sindona, would strip the bishop of his major jobs and shuffle him off into some dead end where he could do no more harm. Pope John Paul I, of course, had no time to do anything. But, many Vatican experts agreed, it would not take long for Pope John Paul II to look over the records of the past and do what ought to be done. Nevertheless, time went by, and Marcinkus remained in charge of the Vatican Bank, and acted as the new Pope's bodyguard as he had for Pope Paul.

In the late fall of 1979, Pope John Paul II arrived in New York on his jubilant and triumphal tour of the United States. Joe Coffey was assigned to be one of his bodyguards. At the airport, as the Pope descended from his plane, Police Commissioner Robert Maguire stepped toward him from among the waiting dignitaries, to make him welcome and to assure him that the New York police were at his command. A large, burly bishop moved quickly forward to block the approach, put a massive hand on Maguire's chest and shoved him forcefully away. Maguire was enraged. He turned to Coffey, who was standing nearby. "Who is that man?" Maguire demanded. "I want to know his name."

"Oh," Coffey said, "I can tell you that. That's Bishop Paul Marcinkus. Give me some time and I'll tell you all about him."

There was one more confrontation at the very end of the visit. As the Pope was leaving, he beckoned those who had been near him through his stay, to give them a personal blessing, to permit them to kneel and kiss his ring. As Coffey started toward the Pope, Marcinkus blocked his way. "No cops," the bishop said.

It appeared that the Vatican watchers were wrong. If anything, Marcinkus's power and influence seemed to be growing and he had successfully deflected all the charges and rumors that had swirled around him and his rule over Vatican finances. Constantly at the Pope's side during the unceasing papal journeys around the world, Marcinkus was the man in charge of making all the arrangements. And in the fall of 1981, he moved up into an even more powerful position in the Vatican hierarchy. Pope John Paul II promoted him to archbishop and named him pro-president of the pontifical commission for the Vatican city-state. He had become the mayor of Vatican City, had total command of all its finances and general administration and was responsible for the Vatican's buildings, museums, newspaper, radio station, bureaucracy and three thousand employees. He had become the third most powerful man in the Vatican, behind only the Pope and the cardinal secretary of state, and his elevation to cardinal and the donning of the red hat seemed imminent.

But, early in the summer of 1982, the Vatican was suddenly awash with a new scandal and at last Marcinkus's role could no longer be ignored; his position was becoming untenable. The scandal, with echoes of the Sindona affair, surrounded Milan's Banco Ambrosiano, the country's largest private bank. As the result of more than $1.25 billion in unsecured loans to Latin American subsidiaries, the bank was on the verge of collapse. The bank's president, Roberto Calvi, suddenly disappeared from Milan, turned up in Vienna and then in London, where he was found hanging from Blackfriars Bridge, his pockets stuffed with bricks and a ticket for a flight to Rio de Janeiro.

Investigators from the Bank of Italy moved in, and were soon using the words "swindle" and "fraud" to describe what had been going on. And they began to unearth some strange connections. Control of Banco Ambrosiano had only recently been acquired by four unidentified Panamanian companies through Ambrosiano's Bahamian subsidiary, the Cisalpine Overseas Bank of Nassau. On the board of Cisalpine sat Archbishop Paul Marcinkus. And his Vatican Bank not only had been a shareholder in Banco Ambrosiano and engaged in several joint ventures with it, but had guaranteed those dubious Latin American loans through a letter of patronage. But once the Italian investigators arrived at Vatican City, Marcinkus was unavailable. He "preferred," said one Italian report, "to remain in hiding," issuing only his opinion that "these are things that happen only in Italy." His aides at the bank agreed to be interviewed, and then flashed a letter from Calvi—though they would not hand it over—that relieved the Vatican Bank of its pledge to guarantee those $1.25 billion in loans.

In the Vatican, there were reliable reports that the Pope's confidence in Marcinkus had been badly shaken as a result of the revelations about this affair—so shaken that he was planning a drastic revision in the structure of the Vatican Bank's administration, with control removed from Marcinkus and put in the hands of the secretary of state, and that he was considering ordering that the bank honor at least part of its commitment to Banco Ambrosiano.

As for Marcinkus himself, his reign appeared at an end. "It is becoming more and more likely," Vatican sources said at the end of the first week in July, "that the Holy Father will dispose of the good bishop," the disposition possibly taking the form of a promotion to some higher, if less responsible, position far removed from the Holy See.

It had, then, taken nearly a decade before anyone in authority in the church took credence in the stories and the mounting evidence about Marcinkus. But the day had come at last. And in New York, Joe Coffey finally smiled just a little.

For instance: One day in the late spring of 1981, a friend from the FBI called Coffey. "I thought I ought to tell you," he said, "Rizzo's out. He was just paroled. He's back in New York." No one convicted in the tangled affair that had begun on a cold rainy night so long before remained in prison now.

"Should I be worried?" Coffey asked.

"I don't know," his friend said. "If I were you, I might be."

I N D E X

• • • • • • • • • • • • •